Raising Cartographic Consciousness

Raising Cartographic Consciousness

The Social and Foreign Policy Vision of Geopolitics in the Twentieth Century

MARK POLELLE

LEXINGTON BOOKS
Lanham • Boulder • New York • Oxford

LEXINGTON BOOKS

Published in the United States of America
by Lexington Books
4720 Boston Way, Lanham, Maryland 20706

12 Hid's Copse Road
Cumnor Hill, Oxford OX2 9JJ, England

British Library Cataloguing in Publication Information Available

Library of Congress Cataloging-in-Publication Data

Polelle, Mark, 1964–
    Raising cartographic consciousness : the social and foreign policy vision of
geopolitics in the Twentieth Century / Mark Polelle.
        p.   cm.
    Includes bibliographical references (p.   ) and index.
    ISBN 0-7391-0011-4 (c : alk. paper)
    1. Geopolitics.   I. Title.
JC319.P582 1999
320.1'2—dc21   99-21214
                                                                                    CIP

Printed in the United States of America

⊖™ The paper used in this publication meets the minimum requirements of American
National Standard for Information Sciences—Permanence of Paper for Printed Library
Materials, ANSI/NISO Z39.48–1992.

I would like to thank my family and Professor Lloyd Gardner for their faith in my project. Thanks also to John Tracy and Jay Marquart of UPPERCASE Solutions, Inc. in Findlay, Ohio for their indispensable help in seeing this project to completion. I would also like to thank the University of Findlay for helping to make the publication of this book possible. All my love to Beth and Tim.

Contents

Chapter 1:
Geopolitics: A Spatial Science of the *Fin de Siècle*

It is what we think the world is like, not what it is really like, that determines our behavior.

–K. E. Boulding

Now when I was just a little chap I had a passion for maps. I would look for hours at South America, or Africa, or Australia, and lose myself in all the glories of exploration. At that time there were many blank spaces on the earth, and when I saw one that looked particularly inviting on a map (but they all look like that) I would put my finger on it and say, "When I grow up I will go there."

–Joseph Conrad, *Heart of Darkness*

This work is inspired by the desire to reflect upon the meaning of the 21 December 1942 article in *Life* entitled, "Geopolitics: the Lurid Career of a Scientific System Which a Briton Invented, the Germans Used, and the Americans Need to Study." More specifically, the goal of this work is to help elucidate the origins and effects of geopolitical discourse during the period 1870-1945 as viewed through the careers of the British geographer Halford Mackinder (1861-1947), the German geographer Karl Haushofer (1869-1946), and American geographer Nicholas Spykman (1893-1943).[1] In achieving this goal, I would like to offer an introductory overview of the life and thought of these figures to readers unfamiliar with the subject of geopolitics. My modest hope is to extend the range of possible interpretations of what, in most instances, is already well known by experts of what I call the geopolitical era. This geopolitical era, I will contend, was shaped by the rise and fall of formal European imperialism, Germany's rise as a threat to the old balance of power system in Europe, and, finally, by changes in the perception of time and space brought about by scientific discovery, technological change, and capitalist expansion. Such changes made possible, I will argue, the rise of a civilian militarist tradition in which the geopoliticians under examination played a crucial founding role. Geopoliticians were also motivated to construct integrated foreign and domestic defense strategies in response to the perceived crisis of the mid-sized European nation-state in an era of continental superstates. Finally, I wish to show how the "dialectical spatialism" (the view that history is propelled forward by the struggle of nations for the accumulation of territory) of the geopoliticians under review highlights their near aesthetic commitment to an apocalyptic narrative in which wars over space inevitably lead to a more natural ordering of states in international politics. Although Mackinder, Haushofer, and Spykman ultimately failed to see their programs fully implemented, all were at least successful in raising the "cartographic consciousness" of their respective societies.

Mackinder, Haushofer, and Spykman utilized the professional authority of geography (itself fostered by the practical needs of the imperial project) to speak out publicly on what they considered to be the realistic domestic and foreign interests of their states. In expounding upon the great issues of the day by applying an academically based rational expertise to domestic and foreign policy questions, these figures were fulfilling roles associated today with the defense intellectual. Sociologically, these three figures shared the quality of being institutionally based in university life and of having professional status of one kind or another within the discipline of geography. These institutional bases aided their interest in being viewed as neutral experts when speaking out on foreign and domestic policy concerns.

Their careers as university-bred experts help us to see that the defense intellectuals (also referred to here as civilian militarists)—assumed only to have arisen after World War Two in the U.S.—actually have a lineage that extends back into the late nineteenth century. The point of finding precursors to the American civilian militarist tradition is not crucial for its own sake. What is important are the questions raised by the existence of these precursors to begin with. Why, for instance, in the late nineteenth century do we see the kind of nexus between knowledge and power expressed in the form of university-supported intellectuals serving state expansionist aims? Why are such intellectuals accorded respect and deference when their success has been so spotty?[2] We may also ask the question of whose interests are served by the work of such individuals.

The other main theme that I wish to develop in the course of examining the careers of these geopoliticians concerns the role of domestic politics within national traditions of geopolitical thought. Too often, geopolitics is taken to be synonymous with realism in foreign policy analysis while the domestic and social policy implications of geopolitics are ignored. Ironically, this way of conceptualizing things is shaped by the mystifying anthropomorphic rhetoric of geopolitics itself; a rhetoric which defines the state as an organic entity acting with single-minded purposiveness on an international scene dominated by other, similarly unified, actors.

In reality, the geopolitical postulates of Mackinder, Haushofer, and Spykman were suffused with *presuppositions* concerning domestic political order and purpose. The term "man-power," for example, was coined by Mackinder to describe a particular management of Britain's social order that would result in the social efficiency needed to combat geopolitically defined threats from abroad (namely Germany and Russia) in his paper "Man-Power as a Measure of National and Imperial Strength" (1907). The elitist and anti-democratic assumptions embedded in the geopolitical enterprise could also be seen in the distrust Spykman and Haushofer had in the abilities of democracies to effectively pursue geopolitical aims with requisite unity of purpose. Indeed, geopolitics in its classical exposition (1870-1945) relied on a core set of *geo-domestic* suppositions that were overshadowed by the geopoliticians' rhetorical focus on external threats and opportunities rather than on the domestic costs involved in such adventures.

While my concern is to focus on the themes of the advent of the civilian militarist tradition and the domestic component of the geopolitics of this era that contribute to the growing literature on geopolitics and its history, in the introduction I would like to situate my approach to the subject *vis à vis* other relevant accounts.[3] I would then like to turn to the contested background of my subject and its time period by discussing at greater length the critical relationship between a newly professionalizing geography (and its geopolitical offshoot) and: 1) the rise of the *Deutschefrage*, or German question, in European affairs; 2) the European imperialism of this era; 3) the changes in the perception of time and space; and 4) the social fissures being experienced on the home front. In the background of the discussion will hover the question of how the model of science in the nineteenth century influenced the aims and methods of geographers and geopoliticians of this period.

Scholarly Treatments of Geopolitical Discourse and Practice

One can divide writings on the history of geopoliticians and geopolitics into roughly four categories. Such categories are, admittedly, arbitrary and employed here simply for heuristic purposes. First, there is a tradition represented by E. W. Gilbert and W. H. Parker which takes what might be called a "great man" view of geographers of the past. W. H. Parker therefore believes that:

> the 1904 statement [concerning Mackinder's "The Geographic Pivot of History"] is a work of genius independent of the nationality of its author, free from the preoccupations of its time and from the stigmata of geopolitical propaganda … [it is] conceived wholly from a detached viewpoint.[4]

This line of interpretation is filiopietistic in treating individuals such as Mackinder as heroes working to advance knowledge and the fortunes of geography as a professional discipline. This school is largely uncritical of Mackinder's life and work, seeking as it does to defend him against his critics while assuming that his geopolitical analysis "mirrors" the reality of world politics.

A variation of this view is that Anglo-American geopolitical tradition is separable from it associations with Haushofer and the Nazis and is a useful component of modern political geography. Most standard accounts, such as that provided by M. I. Glassner and H. J. de Blij in their *Systematic Political Geography*, treat geopolitics as a subfield within the larger field of political geography. Glassner and de Blij, for example, define geopolitics as "concerned basically with the application of geographic information and geographic perspectives to the development of a state's foreign policies."[5] The authors then take care to differentiate between Anglo-American and German contributions to geopolitics by arguing that the German political geographic tradition relied more heavily upon an organic model of the state than did the Anglo-American school.

Friedrich Ratzel (1844-1904) in his *Politische Geographie* (1896) thus argued that states required *Lebensraum* and perpetual growth in order to maintain their existence lest they decay and die. Ratzel was, like many of the geopoliticians, greatly influenced by Social Darwinism, and this influence continued in the work of his disciples, the American environmental determinist Ellen Churchill Semple and Rudolf Kjellèn. Kjellèn (1864-1922), a member of the Swedish parliament and a professor at Uppsala University, was the first to use the term *Geopolitik* in his book *Stäten som Lifsform (The State as an Organism* [1916]) which envisioned a united Europe under the leadership of a victorious Germany at the conclusion of World War One.

Glasner and de Blij see Alfred Thayer Mahan (1840-1914) and Halford J. Mackinder as contributing to geopolitical thought legitimate ideas to an Anglo-American tradition "based more on geographic facts and the policies that should be based on them" than those of their continental brethren.[6] Glassner and de Blij further claim that "in a broad sense his [Mackinder's] assumptions about the heartland were later substantiated."[7] This interpretation of the history of geopolitical thought therefore seeks to differentiate between Anglo-American geostrategists who rely on the "objective facts" of geography and continental geopoliticians who are ideologically biased in their selection and interpretation of geographic facts.

A third school of interpretation holds that geopolitics and geopoliticians largely reflect the material conditions of the social structure in which both are produced. Useful insights derived from this kind of analysis remind us of the material interests served by bourgeois intellectuals such as the geopoliticians under review here. Brian Hudson's important article "The New Geography and the New Imperialism: 1870-1918" (1977) illustrates the way in which geographers served as intellectual midwives to the formal European imperialism of the late nineteenth century by focusing on the need to acquire territory. For observers such as Hudson, the:

> new geography [i.e., modern and professionalized of the 1870s] was vigorously promoted at that time largely, if not mainly, to serve the interests of imperialism

in its various aspects including territorial acquisition, economic exploitation, militarism and the practice of class and race domination.[8]

Under this view, Mackinder, Haushofer, and Spykman can be understood as facilitators and apologists for a territorial expansionism that is inextricably linked with capitalism at its various stages of development.

More recently, the view that geopoliticians' geopolitical discourse is socially constructed or shaped has opened up whole new lines of inquiry and debate. As Neil Smith and Anne Godlewska write in the introduction to *Geography and Empire* (1994), "among the most powerful agendas in human geography today is a sustained commitment to understanding the social construction of geographic space and environment... ."[9] What is now called the critical geopolitical school offers one approach that attempts to meet this agenda and that informs this study as a starting point. Various definitions have been offered for this particular social constructionist approach to the history of geopolitical thought. In their article "Geopolitics and Discourse" (1992), John Agnew and Gearóid Ò'Tuathail stated this group's goals in programmatic fashion when they stressed the need for:

> Geopolitics ... [to be] critically re-conceptualized as a discursive practice by which intellectuals of statecraft 'spatialize' international policies in such a way as to represent it as a 'world' characterized by particular types of places, people, and dramas.[10]

The critical geopolitics program thus posits that the language deployed by such experts (be they geopoliticians or RAND analysts) is, above all, a political tool or resource used to achieve authoritative status for the expert and his views through largely rhetorical effects. This school shows that language is not transparent and that language is important to take into account when studying geopolitical thought because of its effects on the very categories through which we understand world politics.[11] In the chapters which follow, we shall see that for all their dissimilarities, Mackinder, Haushofer, and Spykman took care throughout their careers to couch their foreign policy recommendations by embedding them in the language of the "new" geography.

Thus the heartland for Mackinder was transmuted into a geographic fact through the use of symbolically effective maps which made the location of the heartland appear to be as naturally existing as the surrounding lakes, rivers and cities portrayed on the same map. The like could be said in regard to Haushofer's four "pan-regions" or Spykman's "rimland" concept. The critical geopolitics approach aims to make problematic such objects of analysis and methods as they are employed by the geopoliticians. Critical geopolitics seeks not only to understand the past for its own sake through careful analysis of the language used in expert discourses, but to alter present practices by criticizing current and unjust geopolitical orderings of the world.[12] Agnew and Ò'Tuathail express the concern of this school to link study of the past with the foreign policy practices of the present when they assert a desire to understand, "How are places reduced to security commodities, to geographical abstractions which need to be 'domesti-

cated,' controlled, invaded or bombed rather than understood in their complex
reality?"[13] Geopolitics, therefore, will be considered here as part and parcel of
the very world it purports to explain objectively.

Of course, such aims might be themselves critically analyzed. While practitioners of critical geopolitics desire to see the present materially altered, their
analyses run the risks of adopting a kind of philosophical idealism by being so
heavily focused on discourse at the expense of historical and material contexts.
The problems of idealism enter the discussion to the extent that critical geopolitics is practiced uncritically, such that language is accorded unique status as a
purposive and independent actor in its own right. The potential problems implicit
in a reification of language are perhaps attributable to this approach's self-conscious embrace of an often ethereal postmodern social theory.

Thus Simon Dalby, another important contributor to critical geopolitics,
argues for the centrality of discourses as actors in their own right when he argues
that they:

> are linked to specific claims to speak legitimately or correctly about the world.
> They work to exclude other ways of thinking and specifying the world.
> *Discourses also create* and then specify the relationship of the speaker to the
> object of knowledge the external 'other' of the discourse ... delegitimizing
> other forms of this relationship [emphasis mine].[14]

While it is important to avoid the dangers implicit in reifying language at the
expense of critically examining the users of a particular language, it is also
important to appreciate the central contribution of critical geopolitics for the
purposes of this project. This approach is ultimately informative here for showing how geopolitical discourses can lull the unwary or passive interpreter of a
map or verbal account of a geographically defined enemy into enacting a role
scripted by the makers of this socially constructed discourse.[15]

Read uncritically, Mackinder's writings assign to Britain the inevitable role
of the sea power perpetually in conflict with the great land powers on the continent. Indeed, a whole series of geopolitically informed dichotomies—democracy
versus totalitarianism, developed versus undeveloped, land power versus
seapower, etc.—are revealed by critical geopolitics to be categories that, at certain points in their historical use, merely mystify what they were once created to
clarify and explain.[16] It is in this sense that specifically situated *historical actors*
shape reality through the use and abuse of the discourses at their disposal. In this
account, I will attempt to show how Mackinder, Haushofer, and Spykman used
the domain of professionalized geography as a resource to develop a particular
geopolitical identity for their respective nations. Thus Britain was conceived of
as a socially efficient and organically united "going concern," Germany as a
natural hegemon on the European continent, and the U.S. as a perennial defensive fixer of the dikes along the rimland of a naturally expansive U.S.S.R. Just as
Mackinder and later geopoliticians historicized the old parochial European balance of power system, it is time for us to historicize the geopolitical age as well
(*contra* the wishes of current foreign policy experts such as Henry Kissinger and

Zbigniew Brzezinski). As the political scientist Peter Liberman argues, although one may make a case that territorial conquest could be made to pay as late as 1945, one can no longer—empirically or morally—make this argument today, especially in regard to the most developed nations.[17]

Such an account will, in summation, have to utilize the nuanced appreciation of the strategic use of language brought to the fore by practitioners of critical geopolitics. However, it will also have to avoid the danger of reifying language by showing concern for the way in which geopolitical discourse was shaped by a new social type, the defense intellectual. For it is the defense intellectual who has defined a problem—the crisis in measuring national power—and offered solutions (geopolitics in the period 1870-1945, and a host of theories centered around the atomic bomb in the postwar era) that legitimize early resort to conflict when national security interests are deemed to be threatened. Where David Livingstone argues that geography is not simply an epiphenomenon of empire, so too must it be said for the purposes of the present work that geopolitics is not simply an epiphenomenon of language.[18]

Coming to Terms with Space in the Geopolitical Era

The task of contextualizing the geopoliticians under review here must include consideration of the relevance of what has been called the revolution in perception of time and space occurring some time during the middle of the geopolitical era. Henri Lefebvre notes for instance that:

> around 1910 a certain space was shattered. It was the space of common sense, of knowledge (*savoir*), of social practice, of political power, a space thitherto enshrined in everyday discourse, just as in abstract thought, as the environment for any channel for communication; the space too, of classical perspective and geometry, developed from the Renaissance onwards on the basis of the Greek tradition (Euclid, logic) and brought forth in Western art and philosophy, as in the form of the city and the town.[19]

Where Stephen Kern in his *The Culture of Time and Space* offers suggestive descriptions concerning how changes in the technology of everyday life greatly affected perceptions of time and space, observers such as Lefebvre go further in stressing the notion that space itself is a social production of sorts; a space that is not simply a static stage, but a malleable entity that reflects a larger society acting upon it. For Lefebvre, in short, social space is a social production; social relations are embedded in space; and every society produces its own space according to its particular mode of production.[20]

It is thus possible to see how specific representations of space might be imposed on others. Mackinder offers an example susceptible to this kind of analysis when he notes that "the extent of the red patches of British dominion upon the map of the world ... [is] the cartographical expression of the eternal struggle for existence as it stands at the opening of the twentieth century."[21] The presupposition here about the nature of space is that it is a passive, open container into which British power must flow lest that of some other competing power do so. Britain, France, and Germany here are assumed to be active spatial actors as each nation expanded outward to act on passive, malleable colonial space.

The conflict exists, therefore, between a Western geopolitical conception of space and a non-Western conception of space. It could be argued, in fact, that one of the ironies surrounding geopoliticians and their discourse (dating from Mackinder's 1904 enunciation of the heartland thesis to Spykman's World War Two era ruminations on the possible shapes of a postwar geography) is the idea that they had become imprisoned by their own language into holding on to a static conception of space. During this half century, needless to say, epochal changes in economy and society were producing a new kind of space that no longer necessitated the old territorial imperialism that geopoliticians had been so inspired by. For example, the kind of indirect imperialism exercised by the International Monetary Fund or other international agencies has obviated the need to resort to direct control.[22] Although Mackinder had glimpsed how technology was transforming the conditions of space and time (as in the invention of the railroad, thereby giving a land power such as Russia more chances to exploit its power potential), he—along with our other geopoliticians—never pushed his analysis onward toward seeing the dynamics of the relationship between space, society, and economy. Thus Mackinder never envisioned that after 1945 geopolitics and its obsession with the military use of space could be superseded by geoeconomics and its focus on shaping space according to the needs of an increasingly globalized capitalism.

Thus, between international relations theory (which traditionally simplifies under realist doctrine the ways states are seen to act on the homogenized space of world politics) and classical geopolitics (which equates control of territory with security), we continue in the grip of what Neil Smith describes as a situation in which even "today we all conceive of space as emptiness, as a universal receptacle in which objects exist and events occur... ."[23]

Critical awareness of space thus inoculates us from accepting the static, deterministic conception of space propounded by the geopoliticians discussed here. It also points out the need to historicize these figures so that we may move beyond being hamstrung by their confining categories. By thinking about their individual backgrounds, we may better understand their geopolitical discourses as products not only of national and material ambitions, but as reflective of personal aspirations as well in the sense that the geopoliticians were forging new social roles for themselves. A study of these figures shows that there is liberating power in Neil Smith's conception that "Different societies use and organize space in different ways and the geographic patterns which result bear the clear imprint of the society which uses and organizes the space."[24] The geographers we are looking at here can be interpreted as political *advocates of how various spaces should be used* rather than as neutral describers of eternal verities concerning a static, unified world space. Their advocacy for a monolithic conception of space could only benefit a select few at home since their foreign policy projects required large sacrifices on the part of the average citizen on the home front. For Mackinder, this meant limits at home on traditional freedoms for the sake of national efficiency. For the Nazi sympathizer Haushofer, this meant the need for an authoritarian government to achieve "natural" expansion in Europe and abroad. Finally, for the American Spykman, it meant sacrificing a populist conception of democracy in order to keep the rimlands free of Soviet power.

The Geopolitician as the Prototype of the Defense Intellectual

Mackinder advanced the idea as early as 1917 in Parliament that Britain had a duty "to supply a thinking staff, a general staff of civil affairs, which will prevent our drifting into a dangerous position" because "democracy is in no position to cope with the wiles, calculations, and organizations of autocracy and bureaucracies."[25] Later, he talked of the need to organize the nation's "biomass" to be better prepared for international conflict.[26] Here is expressed the quintessential advice of the defense intellectual that to meet the enemy's challenge, one has to become more like the enemy. There is evidence that Mackinder took the opportunity to share his ideas on national security with the British military in the form of classes that he offered to officers before World War One. Mackinder mentions in the fragments of an autobiography that he was working on before his death that:

> about fifty Captains and Majors passed through them [the courses], some of whom are now Generals. In this connection I visited most of the Army & Navy centres of Education from the Staff College at Camerley, and the War College at Portsmouth to Osborne and the Duke of York's school. I lectured to many hundred Officers.[27]

There is also evidence that American envy for Haushofer's mythical geopolitical institute would lead the U.S. to organize its own World War Two version of an institutionalized structure housing academically trained defense intellectuals.[28] The influential geographer Isaiah Bowman argued the need for expert analysis of foreign policy problems as early as 1921 in his book, *The New World: Problems in Political Geography:*

> To face the problems of the day, the men who compose the government of the United States need more than native common sense and the desire to deal fairly with others. They need, above all, to give scholarly consideration to the geographical and historical materials that we call foreign policy. As we have not a trained and permanent foreign-office staff, our administrative principles are still antiquated. Thus even the loftiest intentions are too often defeated. To elevate the standards of government there is required a continuous examination of contemporary problems by citizens outside of the government service. In this way new points of view are set up and independent judgments made available.[29]

Work therefore needs to be done on finding the roots of a civilian militarist tradition; one that is typically associated with the development of the atomic bomb and the attempt to devise rational strategies to use it. Herken summarizes this view as follows:

> Since 1945, American policy on nuclear weapons has been sometimes determined—and always influenced—by a small nucleus of civilian experts whose profession it has been to consider *objectively* the fearful prospect of nuclear war [emphasis mine]. Scientists, think-tank theorists and cloistered academics have traditionally formed this elite fraternity of experts … who study a subject that did not even exist before Hiroshima.[30]

Yet civilian experts did exist before this time in the form of geopoliticians. In the case of Mackinder, Haushofer, and Spykman, one can also find elements in their careers that evince, on one level at least, an aesthetic satisfaction in imposing geopolitical rationality (and thereby order, stability, balance, and harmony) on what they saw as a recalcitrantly unbalanced and "irrational" international system.

Mackinder's conception of the heartland as the fulcrum of modern world politics shows one such intellectual imposition on the complexity of the international system. Similarly, the very maps of the world constructed by Haushofer and Spykman to express their respective world views end up showing the world divided into balanced organic units (witness the bipolar world envisioned by Spykman and Haushofer's imagined division of the world by four great powers). Such a rationalistic ordering of the world bespeaks a concern to find underlying models and regular causal mechanisms beneath the surface of international relations; i.e., the very qualities that we find in today's defense intellectual. The exigencies of professionalism and interstate competition supported, for example, the call of the geographer A. J. Herbertson as early as 1910 to form an imperial intelligence department for the British Empire that would be made effective *via* the expertise offered by university-trained geographers.[31]

Institutionally, of course, we are talking about intellectuals developing theories and other helping aids designed to facilitate state planning to fight and win wars. In dealing with the genealogy of this type of figure, it must be recalled that intellectuals were only named as such in the modern sense beginning in the late nineteenth century.[32] Mackinder and Haushofer, in particular, were thus among the first intellectuals interested in using the prestige they enjoyed from holding university posts as vehicles for the public expression of their views on international affairs. By laying down the mold through the example of their careers, figures such as these could establish institutional precedents for a civilian militarist tradition long after they were gone. Thus, in the case of Haushofer, we will see how elite and popular interpretations of his career in America led to a kind of schizophrenia in which he was on the one hand repudiated for his links to Nazism, but on the other hand emulated as an example of what could be achieved through the marriage of university-bred expertise and foreign policy analysis. This was witnessed in the call for American geopolitical institutes and the mushrooming of geopolitics courses in universities during and after World War Two. Indicative of state interest in expert-produced knowledge during the geopolitical age is the following anecdote concerning the actions of the British government in 1874:

> the military and civil servants of Her Majesty well appreciate the value of the [Royal Geographical] Society's map room. No sooner does a squabble occur—in Ashanti, Abyssinia, or Atchin—than government departments make a rush to Savile Row and lay hands on all matter relating to that portion of the globe which happens to be interesting for the moment.[33]

Lawrence Freedman in his *Nuclear Strategy* and Gregg Herken in his *Counsels of War* (1987) also empirically show the symbiosis between the defense intellectual and the modern university. The dean of American strategists—Bernard Brodie—came from the same realist-minded Yale Political Science Department that provided intellectual sustenance for Spykman.[34] Thus Oxford and the London School of Economics served for Mackinder—as Munich and Yale did for Haushofer and Spykman respectively—as necessary institutional bases for the development and expression of their ideas. To the extent that the university could be associated with a tradition of disinterested inquiry, such thinkers stood to gain a more respectful hearing as bearers of university-sanctioned truth when issuing geopolitical nostrums.

In terms of institutions, we also associate the term "defense intellectual" within the context of the specialized think tank. According to the *Oxford English Dictionary*, "think tank" originally constituted turn of the century English slang for brain. By the 1960s the term had come to be associated with defense planning institutes when Kennedy's "best and the brightest" arrived in the Pentagon under the leadership of Secretary of Defense Robert McNamara. The pervasiveness of the term in the 1960s was recognized by Theodore White in his *Life* magazine article "Action Intellectuals."[35] *Business Week* marked the new public appreciation for these types as well in 1963 by claiming that:

> Today's great national security problems involve an interaction of scientific, technical, economic, and political factors. They demand a type of abstract thinking that is both disciplined and inspired, a type of thinking that has always been associated with a very unmilitary type of person. For lack of a better name, this sort of person usually is called an 'intellectual.' For many it has been a shock just how important the intellectuals have become ... Traditionally they have been outsiders, social critics, idealists. But now, they are insiders and forced to come to grips with reality.[36]

While no exact equivalents to RAND or the Hudson Institute can be found in the Britain of Mackinder's days, one can trace institutional antecedents to the rise of what are, at their basis, groups of university-trained experts devoted to applying particular professional skills (i.e., cartography or mathematical analysis) to government-defined social, domestic, and foreign "problems."

James Allen Smith has traced some of the American antecedents to the application of expertise to domestic issues in his *The Idea Brokers: Think Tanks and the Rise of the New Policy Elite* (1991). He develops a genealogy of these types stretching back to groupings such as the Progressives, Hoover's technocrats, Roosevelt's New Deal brain trust, Truman's Cold War liberal advisers, Kennedy's defense intellectuals, and Johnson's Great Society workers.[37] One task of this project is to reckon with Mackinder's connection to the Coefficient Society, a grouping well connected (socially and by birth) to the British government of the day. We will later examine how this group touched on nearly every great issue of the day with the opportunity to "imagine the unimaginable," or at least think through hypotheses that politicians felt they could not consider in the face of an increasingly democratic public life.[38] Another germane example is Isaiah Bowman's participation in the Council of Foreign Relations, as well as his work on the World War One era Inquiry designed to collect information relevant to the upcoming Paris Peace Conference.[39]

The general public's reaction to such experts was, from the beginning, marked with distrust. Just as Mackinder's on-the-spot reporting from post-revolutionary southern Russia and his politically unviable advice on the subject of stopping communism was looked at with disdain by the British Cabinet who thought it out of touch with political reality, so too do we find in modern America a tension between the theoretical focus of defense intellectuals and the political concerns of civilian leaders. We have already alluded to the fact that part of this tension has to do with the greater number of constituencies that "practical" politicians and armed services are typically beholden to. Also, institutional inertia and ideological fixity in these institutions can conflict with the application of the recommendations of defense intellectuals. Haushofer's own ideological commitments—his Machiavellianism and aristocratic conservative loyalties—prevented him from seeing that Nazi ideology was not just pablum for the masses (behind which to institute a serious geopolitical program), but was taken seriously by leading elements of the very same Nazi elite he staked his career on as potential implementers of his geopolitics. The geopolitician's expert disdain of the "half-educated masses" (as expressed by Mackinder in his mistitled *Democratic Ideals and Realities*) and ignorance of the political necessities that had to be attended to before abstract theory could be put into practice often made the geopoliticians more idealistic than realistic.

Geopoliticians believed that the nation-state as it entered the twentieth century required more than birth and breeding in leaders. The events being described here are all representative of the crisis of Europe's old regime. This crisis was manifested in the popularity of the politics of national efficiency; the palpable fear of what the twentieth century might mean for European nation-states in an age of continental superstates; the military consequences of the second industrial revolution that threatened to change the nature of war and the very measurement of power upon which rational war planning depended; the rise of working class parties that challenged the legitimacy of the traditional hierarchical ordering of the nation-state at a time when domestic harmony was increasingly seen as a *sine qua non* for the effective defense of the nation-state's interests abroad; and, finally, crises concerning the revolution in the European perception of the world (caused in part by tensions previously exported *via* imperialism now being imported back to Europe).

One such catalyst for this European-wide crisis was Germany. Germany's nineteenth-century triumphs on the battlefield led states with any pretension to importance to emulate what was perceived to be Germany's scientific approach to war and war planning.[40] Thus, in planning to build its modern armed forces, Japan chose the German model while still continuing to use Britain as a model for its own naval ambitions. Precisely because of the speed-up in the tempo and violence of international relations between the great powers in the late nineteenth century, traditional methods of war planning and diplomacy were being put into question. Improvements in communications and transport had, for example, made it seem logical to rely on rigid advance war planning preparation in order to avoid having to improvise in a crisis while the other side mobilized according to a set battle plan. Classical geopolitics offered itself as a clarifying guide to the "real" distributions of power in the world and so promised to simplify the complexities inherent in such planning.

The creation of abstract concepts such as the heartland, *Lebensraum*, rimlands (or even certain elements of nuclear strategy) have the virtue of offering a simplification of a complex world picture to the state's caretakers. Democratization, arms races, improvements in communications, and the like not only produced a new sense of space and time, but ushered in a crisis in the measurement of power itself. Mackinder and future defense intellectuals would take advantage of doubts caused by these changes by coming to the fore of public life with answers designed to alleviate doubts about the methodology of measuring newly complex balances of power. When governments and publics came into doubt about such fundamental questions, a space was opened up for the bourgeois civilian militarist to market actively strategic ideas to both the general public and the policymaker. The publisher George Philips, for example, sold a half million copies of Mackinder's works before World War One, while Haushofer and Spykman enjoyed similar recognition in their own respective markets.[41]

The geopoliticians under discussion were all active in seeking to supply answers to the thorny questions posed by these changes in an era of mass political mobilization. In the chapters that follow we will see Mackinder seek a seat in Parliament, Haushofer cultivate contacts with the future Nazi elite at Landsberg prison (and voice his opinions nationwide *via* regular radio broadcasts), and Spykman write books aimed at a large general audience in his attempt to sway public opinion toward his vision of a postwar geographical order. They too shared with Robert McNamara's "whiz kids" or Theodore White's "new priesthood" of action intellectuals a desire to shape opinion based on what they thought was the expertise underlying their propositions. These three geopoliticians may not have seen their respective geopolitical visions wholly realized, but they were strikingly successful in public relations and in hawking their wares to a large book-buying, map-viewing, and radio-listening audience.[42]

Ultimately, we could trace the application of expert reason to affairs of state back to the Enlightenment. The early nineteenth-century strategic thinker Jomini thus proposed that war could be reduced to fixed rules and even mathematical formulae. Interstate conflict did not have to be left to chance, divine intervention, or the social prejudice of armies run by amateur aristocrats. Rather, it could be conceived of for the first time as a meritocratic struggle between entire social systems in which, in true Enlightenment (later, Darwinian) fashion, the most rationally constituted forces would emerge victorious. Mackinder thus thought it necessary to warn his nation's elite against the objective fact of the heartland and the barbarian authoritarianism it could support (i.e., that of Germany, Russia, or even China). This leitmotif of a civilized West pitted against a barbarous East is also discernable in the whole of Haushofer's thought. Pan-regionalism was, among other things, intended to allow Europe to compete effectively against the U.S. and Russia at the same time. Finally, we find in Spykman's rimland notion yet another binary opposition between a U.S. conceived of as the defender of the West and its Enlightenment norms against the irrational despotism beyond the rimlands.

With these ultimately deterministic world views, we can appreciate how Lawrence Freedman's remark concerning defense intellectuals and their reliance on the methodology of game theory can be extended to the geopoliticians: "[game theory is] a means of reducing strategic problems to a manageable form in which the dilemmas and paradoxes of the age could be bared and solutions explored."[43] Instead of the language of game theory, of course, geopoliticians exploited the power of visual symbols on specialized maps. And maps, far from being unproblematic containers of meaning, are aptly described by Mark Edley in *Mapping and Empire* as:

> representations of knowledge; as representations, they are constructed according to culturally defined semiotic codes; the knowledge is constructed using various intellectual and instrumental technologies; the knowledge and its representation are both constructed by individuals who work for and within various social institutions, according to cultural expectations.[44]

Strategic man was—like economic man—born under that aspect of Enlightenment thought which emphasized a utilitarian conception of the sources of individual behavior. States in this conception are, therefore, rigidly thought to follow incentives to maximize their growth and strength *vis à vis* other nation-states. Still, the bourgeois model of strategic man or the civilian militarist was never universally accepted. Certainly North Vietnam failed to act according to his predictions while the Soviets never accepted this model in their thinking about international conflict.

Obviously, a geopolitical mode of thinking depoliticizes conflict into a game, making the issue of what kind of culture actually held sway over the heartland moot before Mackinder's environmental determinism. Whatever entity controlled this territory was ipso facto a threat in the mind of the self-proclaimed "landscape gardener" of civilizations. Indeed, when Mackinder wrote of himself as a "landscape gardener of civilization, with his organic remedies" for problems in British domestic and foreign policy, he was foreshadowing similar concerns on the part of such future geopoliticians as Haushofer and Spykman to rectify their own nations' social and foreign policies.[45]

Social Geopolitics

The second major theme I wish to introduce concerns the domestic geopolitics enfolded within foreign geopolitics. Where the German historiographical school led by Fritz Fischer struggled to show that German foreign policy (*Aussenpolitik*) was never isolated from domestic concerns (*Innenpolitik*), in a similar vein I would like to examine critically the domestic agendas undergirding the foreign geopolitics of Mackinder, Haushofer, and Spykman.

The first fundamental fact of the social or domestic side of geopolitics is its deep distrust for democracy. This is explicitly seen whether it is Mackinder talking about the dangers of Bolshevism in influencing Britain's working classes, Haushofer ruminating on Bolshevik threats to German conservatism, or Spykman disdaining the ability of democracy to maintain a constant course in pursuing geopolitical aims. Democracy was to be distrusted by these figures because their understanding of constants and patterns of the geography underlying international relations (manifested in such phrases as "he who rules the heartland ... controls the world") made them see average people as, by and large, fickle, emotional, and pacifist in nature. For Mackinder they were the "half-educated masses" who needed the guiding hand of hardheaded realists such as himself.[46]

The Anglo-American geo-strategic tradition could not, contrary to the efforts of American geographers such as Isaiah Bowman, ever be successfully separated from the anti-democratic leanings represented most extremely in German geopolitical thought. Geopoliticians believed that only strong governments would be capable of adopting their programs over the objections of public opinion. Mackinder and Spykman had a distrust of democracy that was also shared by another forger of the Anglo-American geo-strategic tradition, A. T. Mahan. Mahan also questioned:

> Whether a democratic government will have the foresight, the keen sensitiveness to national position and credit, the willingness to insure its prosperity by adequate outpouring of money in times of peace, all of which are necessary for military preparation, is yet an open question. Popular governments are not generally favorable to military expenditure, however necessary, and there are signs that England tends to drop behind.[47]

While democracy was disdained, social efficiency and social sacrifice were honored by these geopoliticians. In Mackinder's case, this is explicitly obvious. His very development of the concept of "man-power" demonstrates his concern that Britain exploit every power resource available to it. Absent healthy, efficient and productive man-power, Mackinder warned that the British Empire might not

have the strength to hold off its rivals. Entailed in such a vision was the implication that what were considered virtues by others—namely, Britain's relatively
weak central government and its relative tolerance for individual liberties—were
luxuries or perhaps vices in the geopolitical era when mass mobilization of
population for the acquisition of broad swaths of territory could still be seen as a
rational goal. To raise Britain's power potential, a kind of *internal colonization*
would have to occur whereby a stronger central government would be empow-
ered to extract more and more from the polity with the intent of warding off its
enemies. Thus the symmetry between external and internal colonization, or
between geopolitics and geo-domestic policy. With the rest of the world
increasingly divided up between Europe by 1914, competitive tensions could no
longer be dissipated in foreign colonial ventures. Instead, "have-not" powers
such as Germany sought the answer to the problem of the mid-sized nation-state
through expansion within Europe itself. Planning such ventures meant a concomitant militarization of society that incorporated much of the organic conservative philosophy espoused by the geopoliticians.

   Mackinder had Germany mostly in mind as both enemy and model at the
same time. Mackinder in his "Modern Geography, German and English" (1895)
idealized the German model in geography, social structure, and military affairs
while finding Britain wanting in these areas. The social component of
Mackinder's geopolitics was more than social imperialism in the sense that
Bernard Semmel discusses.[48] Mackinder, as a self-proclaimed landscape
gardener of civilization, looked critically at the very geographic distribution of
social, political, and economic activity within Britain itself. Above all, he
thought London too big and representative of an unfettered capitalism's emphasis on change, materialist values, and individualism. Such values did not comport
with his idealization of past epochs in history as represented by the cases of classical Greece, Florence, and certain aspects of the organic societies of the Middle
Ages. In his *Democratic Ideals and Reality*, he extracted from his understanding
of these periods values such as social balance and harmony that he found sorely
lacking in modern Britain.

   London and all that it represented in the way of capitalistic modernity trou-
bled Mackinder because such modernity represented for him the advent of an
increasingly unrooted society that violated his organic model. While he pushed
for protectionist measures as a member of Parliament, the London establishment
advocated free trade; a free trade that he saw as wreaking havoc with British
(non-urban) traditions and values. Mackinder's views on domestic policy were
never hermetically sealed from his views of international relations. His dislike of
an internationalized capitalism (shared by Haushofer), for instance, reflected his
concern for balanced economic development, but it was part of his overarching
dislike of a phenomenon that weakened national borders and loyalties while
stimulating an equally detested social movement, working class political organization. While Mackinder showed budding awareness of new possibilities concerning the relationship between space and social change in his pivot paper, he
still remained largely wedded to a static vision of space. In reality, however, im-

perial territorial expansion would increasingly be coterminous with the nation's capitalistic growth.[49]

Haushofer and Spykman never explicitly expressed an ambition to be "landscape gardeners" of civilization. The two relied, however, on particular visions of domestic social order that needed to be in place in order for their foreign geopolitical program to be implemented. We will see that Haushofer—although not the rabid Nazi he was made out to be by foreign observers—could never abandon his loyalty to the autocratic and hierarchical society embodied in the Second Reich of his youth. For him, there was no question that individuals such as himself must provide the leading ideas and policies by which Germany should be guided. His practical experience as a veteran officer in World War One— coupled with the doctorate in geography he had earned at Munich—ensured him the prestige and authority to enable him to be heard respectfully in an era of general staffs and university experts. He took for granted the need for society to be organized around the principle of willingness to sacrifice the individual interest for the collective good of the attainment of *Lebensraum*. The latter goal, once achieved, would, according to Haushofer, cure the social ills stemming from overcrowding and the unhealthy tendency to concentrate in the cities. With these basic assumptions in mind, Haushofer could afford to be flexible as to what kind of right wing movement he could support so long as it would help Germany be rid of the (relatively) territorially unambitious Weimar Republic.

Such a democracy was viewed by Haushofer as incapable of pursuing *Lebensraum* and leading a healthy, growing nation because of its inherently pacifist impulses, emphasis on individual rights, and distrust of nationalist goals. Thus the Nazis appeared to Haushofer as effective a force to back as any in the race to undo both Weimar democracy and the Versailles Treaty. As was the case with German conservatives of the old school, he believed that the excesses of Nazi ideology were not meant to be taken seriously. Surely, he thought, the Nazis would accede to the dictates of bedrock geopolitical logic and not invade the U.S.S.R. out of mere ideological pique. By the end of his life there was some truth to his apologia concerning his wartime activities when he told Father Edmund Walsh (who was charged with the task of examining Germans who might merit prosecution as war criminals) that he was not a Nazi and that his influence on policy was minimal, especially after the Munich conference of 1938 when he advocated a slowdown in German expansionism.

The outlines of a social philosophy can be gleaned from Spykman's work as well. This is so even though he died at a relatively young age after having published only two major works. Furthermore, these works were published at a time when the natural aversion between geopolitics and democratic sentiment had to be sublimated during wartime conditions. The political geographer George Renner, after all, faced great opprobrium for suggesting in the pages of *Collier's Magazine* (1942) a "realistic" postwar map of Europe that would have treated Germany fairly generously (in terms of territory) on the theory that future conflict might thereby be avoided.[50] During World War Two, geographers and geopoliticians were sensitive to the charges of being mere American imitations of

Haushofer. The problem faced by Bowman, Spykman, and other American geographers lay in trying to separate a democratic, scientific, and American geography from the ideological crudities of German geopolitics. We will see that this problem was never to be solved satisfactorily because of the inherent anti-democratic path that a commitment to classical geopolitical discourse entailed. Spykman feared that the U.S. would be unwilling to sacrifice its citizens to rectify abstract imbalances in geopolitically measured balances of power. The typical individual in a democracy, he believed, stubbornly "preferred dying on his own soil instead of abroad [which] is a serious handicap to the democratic state."[51]

Civilian militarist experts such as himself would have to bear the burden not only advising governments of their geopolitical views, but would have to sell them to the public as well in an age of mass media. As he put it, "unless public opinion is educated to the strategic advantages of offensive action or inspired by a messianic ideology, the nation will offer the lives of its sons only for national defense."[52] Autocracies were seen as having the advantage in not having to mobilize their citizens to pursue the state's geopolitical goals. Such was the kind of thinking that the writers of NSC-68 and a good part of the postwar American security establishment shared. Spykman merits attention in this context as someone attempting to contribute to an Anglo-American tradition in foreign policy theory based on the constants of a deterministic geography. He claimed therefore that:

> Because the geographic characteristics of states are relatively unchanging and unchangeable, the geographic demands of these states will remain the same for centuries, and because the world has not yet reached that happy state where the wants of no man conflict with those of another, these demands will cause friction. Thus at the door of geography may be laid the blame for many of the age-long struggles which run persistently through history while governments and dynasties rise and fall.[53]

Geopolitics and the Professionalization of Geography: Science, Imperialism, and War

Some words must be said about the professional milieu of geography in which these geopoliticians operated. To the extent that geography was recognized as a professional discipline—an autonomous interpretive community—harboring experts with practical and theoretical skills that required a specialized education to achieve, geopolitical thinkers could enjoy credibility by maintaining a close connection to mainstream geography. As we have seen, such expertise was not politically neutral. Indeed, the empowering professional contexts from which Mackinder, Haushofer, and Spykman drew intellectual and institutional sustenance could not help but reflect the social context in which they existed.

David Livingstone, a recent commentator on geography's professionalization in the nineteenth century, thus notes how "geographers' traditional craft-skills—such as cartography and the regional survey—turn out to be rhetorical devices of persuasion by which geographers have reinforced the authority of their assertions."[54] Thus does critical geopolitics and its nuanced focus on language become entwined with the history of geography as a discipline. Behind Livingstone's statement lies the assumption that folk wisdom still induces us to see such rhetorical devices as helping to produce an objective knowledge untainted by larger social concerns.

Commentators on the history of professions and professionalization offer a starting point for critically examining the careerism of the geopoliticians under review and the social uses to which such devices have been put.[55] In the important work *The Rise of Professionalism*, M. S. Larson relates modernization to its effect on the professions in the late nineteenth century and notes that it represents the "advance of science and cognitive rationality and the progressive differentiation and rationalization of the division of labor in industrial societies."[56] Professionalization, in this account cannot be reduced to the simple model of: 1) the norm of a service ethic to justify the autonomy granted by society to a particular discipline, and 2) a theoretical core of the discipline that must be mastered in advanced training. Rather, Larson suggests that professionalization—taken as a whole—be considered "as the process by which producers of special services sought to constitute *and control* a market for their expertise."[57] As we will have further occasion to note, geopoliticians were entrepreneurial in the way in which they capitalized on the governmental and popular fears surrounding the tumultuous changes occurring at the level of international relations in the period 1870-1945, a period unique for the importation back into Europe of energies previously directed abroad, the rapid industrialization of warfare, and the advent of mass politics. Geopoliticians were therefore particularly interested in exploiting the professionalization of geography for civilian militarist ends.

Geopoliticians may have thought they were purveying intellectual goods based on the underlying realities of world politics. But for observers such as the historian of geographic thought David Livingstone (who finds useful the Edinburgh school's strong program of seeing science as above all a cultural practice), geographers in reality make the world through their interpretations of the world rather than simply by discovering aspects of it.[58] This emphasis on the merits of examining science as a cultural practice will prove useful in the attempt to illuminate just what it was geopoliticians *qua* civilian militarists were trying to accomplish. The use of first-hand exploration narratives (Mackinder was the first to climb to the summit of Mt. Kenya in 1899 while Haushofer spent time in Japan beginning in 1909) legitimated geopoliticians in the minds of professional geographers who valued first-hand observation as well as theoretical acumen.

For example, professional affiliation in particular enabled these geopoliticians to take advantage of public trust in maps and mapmaking. A map labeling a large part of Eurasia as an inevitably aggressive heartland can overawe the viewer just as the prisoner's dilemma logic beloved by game theorists can be used to demonstrate the inevitability of arms races.[59] In either case, expert claims to authority—whether concerning mapmaking or game theory—can lead to claims about the true nature of reality such that further debate on the matter is artificially cut off. Such *depoliticization* of what are at heart inherently political choices is a theme that will recur throughout the following pages as we see one form or another of geopolitical logic indubitably leading its adherents to a very narrow range of conclusions.

But what is the connection between professional geography and science as our geopoliticians understood these terms? Mackinder himself pointed out the tension between the old and the new geography when he reflected that he had been a pawn in what he termed a

> battle royal that was being waged within the Council of the [Royal Geographical] Society, between a hitherto dominant part of explorers, navigators, and mapmakers on the one hand, and on the other hand a small group of scientific men led by Douglas Freshfield and Francis Galton who saw in geography something more than mere inventory of facts arranged upon a map.[60]

Mackinder's professional task in the "On the Scope and Methods of Geography" (1887) was therefore in large measure to show the unity of his discipline. In this paper delivered before the Royal Geographical Society, Mackinder confronted the issue by stating that:

> At the moment we are suffering under the effects of an irrational political geography, one that is, whose main function is not to have causal relations, and which must therefore remain a body of isolated data to be committed to memory. Such a geography can never be a discipline, can never, therefore, be honored by the leader.[61]

Certainly for Mackinder and Haushofer (as translated in German terms through the biologist Ernst Haeckel), the Darwinian revolution loomed large as a cultural marker separating earlier religious teleological arguments (such as those of William Paley) about the nature of the earth and its history from later nineteenth century evolutionary and materialistic theories. The geographer and one-time RGS librarian H. R. Mill (1861-1950) thus reflected that "evolutionary theory ... has become the unifying principle in geography" with the reception of Darwinism in the intellectual life of late nineteenth century Europe.[62] Mill went even further by describing how:

> Charles Darwin, not so much by his research in physical geography, ... as by his service in establishing and popularizing the theory of evolution has done more than any other geographer of the nineteenth century to advance the science by supplying the co-ordinating glue which unifies it.[63]

What was at stake here was where intellectual authority in Victorian Britain would lie. This is nicely captured by David Livingstone's statement that "professionalization of science in late Victorian England was merely part of an ideological transfer from religion to science as the basis of social validation."[64] William

Morris Davis, the first president of the Association of American Geographers, thus believed the old teleology of Ritter had been superseded by the evolutionary principle in nineteenth century geography.[65]

In Britain as in the similar cases of Germany and the U.S., the impulse to professionalize geography thus had both intellectual and political roots. In Britain, however, the confidence in national abilities symbolized by the Great Exhibition of 1851 had given way by the 1870s to a nervous sense that Britain was falling behind Germany in the natural sciences and in the education of its populace. In 1870 the Education Act was passed while a Royal Commission on Science Instruction was in existence between 1870-1875. Similar concerns about continental superiority in geographical studies resulted in Scott Keltie being appointed inspector of geographical education by the Royal Geographical Society in 1884.

The importance of the Keltie's report for geography's professionalization is underlined by the British professor R. Brown's judgment that it "may be regarded as inaugurating the scientific study of geography in the schools and universities of Great Britain."[66] Keltie himself believed in the necessity of a unified body of knowledge by which geography could be turned into an autonomous professional discipline. As he stated in his report:

> Were geography taught by qualified teachers as one single subject, all the points of which are intimately connected, it would not only form a body of knowledge of high value, and cease to be the barren task which it is now ... [and] it could not fail to be a real discipline.[67]

The focus on the making of a viable discipline is important since Mackinder met Keltie in 1885 and was found by the latter (as well as by the Royal Geographical Society) to be the proper person to offer a definitional synthesis of the new geography.

While the Darwinian revolution offered one important impetus leading toward geography's elevation to professional status in Britain and elsewhere, imperialism constituted another important strand in the story. David Livingstone claims that geography is the quintessential science of imperialism because the early practices that made a geographer unique—his capacity for exploration of the unknown, ability to perform topographic surveys, create and interpret maps and the like—were all put willingly in the service of overseas expansion.[68] In its strongest form, this thesis is well expressed by Brian Hudson when he states that "It was not the 'grand old men' [such as Mackinder] who made the new geography. Rather, it was the new geography [in the service of the state] which made their careers as geographers."[69]

This new geography was greatly shaped by the imperialism so strongly supported by the Royal Geographical Society. After all, the RGS, which played such a great role in the professionalization of geography in Britain, started out as a society consisting largely of non-academic travelers and explorers who wanted to see their values—support for empire, exploration, and the individual testing of character—reflected in the Oxford readership the Society helped fund for

Mackinder at Oxford in 1887.[70] These imperial values were made explicit in the first issue of the *Journal of the Royal Geographic Society* of 1831. The aims of the Society were stated as follows:

> That a new and useful society might be formed, under the name of THE ROYAL GEOGRAPHICAL SOCIETY OF LONDON. That the greatest interest excited by this department of science is universally felt; that its advantages are of the first importance to mankind in general, and paramount to the welfare of a maritime nation like Great Britain, with its numerous and extensive foreign possessions.[71]

In return for the services rendered by the new geography in the late nineteenth century, these governments provided a military shield for geography behind which geographers could expand their discipline's intellectual capital through colonial exploration. Geographic knowledge could therefore grow hand in hand with the territorial growth of the state. Geography's role here was reduced to describing and mapping the inevitability of struggle between states for spaces waiting to be filled in by the expanding nations.

The German Problem in European Politics and the Response of Geopolitics

The struggle Mackinder and others were describing did not just have to do with the definition and conquest of extra-European space, however. The question concerning Germany's role in Europe (and the world) after its successes in becoming unified through *Realpolitik* diplomacy and military aggression between 1864-1871 raised the issue of a contest of spatial conceptions taking place in Europe as well. The German model in war, politics, economics, and in individual disciplines (such as geography) had a powerful influence on geopolitical thought. In terms of geography's professional status, the German model was seen as having proved its superiority by dint of its apparent connection to the decisive German victory over the French in 1871. The aforementioned William Morris Davis had declared that the Franco-Prussian clash was a "war fought by maps" and won by officers who had studied under the great Ritter.[72] The fact that chairs in geography were established in Prussian state universities in 1874 only helped cement the arguments being made for the professionalization of geography in competing states such as Mackinder's Britain. Indeed, similar dynamics could be seen at work during World War Two when the apparent connection between Hauhshofer and Nazi successes stimulated a desire to emulate the geopolitical institutes assumed to exist in Germany.

Mackinder's paper "On Geography, German and British," along with Scott Keltie's 1885 report on geographic education, allowed leading advocates for geography's professionalization to point to Germany as the model for how practical benefits would follow the integration of geography within the universities. Always hovering in the background of such discussion was the possibility that war in Europe (one likely to involve Germany) would require mobilizing the public's cartographic consciousness in an era of mass warfare and politics.

On the specifically practical benefits to be had from supporting geography's professionalization, Sir George Goldie, a strong supporter of geography's military uses, told the RGS in a 1907 speech that it was "a moot point whether war is more useful to geography or geography to war," and that "war has been one of the greatest geographers."[73] The theme concerning the relationship between geography and military science was one that subsequent geopoliticians would later exploit. That this was easy to do is in part attributable to the long-standing connection between the two. As early as 1842, W. R. Hamilton delivered a presidential address to the RGS in which he maintained that geography:

> is the mainspring of all the operations of war, and all the negotiations of a state of peace; and in proportion as no one nation is the foremost to extend her acquaintance with the physical conformation of the earth, and the water which surrounds it, will ever be the opportunities she will possess, and the responsibilities she will incur, for extending her commerce, for enlarging her power of civilizing the yet benighted portions of the globe, and for bearing her part in forwarding and directing the destinies of mankind.[74]

The *Deutschefrage*, or German question, underlines many of the disparate issues and concerns adumbrated here as it constituted the focal point around which discussion of imagined wars increasingly centered.[75] In sum, the relationship between the rise of geopolitics and the playing out of German expansionist ambitions between 1870-1945 must be explored. So much of geopolitical writing at this time concerned Germany as either constituting an inevitable threat to peace (or, in Haushofer's view, as a geographically mistreated actor on the world political stage) that it is hard to imagine geopolitical thought developing the same way without the existence of a territorially expansionist Germany during this time period.

As we have seen, Mackinder's energies were largely devoted to using the example of Germany as a warning to professionalize British geography. Furthermore, the threat of Germany provided Mackinder a rationale for implementing a social (as well as foreign) geopolitical program that could prevent the heartland's resources from coming under German organizational sway. In particular, Germany constituted a *necessary* external enemy that might prove a positive force in waking up a Britain that he saw as already decadently susceptible to the moral and political confusion stimulated by *laissez faire* capitalism. To paraphrase Voltaire, if Germany did not exist, it would have to be invented if Mackinder and other civilian militarists in the West were to awaken their fellow citizens to the rigors and perils of world politics in the twentieth century, all the while maintaining social hegemony at home for geopolitically-minded elites bent on economic and territorial expansion abroad.

By extension, during the geopolitical age and the subsequent Cold War era, civilian militarist defense intellectuals could thrive only when well-defined enemies such as Germany and Soviet Russia existed. Geopoliticians admired the ability of these rival powers to pursue their interests abroad without apparent need to worry about placating public opinion or special interests at home. Such powers were thought to enjoy an advantage as well in not having to worry about individual rights at the expense of the collective good of the social organism. Mackinder, for example, referred to society as a "Going Concern" by which he meant an idealized organic community that was not paralyzed by debates or procedures on such fundamental issues as foreign policy. Spykman, as we have discussed, expressed similar feelings when he stressed the divisive anti-geopolitical forces represented by "hyphenated-Americans" and the inherent pacifism of democracy.[76]

Institutionally, the focus on Germany as both model and anti-model in this classical geopolitical era provided the impetus by which governments began to rely increasingly on experts for the conduct of foreign affairs. Besides the role of geography in the Franco-Prussian War, one can cite the examples of the post-World War One Inquiry under Isaiah Bowman's leadership, Mackinder's participation in the Coefficient Society and his fact-finding mission to southern Russia in 1919, the uses made by the Nazis of Haushofer's brand of geopolitics, and the work of the American OSS under the geographer Richard Hartshorne during World War Two as indicative highlights for this shift. Thomas Holdich, a military surveyor and a president of the RGS, captured the fluidity in territorial definition of this geopolitical era (defined, in part, by an expansionist Germany) when he remarked that this was a:

> period in our history [which] has been well defined as the boundary-making era. Whether we turn to Europe, Asia, Africa, or America, such an endless vista of political geography arises before us, such a vast area of land and sea to be explored and developed; such a vision of great burdens for the white man to take up in far-off regions, dim and indifferent as yet.[77]

Germany as an anti-model, of course, allowed Mackinder or Spykman to fall back on an essentialist notion of what it meant to be British or American in an era of geopolitical struggle. Thus the domestic component of geopolitics emphasized the patriotic need to depoliticize decisions concerning national economic policy or strategy to meet the enemy. In interpreting the threats posed by Germany during this period, such figures were poised to benefit as privileged and professional interpreters of a German phenomenon that was both beguiling and threatening. It is in this sense that—beginning in this geopolitically defined era—we become aware of the fact that, in Klaus-John Dodd's words, "Foreign policy professionals are ... [the] state's privileged storytellers."[78] In sum, the hierarchy of Germany's social structure, its perceived application of scientific expertise to warfare, and its apparent obeisance to geopolitically inspired realism in its approach to foreign policy sparked the elements of an intellectual arms race that was to continue into the Cold War.

Notes

1. I would especially like to acknowledge my debt to such commentators on geopolitics as Neil Smith, Gearóid Ó'Tuathail, Geoffrey Parker, Brian Blouet, and many others mentioned throughout in my endnotes and bibliography. I can at best hope that this essay makes use of their insights and research to extend the range of possible interpretations of the geopolitical phenomenon.

2. Witness Mackinder's erroneous prediction about what control of the heartland would necessarily entail or the myriad failures of defense intellectuals in regard to predicting the behavior of North Vietnam or the strength of the Soviet Union during the Cold War.

3. The recent publication of *The Dictionary of Geopolitics* and its attendant bibliography offer an overview of recent scholarly approaches to the subject. J. O'Loughlin, ed., *Dictionary of Geopolitics* (Westport, Conn.: Greenwood Press, 1994).

4. W. H. Parker, *Mackinder: Geography as an Aid to Statecraft* (Oxford: Clarendon Press, 1982), 161. E. W. Gilbert's view of Mackinder is represented in *Sir Halford Mackinder 1861-1947: An Appreciation of His Life and Work* (Oxford: Clarendon Press, 1961).

5. M. I. Glassner and H. J. de Blij, *Systematic Political Geography* (New York: Wiley, 1980), 263. *The Oxford English Dictionary* first identifies the use of the term "geopolitics" with Rudolf Kjellèn in 1900.

6. Glassner and de Blij, *Systematic*, 263.

7. Glassner and de Blij, *Systematic*, 267.

8. B. Hudson, "The New Geography and the New Imperialism: 1870-1918," *Antipode* 9 (1971): 12.

9. A. Godlewska and N. Smith, eds., *Geography and Empire* (Cambridge, Mass.: Blackwell, 1994), 3. On the attempt to reassert the centrality of space in critical social theory (i.e., to "compose a new critical human geography, an historical and geographical materialism attuned to contemporary political and theoretical challenges"), see E. W. Soja, *Postmodern Geographies: The Reassertion of Space in Critical Social Theory* (London: Verso, 1989), 6.

10. J. Agnew and G. Ó'Tuathail, "Geopolitics and Discourse: Practical Geopolitical Reasoning in American Foreign Policy," *Political Geography* 11 (1992): 192.

11. For the way in which a discourse (in this case that of art history) can mystify the very subject it seeks to elucidate, see J. Berger's *Ways of Seeing* (New York: Viking, 1973).

12. For a creative utilization of this approach as applied to the IMF, see E. J. Popke's "Recasting Geopolitics: The Discursive Scripting of the International Monetary Fund," *Political Geography* 13 (1994): 255-269.

13. Agnew and Ó'Tuathail, "Geopolitics," 195.

14. S. Dalby, "American Security Discourse and Geopolitics," *Political Geography Quarterly* 9 (1988): 174.

15. On the rhetorical power of maps, Y. Lacoste has written of maps that they "define space along the lines set within a peculiar epistemological experience; ... [they] actually transpose a little known piece of concrete reality into an abstraction which serves the practical interest of the state machine." Cited in G. Ó'Tuathail, "The Critical Reading/ Writing of Geopolitics," *Progress in Human Geography* 18 (1994): 327.

16. Klaus-John Dodds and J. D. Sidaway speak of how "the division of the world into heartlands, pivot zones, or inner crescents was underwritten by the epistemological

assumption that the world could be flawlessly represented ... " in "Locating Critical Geopolitics," *Environment and Planning D: Society and Space* 12 (1994): 519.

17. P. Liberman, *Does Conquest Pay? The Exploitation of Occupied Industrial Societies* (Princeton U. Pr, 1996).

18. D. Livingstone, *The Geographical Tradition* (Oxford: Blackwell, 1992), 220.

19. H. Lefebvre, *The Production of Space* (Oxford: Blackwell, 1991), 25.

20. Lefebvre, *Production*, especially 26, 31, 404.

21. H. J. Mackinder, *Britain and British Seas* (Oxford: Clarendon Press, 1902), 343.

22. E. J. Popke, *op. cit.* N. Smith notes that in the last hundred years, the production of space has been "accomplished not through absolute expansion in a given space but through the internal differentiation of global space ... " N. Smith, *Uneven Development: Nature, Capital and the Production of Space* (Oxford: Blackwell, 1984), 88.

23. Smith, *Uneven Development*, 68.

24. Smith, *Uneven Development*, 76-77.

25. *Hansard's Parliamentary Debates*, Fifth Series, House of Commons, 16 May 1917.

26. P. Taylor, *Political Geography of the Twentieth Century: A Global Analysis* (Belhaven Pr., 1993), 24.

27. Mackinder Papers, Oxford School of Geography.

28. G. Ò'Tuathail, *Critical Geopolitics* (Minneapolis: U. of Minnesota Pr., 1996) 50.

29. Isaiah Bowman, *The New World: Problems in Political Geography*, 4th ed. (New York: World Books, 1928), iii.

30. G. Herken, *Counsels of War* (New York: Oxford U. Press, 1987), xiv.

31. A. J. Herbertson, "Geography and Some of its Problems," *Geographical Journal* 36 (1910): 468-79.

32. T. W. Heyck, *The Transformation of Intellectual Life in Victorian England* (1987) locates the rise of these figures in the period 1870-1900.

33. Cited in F. Driver, "Geography's Empire: Histories of Geographical Knowledge," *Environment and Planning D: Society and Space* 10 (1992): 29.

34. See W. Fox's "Geopolitics and International Relations," in C. E. Zoppo and C. Zorgbibe, eds., *On Geopolitics: Classical and Nuclear* (Dordrecht: Martinus Nijhoff Pubs., 1985).

35. T. H. White, "Action Intellectuals," *Life*, June 9, 16, 23, 1967.

36. "The Problem Solvers of National Security," *Business Week*, July 13, 1963.

37. J. A. Smith, *The Idea Brokers: Think Tanks and the Rise of the New Policy Elite* (New York: Free Press, 1991), 22.

38. In one early Coefficient club meeting, Bertrand Russell quit the organization after Leo Amery suggested sending the bulk of Britain's population over to Canada in case of a war with the United States. Minutes of the Coefficient Club, Oxford School of Geography.

39. N. Smith, "Isaiah Bowman; Political Geography and Geopolitics," *Political Geography Quarterly* 3 (1984): 69-76.

40. On the perceptions and realities surrounding this German model, see A. Gat, *The Development of Military Thought: The Nineteenth Century* (Oxford: Clarendon Press, 1992) and T. N. Dupuy, *A Genius for War: The German Army and General Staff, 1810-1945* (Fairfax, Va.: Hero Books, 1984).

41. On the sales figures for Mackinder, see R. Symonds, *Oxford and Empire* (New York: St. Martin's Press, 1986), 145. On Spykman's public reception, see below.

42. The political scientists Harold and Margaret Sprout said of Spykman's book: *"America's Strategy in World Politics* was probably read by more people in America during World War Two than was any other book on international politics ... This book represents a crucial turning point in American thinking about foreign affairs, and its imprint on American thinking is still discernible." H. and M. Sprout, *Foundations of International Politics* (Princeton: Van Nostrand, 1962), 111.

43. L. Freedman, *The Evolution of Nuclear Strategy* (New York: St. Martin's Press, 1981), 12.

44. M. Edley, *Mapping an Empire: The Geographical Construction of British India,1765-1843* (Chicago, Il.: U. of Chicago Pr., 1997).

45. H. J. Mackinder, *Democratic Ideals and Reality* (New York: Holt, 1962), 196.

46. Mackinder, *Democratic Ideals*, 146.

47. A. T. Mahan, *The Influence of Sea Power on History: 1660-1805* (Englewood Cliffs, NJ: Prentice Hall Inc., 1980), 56.

48. B. Semmel, *Imperialism and Social Reform* (Garden City: Doubleday, 1968).

49. N. Smith states in *Uneven Development*, for example, that the "absolute expansion of nation states and of their colonies came to an end with the final partitioning of Africa in the 1880s" (87).

50. K. De Bres, "George Renner and the Great Map Scandal of 1942," *Political Geography Quarterly* 5 (1986): 385-394.

51. N. Spykman, *America's Strategy in World Politics: The United States and the Balance of Power* (New York: Harcourt Brace, 1942), 27.

52. Spykman, *America's Strategy*, 27

53. N. J. Spykman, "Geography and Foreign Policy, I," *American Political Science Review* 32 (Feb. 1938): 29.

54. D. Livingstone, *Geographical*, 29.

55. On this topic, I have especially relied on M. S. Larson, *The Rise of Professionalism* (Berkeley: U. of Calif. Press, 1977), T. L. Haskell, *The Authority of Experts* (Bloomington: Indiana U. Press, 1984), and H. J. Perkin, *The Rise of Professional Society: England Since 1880* (London: Routledge, 1989).

56. M. Larson, *Rise*, xiii.

57. M. Larson, *Rise*, xvi.

58. D. Livingstone, *Geographical*, 15, 168.

59. On the methodologies employed by the modern defense intellectual, see S. J. Heims, *John Von Neumann and Norbert Weiner: From Mathematics to the Technologies of Life and Death* (Cambridge, Mass.: MIT Press) and A. K. Dixit, *Thinking Strategically* (New York: Norton, 1991). For a critical look at the objectivity of science underlying many of the claims of geopoliticians and contemporary defense intellectuals, see S. Woolgar, *Science, The Very Idea* (New York: Tavistock, 1988).

60. Cited in P. Coones, "Mackinder's 'Scope and Methods of Geography' After a Hundred Years," (copy consulted at the Oxford School of Geography).

61. H. J. Mackinder, "On the Scope and Methods of Geography," *Proceedings of the Royal Geographical Society* 9 (1887): 143.

62. H. R. Mill, "Geography," *Encyclopaedia Britannica* (London, 14th ed., 1929), 147.

63. H. R. Mill, ed., *International Geography* (London, 1907), 12.

64. D. Livingstone, *Geographical*, 17.

65. D. Livingstone, *Geographical*, 212-213.

66. Cited in M. J. Wise, "The Scott Keltie Report of 1885 and the Teaching of Geography in Great Britain," *The Geographical Journal* 152 (1986): 380.

67. Wise, "Scott Keltie," 371.

68. D. Livingstone, *Geographical*, 170.

69. B. Hudson, "New Geography," 13.

70. On the history of the RGS, see D. R. Stoddart, *On Geography and its History* (Oxford: Basil Blackwell, 1986), 59-77.

71. *Journal of the Royal Geographical Society of London* 1 (1831): vii.

72. B. Hudson, "New Geography," 13.

73. G. T. Goldie, "Geographical Ideals," *The Geographical Journal* 29 (1907): 8.

74. W. R. Hamilton, "Presidential Address," *Journal of the Royal Geographical Society* 12 (1842): lxxxviii-lxxxix.

75. I. F. Clarke, *Voices Prophesying War: 1763-1984* (London: Oxford U. Press, 1966).

76. Spykman, *America's Strategy in World Politics* (New York: Harcourt Brace, 1942), 212.

77. Cited in Driver, "Geography's Empire," 27.

78. Klaus-John Dodds, "Geopolitics and Foreign Policy: Recent Developments in Anglo-American Political Geography and International Relations," *Progress in Human Geography* 18 (1994): 194.

Chapter 2:
From Balance of Power Politics to Geopolitics

Concerns for the future among the elites in Britain and Germany was, in an important way, linked to the crisis in the five-hundred-year-old tradition in European balance of power politics. The consequences of what Eric Hobsbawm has termed the dual revolution in politics and economics (essentially, the consequences of the French and Industrial revolutions), coupled with the clash between European imperial aspirations and the rise of non-European centers of power, combined by the end of the nineteenth century to usher in a "geopolitical age." Political elites who had managed to identify their interests with the greater interests of the state since the Middle Ages now had to yield control to largely middle class professional caretakers of the modern state apparatus.[1]

The effect of the revolution in Europeans' perception of the world was manifested in a demand for a more modern form of government and social hierarchy. Just as international competition in a new global system was upsetting the parochial European balance of power at the end of the nineteenth century, so too—on the societal level of European nation-states—the principle of governing hierarchy based on birth was continuing to give way, however slowly, to a new hierarchy based on the principles of meritocracy and expert professionalism (i.e., the social and economic change forced upon even less developed European societies attempting to participate in—or defend against—the competitive European state system).

The competitive dynamic in economics and politics—heretofore advantageous for Europeans—became something of a problem by the late nineteenth century.[2] On top of this, the persisting old regime and its methods of maintaining dominance at home and abroad were ceasing to have legitimacy. At home, the ideal of meritocracy threatened social status based on birth, while in interna-

tional affairs the civilian militarist principles embodied in geopolitics were
beginning to supersede an aristocratic and parochial balance of power politics
epitomized by the Austrian statesman Metternich.[3] The professionalization of
geography at the end of the nineteenth century was, after all, intimately connected to the imperialism and intensified international competition beginning in
the 1870s.[4] Even though three major geographical societies were founded only in
the first third of the nineteenth century (the *Société de Geographie de Paris*, in
1821; the *Gesellschaft für Erdkunde zu Berlin*, in 1828; and the Royal
Geographical Society, in 1830), by 1885 there were roughly one hundred geographical societies with a collective membership of fifty thousand.[5]

It has been argued that many of the elements of the competitive dynamic in
economics and international politics described here have uniquely European origins. The classic, parochial European balance of power system (which was being
clearly superseded beginning in the 1890s, according to Geoffrey Barraclough)
had traditionally been defined in Enlightenment terms, as when Edward Gulick
describes the context in which such thinking was born:

> an age of mechanistic philosophy in which Newton was king, Locke, Voltaire,
> and Montesquieu the royal advisers, and in which the religious vogue of Deism
> ... had relegated God to the role of retired watchmaker of the universe [an age
> which] was anything but hostile to the logic of balancing power.[6]

The competitive dynamic in European history was therefore conceived of in
mechanistic terms from the Enlightenment to the late nineteenth century. This
had to do with a competitive state system in which the various states shared fundamental beliefs concerning the "rules" of conflict. As a student of this classical
balance of power notes, the "theory assumed the existence of a state system, an
understood territorial extent for it, a certain homogeneity of the member states,
and a *rational system of estimating power* [emphasis mine]."[7]

The linchpin of the system was the tacit acceptance of the tenets described
above by the landed ruling elites of the various players in balance of power politics. This was relatively painless, given that before the dual revolution, social
structures consisted of relatively static societies of orders (as opposed to classes)
headed by aristocrats who had such values in common as a shared language (by
this time French over Latin), belief in the efficacy of limited war (as witnessed
by the European elite's horror at Napoleon's threat to approximate a kind of total
warfare), and largely feudalistic cultural values.[8] The fundamental purpose of
balance of power politics was to "insure the survival of independent states."[9]
Even the conservative aristocrats at the top of Europe's social pyramids realized
the benefits of (limited) competition at home and abroad. Beginning in the early
modern period, for example, limited competition allowed at home in the form of
mercantilist capitalism provided the new wealth for aristocrats through taxes
which supported and enabled them to finance armies that could compete with
other states in Europe for wealth, power, and prestige in Europe and abroad.

Political scientists argue that there are basically three forms of international
structures: the hegemonic, in which one power dominates all the others; the

bipolar, in which two competing powers tower above all the others; and the balance of power system in which there is a sufficiently diffused spread of power to prevent the emergence of any single over-powering state.[10] The relations among states (as seen at the rarefied level of the political scientist or world historian) are driven by the struggle for power, prestige, and wealth in essentially anarchical conditions. For example, the World War One era German General Bernhardi observed that:

> there is no impartial power that stands above the rivalry of states to restrain injustice, and to use that rivalry with conscious purpose to promote the highest ends of mankind.[11]

In the classic phase of European balance of power politics (1648-1914), the destructive consequences of absolute anarchy were, of course, mitigated by the cosmopolitan values and relatively limited aims of the various ruling elites, not to mention their collective fear of the social upheaval spurred by the extremes of warfare (seen, for example, during the Thirty Years' War).

This classic phase of balance of power politics "worked as well as it did because of its flexibility," according to A. W. DePorte.[12] One of the reasons for this flexibility derived from the relative lack of pressure placed on elites and their cosmopolitanism from below. Before the onset of the nationalism and secularism (that made the nation a focus of almost sacred loyalty in place of institutions such as the Church), "most citizens of the country concerned knew little of its foreign policy and cared even less."[13] The classic balance of power system was not only shielded from attacks from below, but also by the fact that interstate squabbles in Europe could be relieved by exporting them abroad.[14] Thus the Seven Years' War (truly the first world war in many respects) exported Anglo-French conflict to territories as diverse as North America and India, leaving the home territories of the chief warring nations nearly unscathed.

Already by the late eighteenth century this classic balance of power system seemed so effective to its masters that certain observers ascribed to it law-like characteristics. Rousseau, for example, said that:

> The actual [balance of power] system of Europe has precisely the degree which maintains it in a constant state of motion without upsetting it. The balance existing between the powers of these diverse members of this European society is more the work of nature than of art. It maintains itself without effort, in such a manner that if it sinks on one side it reestablishes itself very soon on the other.[15]

The invisible hand that Adam Smith used to describe the self-regulation of internal economic competition was thus ascribed to the relations among states by observers such as Rousseau. Competition, whether on the plane of economics or foreign affairs, seemed capable of self-regulation.

The high point of the system occurred at the Congress of Vienna in the aftermath of the Napoleonic wars. At this congress, Europe's leading diplomats—Castlereagh, Metternich, Hardenbergh, et al.—reinforced the balance of power concept by restructuring Europe so as to prevent any renewed French attempt to gain predominance over the continent. The quarter century of conflict between France and the rest of Europe had severely tested and strained the system's principles of limited war. All the fury of Carnot's nation in arms and Napoleon's military genius could not, however, end European elites' faith in the "managed" competition that balance of power politics offered. The system stressed an ideal balance that could probably only be realized in aesthetically self-conscious similes and metaphors such as the following:

> the system was like an arch in a vault, in which every stone has its function in terms of thrust and counter-thrust, but in which it is the key-stone that ultimately holds them together as a vault. The key-stone here was the fear of hegemony.[16]

How did the classical balance of power system decline in the century after it had apparently shown the immutability of it benefits at the Congress of Vienna? While the diplomats in Vienna showed a renewed faith in the balance of power system, only a century later Woodrow Wilson and Vladimir Lenin were seeking to replace balance of power politics with their own conceptions of international order. In the aftermath of the Vienna settlement, the struggle between France and Britain seemed to be settled once and for all on largely British terms, with France willingly being socialized back into an acceptance of the usual balance of power politics. Britain, for its part, had laid the foundation for the building of a second empire in the period 1793-1815 after the loss of its first empire in America. The nation had reasserted its status as what Ludwig Dehio termed a "flanking power" vis à vis the European continent.

British power, along with that of Russia, occupies a special place in European history for showing a tendency to prevent the political unification of Europe. Such powers as Imperial Spain, France, and Germany had, after all, successively sought to unite the continent against Britain as suggested by the German historian Ludwig Dehio. At the same time, Britain (during Mackinder's post-Columbian epoch) was unique for being a world and European power at the same time. After 1815 Britain, the leading industrial nation, was able to take advantage of its position to instill in the international community its own values of laissez faire capitalism and political liberalism. Britain's very dynamism made likely the universalizing of these values into an ideology.[17] As the international relations scholar A. F. K. Organski points out:

> By 1900, England had conquered 12 million square miles of territory and 360 million people to make up the greatest empire in the world's history and her economic and political influence were felt far beyond the one-quarter of the globe that she ruled formally. Most of the nations of the world were more or less in England's economic orbit. Britannia ruled the waves, and laissez-faire ruled the markets. England and her order were supreme.[18]

The British navy helped to maintain a balance of power system on the European continent that was integrally linked to her empire abroad. Should a continental power arise to attempt the domination of Europe, it could threaten to use the manifold resources of Europe to build a navy that could contest not only British supremacy on the sea, but also the whole nascent international order that Britain stood for.

Britain in its prime was not alone in having vested interests in keeping alive the international system which reflected its own interests.[19] France, for example, became increasingly associated with Britain as both countries built up common ties to political liberalism and developed an antagonism toward the Holy Alliance of Prussia, Austria, and Russia that extolled monarchism and conservatism. By the end of the nineteenth century, of course, the rise of the U.S. to world power could only reinforce the international system Britain had built largely in her own image. The basic ideas behind Britain's international system seemed so powerful that their universality was rarely questioned in an age of progress. Although one might speak of a burgeoning ideological rift between those eastern powers that espoused reactionary domestic policies and those western powers that increasingly espoused the benefits of political liberalism, this rift was relatively minor compared to the role ideology was to play in international affairs after 1917. After all, the ruling elites in post-1815 Britain and France were still dominated by landed aristocracies and their values well up until 1914. A. J. P. Taylor was thus able to note of this period that:

> Ideologies were a minor theme in the seventy years between 1848 and 1918; and the Balance of Power worked with calculation almost as pure as in the days before the French Revolution.[20]

Paradoxically, it was Britain's very preponderance of power that facilitated the efficacy of the "balance" of power system until the 1890s, when the rise of the U.S. and Germany began to challenge this system successfully. As long as Britain's competitors in Europe perceived it as dominant economically and politically, continent-wide warfare was deterred.[21] But what would happen to Britain's position in the world—and the international system with which it was so identified—if such hegemony were challenged within and outside of Europe at the same time?

By the 1890s "contemporary history" may be said to have begun.[22] Britain's position was being eroded in Europe by the rise of German and Russian power in Europe, and by the rise of America and Japan outside of Europe. The "new right" civilian militarist geopoliticians under consideration here, however, did not accept the shift from a Eurocentric balance of power politics to a global system as inevitable. On the contrary, this group's most profound aspiration was that the classical balance of power system could be updated and transformed. If Mackinder and his successors had their way, the survival of the middle-sized European nation-state in the twentieth century would be ensured. This geopolitical conception, in fact, envisioned the world's division between great powers that were "geographically literate," and much smaller powers that were "geographically illiterate" by the standards of geopolitics.

What trends and events of the nineteenth century were causing the balance of power concept no longer to fit the images most European statesmen had when they usually thought about the world of the future? E. V. Gulick argues that:

> The classical balance of power system, based on mechanical premises, cosmopolitanism and the existence of a limited framework, was dated as soon as the great new forces of the nineteenth century gained their feet.[23]

Forces such as nationalism, liberalism, the industrial revolution, mass politics, and even romanticism in this interpretation, are all held to have had a corrosive effect on the system. Nationalism limited the flexibility of statesmen in dealing with one another. Liberals concerned with foreign affairs (most famously represented by Richard Cobden and later Woodrow Wilson) saw such a system as antithetical to the ideals of democracy and as an unnecessarily bloody and hypocritical way of maintaining order in international relations. The industrial revolution, in turn, speeded up technological and social change to the extent that such change threatened the very existence of pre-industrial elites who were experienced and content with the traditional balance of power mechanism.

This interpretation so far ignores the fact that the rational measurement of power, which was an essential enabling assumption of classic balance of power theory, became ever harder to determine. What A. J. P. Taylor has called the "perpetual quadrille of the Balance of Power" depended on the Enlightenment notion that calculation of the balance could be arrived at consensually, in so far as measurements of power were commonly understood and accepted in London, Paris, Berlin, Vienna, and St. Petersburg.

Certainly the course of imperialism was affecting the balance of power system in the nineteenth century, along with such momentous domestic developments as the unfolding of the industrial revolution in Europe. The Berlin Conference of 1885 represented an important turning point in European imperialism. This conference demonstrated Europe's ability to regulate, albeit temporarily, imperial competition. Up until this point, therefore, imperialism abroad was compatible with the smooth running of the balance of power system in Europe.

Earlier in the century the British statesman George Canning was famously able to call "the new world into existence in order to redress the balance of the old." This demonstrated the way in which peace in Europe could be guaranteed by imperial manipulation of the rest of the world. Imperialism could geographically disperse revolutionary impulses abroad that might otherwise have been let loose in Europe itself. George Lichteim, in fact, concluded about this period that "Imperialism abroad [was] an extension of domestic politics at home."[24] But the Westernization of the world was soon threatening to redound negatively on Europe as the space itself in which imperial competition took place became increasingly limited. And, as Lichteim further observes, the "European nation state, after preparing the ground for the emergence of trans-continental imperialism, prompted the destruction of Europe's historic pre-eminence."[25]

Imperialism could only serve as an outlet for the forces embodied in the competitive dynamic up until the point at which the rest of the world was formally divided up. When this competition to expand territorially, culturally, and economically finally turned back upon Europe itself, beginning especially in the 1890s, international anarchy escaped the bounds placed upon it by the balance of power system. While the European nation-state provided ultimate order at home through its monopoly on violence, in relations between states no such higher authority existed to regulate disputes. Traditionally, anarchy had been contained by the explicit and tacit rules of the balance of power system. In the aftermath of the revolutions of 1848, for example, the elites of Europe were anxious not to let the forces of popular politics seriously impede the autonomy of the state, especially in the area of foreign affairs. The examples of Russia's aid to Austria in putting down the Hungarian uprising during the revolutions of 1848 and the care that France took in not spreading revolution across the Rhine demonstrated how relatively unified Europe's political elites were in maintaining the basic cosmopolitan tenets of the balance of power.

By the 1890s, less confidence could be shown for the managed competition represented by the old balance of power system. While the centripetal forces of the balance played their expected role during 1848, the centrifugal forces noted by geopoliticians thereafter gained increasing sway by the 1890s. Traditional balance of power politics assumed that realism:

> an offspring of modern science and the Enlightenment, would offer statesmen the ability to calculate power and national interest ... [to] create order out of anarchy and thereby moderate the inevitable conflicts of autonomous, self-centered, and competitive states.[26]

The crisis felt by Europe's ruling *ancien régimes* in managing domestic and foreign affairs came, therefore, to a climax between 1890 and 1945. F. H. Hinsley describes the themes which dominated this period when he remarks that:

> the international unsettlement which began in the 1890s and continued until the end of the Second World War, ... [make the] years to 1945 the longest stretches of unrelieved disorder in modern times.[27]

This unsettlement, of course, coincided with what Mackinder diagnosed as the onset of a post-Columbian epoch; an epoch in which the outward expansion of Europe had ceased at the very same time non-European centers of power were arising to contest European hegemony. The period 1870 to 1945, then, may be called the geopolitical age in so far as geopoliticians and statesmen began to interpret maps of the world in an increasingly pessimistic manner. This should come as no surprise, since, as P. R. Viotti and M. V. Kauppi maintain:

> Dominant schools of thought in international relations are as much a part of the *Zeitgeist* of their age as are dominant theories of art and literature; all are part of the *ductus* of a culture.[28]

Just as the basic postulates of balance of power politics were so deeply rooted that few felt the need to formalize them, so too in this new geopolitical age would few (outside of the geopoliticians themselves) bother to be self-conscious in articulating the geopolitical assumptions that uniquely marked European international relations in the first half of the twentieth century. The influence of such geostrategic thinkers as Mahan, Mackinder, Haushofer, and Spykman on statesmen as diverse as Theodore Roosevelt and Adolf Hitler attests to this reality. As E. H. Carr put it, "theory, as it develops out of practice and develops into practice, plays its own transforming role in the process."[29] Just as the balance of power had taken on a life of its own in framing the reaction of statesmen in the past to contemporary events, so too in the geopolitical era would concern for such novel phrases and terms as "landpower versus seapower," "manpower," and "heartland" pervade and influence the thinking of this period's statesmen.

Michael Mandelbaum observes that "In arming themselves, states often imitate their putative adversaries."[30] In the race to see who would *geographically* dominate Europe in the period 1870-1945, civilian militarists in Britain and Germany took to envying each other for virtues seen to be lacking at home. In seeking to provide the proper mental armament for the executors of British state interests, Halford Mackinder pointedly recommended and admired German organization, efficiency, and awareness of the importance of landpower in the new century. Karl Haushofer, on the other hand, returned the compliment through his own admiration for the tremendous geographical extent of the British Empire. The question being indirectly asked by these and other geopolitical thinkers was, how (and by whom) in this post-classical balance of power era was Europe to be organized in the twentieth century? Geopolitical thinkers thought through this question in ways that emphasized struggle and competition rather than cooperation.[31] Armed with the new perception of world politics provided by the likes of Mahan, Mackinder, and Haushofer, even non-expert observers of geopolitics could say:

> Statesmen and general staffs rationalized their new preferences with the help of 'geopolitics', a doctrine designed to show that the European nation state had become too small for the new age of empire building.[32]

Just as the Italian city-state had been superseded in favor of the larger entity of the modern nation-state represented in northwestern Europe in the sixteenth century, geopoliticians at the end of the nineteenth century similarly theorized the end of the nation-state in the face of continentally-sized states. Whereas earlier strategists and political theorists from Machiavelli to Mazzini had called for the effective unification of potential nation-states such as Italy, Mackinder, Haushofer, and Spykman now saw world powers in the twentieth century as being necessarily dependent upon the effective unification of whole continents by territorially aggressive states. For all their differences, the old balance of power politics and the new geopolitics assumed the need for enlightened elites to avoid the advent of fully realized democracies, since, as theorists of both schools have historically argued:

> democracy, with its slow moving processes, has been less well adapted to the pursuit of balanced power than absolutism, which has benefited ... from more swiftly moving machinery in foreign policy.[33]

The geopoliticians were united around the idea, as expressed by the historian Michael Geyer, that the "organization of destruction has become a 'primary' means of social integration" in the twentieth century.[34] In preparing to fight future wars, the geopoliticians felt the need to give up the idea of limited war, since it was assumed that all resources would have to be mobilized in ensuring victory in future wars. Geopoliticians, unlike earlier balance of power theorists, saw the need to link domestic and foreign policy in order to make the nation prepared for twentieth century conflict. Geo-domestic organization of the home front would provide the foundation upon which the state could practice a successful geopolitics abroad. In effect, hierarchies had to be reconfigured at home in order to ensure a place in the new international hierarchy. The stakes were indeed high since, with the decay of British power and the classical balance of power which Britain supported, a succeeding power would be able to leave its imprint on the larger European and international orders.[35] As Gramsci pointed out, just as domestic social hierarchies are mediated by culture, so too on the international scene are there great powers seeking to shape to their advantage the rules and language through which international relations are conducted.

In contrast to the geopolitical vision, one of the reasons that the balance worked so well after 1815 is that Europe's statesmen were concerned to regulate their conflicts so as not to incite unrest at home.[36] As is well-known, revolution was anathema to that quintessential representative of Europe's old elite, Metternich. By the 1890s, however, the rise in the power of public opinion was such that new, preferably scientific, rationalizations had to be developed in order to support foreign policy choices that had previously been nakedly made in the interests of *raison d'état*. For, in the unfolding of modern European history, "governments everywhere have become less independent of the societies they govern."[37] The demand was thus created for a geopolitically informed rethinking of interstate rivalry; a rethinking that would take into account the new power of national sentiment and that would try to channel it into geopolitically justified purposes.

The shift from a balance of power politics to a geopolitical management of a heightened interstate competitive dynamic beginning in the 1890s is also linked to the contemporaneous crisis in the ability to measure national power. Changes in war, economics, technology, and assumptions about the future all conjoined to make measurement of power problematical at this time, thereby helping to further erode a balance of power tradition (which had come to depend on at least the perception that accurate power measurement was possible). By the last third of the nineteenth century, the Heraclitean maxim that "all is in flux" seemed to apply with special force to the difficulties associated with measuring the power of nations. It has been said of this period that "states ... became both more pre-occupied with relative power and less confident in their ability to assess it."[38] Certainly the advent of mass armies inaugurated by Carnot's call for a *levée en masse* in 1793 and the subsequent industrialization of European warfare in the next century raised the demands on the state to higher and higher levels.

The Franco-Prussian War (1870-71) indicated to Europeans the importance of railways, mass armies, long-term planning by a general staff, and the use of the most up-to-date technology. This war made clear the new realities of modern conflict and the need to understand them effectively lest one's country risk a defeat on the order that France suffered. It has been said in this regard that the:

> nature of military power changed, especially after 1870, and this contributed to the breakdown of the Vienna system. Steel production and railroads took their place beside territory and population as the sinews of military might.[39]

Yet how was power to be measured after 1870? In an earlier age strategists thought in terms of small professional armies operating under the command of aristocratic officers who had a vested interest in obeying certain tacit rules to limit war and the aims for which wars were fought. Clausewitz represented the apogee of this tradition in his attempt to keep war "rational," professional, and limited through his emphasis on the need for limited political ends to govern military means.

In sum, if it is true that "the formulation of accurate assessments [of power] is widely held to be the single most important prerequisite of successful states-manship," the end of the nineteenth century witnessed a crisis in the ability of European statesmen to assess adequately power relationships.[40] What kind of strategist—what kind of strategical thinking—could simultaneously take into account the fact of industrialization, the existence of railroads, and the role of mass armies in the modern competition between states? While Clausewitz reck-oned with updating military strategy to take into account the effect of Napoleonic innovations, by the end of the nineteenth century civilian militarists (typified by Mackinder and later Haushofer) were coming into their own, armed with a professionally authoritative knowledge that could provide the necessary foundation upon which to theorize about these changes. This expertise was espe-cially of interest, given the "strong organizational forces acting to push modern states away from a unified assessment process and toward a more fragmented appropriation of that ideal."[41] The modern phenomenon of an ever-increasing division of labor affected even the state as it and its activities expanded, making it more difficult for unified decision-making to occur.

With the eclipse of the balance of power system in favor of a geopolitics that took into account an emerging world system, the civilian militarist-cum-geopoli-tician promised to offer not simply a pure military strategy, but a synthetic view of strategy in an age of increasing cultural fragmentation and division of labor. If it may be said that—in the period of contemporary history beginning in 1890—(*pace* Clemenceau) war was becoming too important to be left to the generals, it was also becoming clear to many geopoliticians that thinking about conflict in

the twentieth century was too important to be left to the old ruling class or the
new professional politician (beholden as the latter was to the dictates of popular
opinion). In an age when professional expertise as a rationale for a social hierarchy (a rationale based on efficiency and merit) began to overtake traditional
forms of social hierarchy (those based on birth and tradition), the geopolitician
as civilian militarist came into his own as a purveyor of strategic world views in
a critical transitional period for the middle-sized European state trying to measure power in an uncertain age.

The geopolitician thus strove to update the state's competitive strategy in an
era when the traditional rules of the game no longer seemed to apply. Because
civilian militarists aspired to scientific objectivity, they and their audience rarely
took into account the fact that:

> assessment is clearly a crucial 'intervening variable' between objective changes
> in the structures of the international system and the behavior of individual
> states. Assessments are related to but not directly determined by reality. They
> are themselves, in turn, related to but not fully determinative of policy.[42]

As we have seen, assessments concerning the future loomed large in the thinking
of civilian militarists and statesmen in both Britain and Germany. In trying to
master the competitive dynamic, civilian militarists and geopoliticians sought to
show how their nations could adapt to the competitive dynamic as it appeared to
be evolving in its new twentieth century form. Concerning these civilian militarists, it might rightly be said that:

> The urge to explain is not born of idle curiosity alone. It is produced also by
> the desire to control, or at least to know if control is possible, rather than
> merely predict.[43]

As in the tale of the sorcerer's apprentice, the competitive dynamic sped out
of direct European control in the nineteenth century (exported as it was around
the world through European imperialism). That the geopoliticians sought to
develop strategies founded on the authority of science to gird their nations
through the perilous times ahead merely highlights the fact that "activities like
interpreting, proving, marshalling evidence and making observations have
always been 'social' in the more phenomenological sense of the term."[44]
Mackinder, Haushofer, and Spykman were not disingenuous in their belief that
foreign policy could be founded upon the scientifically based facts of geography.
This belief seemed better than allowing foreign policy to be left in the hands of a
decadent elite. In an age of heightened competition in which power was becoming increasingly difficult to measure, the comparative advantage a seemingly
scientific and coherent strategy could bring to a "knowledgeable state" was
immense.[45]

The meaning of national power itself became a nebulous concept amid the
welter of changes taking place in late nineteenth-century European society. For,
if it is true that a nation's strength depends on what other nations perceive it to

be, then the end of the nineteenth century showed how problematical measuring a state's relative power was becoming. The rise of non-European powers like America, Russia, and Japan—coupled with the threat to British hegemony posed by Germany—greatly clouded such calculations. Statesmen in London and Berlin now not only had to take into account the effects of their actions on a handful of other European powers, but now had to take into account all the new non-European powers engaged in the emerging world system. It has been said, for instance, that "Power ... is not a thing; it is part of a relationship between individuals or groups of individuals."[46] The problems posed by the concept of "power in the eighteenth and early nineteenth centuries was less intricate than it is today, simply because the instruments of power were themselves less complex."[47]

During the same time that H. G. Wells wrote (in his *Anticipations* of 1902) that "war is being drawn into the field of the exact sciences" and that "we must educate or perish in the twentieth century,"[48] Halford Mackinder also showed great concern about the state of British education. Once the old elites demonstrated their obsolescence by plunging Europe into war in 1914—a war that could not subsequently be stopped by the old methods of elite diplomacy—geopoliticians sensed a need for professional management of foreign affairs. It was now the task of self-appointed middle class civilian militarists like Mackinder to mobilize such professional energies on behalf of the great geopolitical project of maintaining British power. In short, geopoliticians promised to fend off the vagaries of Clausewitz's fog of war through the rigors of their analytical technique.

A. J. P. Taylor's aside that "Men began to think statistically in the later nineteenth century" helps make understandable the geopoliticians' attempt to speak in a seemingly more precise and scientific way about the grand strategy of nations.[49] Indeed, thinking about international conflict was becoming more abstract and theoretical as command of actual fighting forces was left to generals who moved farther and farther away from the battlefield. The geopolitician's concern with worst-case scenarios based on the abstract capabilities of a potential opponent (rather than on his intentions) illustrates the general tendency of the age to seek to manage the imponderable through scientific means. The beginning of the first modern arms race between Britain and Germany over naval strength showed that the boundaries between peace and war were themselves eroding, putting the nation in need of the constant war-preparedness advocated by geopoliticians.

Given this trepidation over the future, and the concomitant concern among geopoliticians to control the future through a new spatial science, it is not surprising that:

> there was the idea that learning too must be placed at the service of the nation;
> then the theoretician could provide solutions which, in their end effect, were
> eminently practical.[50]

The power of maps during this period (1870-1945) to shape the cartographic consciousness among citizens of wary middle-sized European nation-states at the turn of the twentieth century should not be underestimated. As is said even today, "Men have already learned to distrust words and figures but they have not yet learned to distrust maps."[51] Geopolitical maps have always been capable of putting forth powerful political messages. Included among the repertoire of visual devices that can be used by a mapmaker are: the manipulation of text to describe the map, manipulation of map scale, willful non-identification of the projection being used, manipulation of emotionally laden symbols and colors, and selectivity in choice in regard to highlighting or downplaying the many possible features of a given reality a map is supposed to represent.[52] The geopolitician offered a new, visualized paradigm of a nation's grand strategy that could make what had appeared in the past as intractable foreign policy problems suddenly amenable to purely technical solutions For example, political scientists have recognized that realism in foreign policy theory owes much to geopolitics and its apparent authoritativeness.[53] The urge to objectify political problems in modern society by framing them in scientific terms is appealing because decisions reached by such a tactic are made to seem indisputable and beyond the messy debates inherent in democratic politics. Indeed, Mackinder and subsequent geopoliticians often believed that authoritarian governments were more capable of adapting to shifts on the international scene than were democracies. Even Woodrow Wilson, a self-proclaimed opponent of *Realpolitik*, believed, according to R. S. Baker, that peace could be achieved in international affairs if outstanding problems were settled "not by diplomats or politicians each eager to serve his own interests, but by *dispassionate* scientists—geographers, ethnologists, economists—who had made studies of the problem involved."[54]

Taken altogether, the unfolding consequences of the dual revolution and the decline of a parochial European balance of power system in favor of a world balance of power system put ever increasing pressure on traditional ruling elites in countries like Britain and Germany. The pressure created an incentive to seek new strategies for maintaining world power aspirations. At home, both the left and the "new" right opposition to mainstream governments in Britain and Germany agreed that government in the hands of the old aristocracy was not efficient enough to grapple with the perceived demands of the day. For the "respectable" left (represented by the Fabians in Britain and the Social Democrats in Germany) government appeared to be conducted for the narrow interests of a small, and still largely landed ruling elite, whose interests did not coincide with those of the nation at large. The new right after the 1890s, on the other hand (represented most stridently by the various army and navy leagues in both Britain and Germany along with a growing contingent of civilian militarists such as Mackinder and Haushofer), had a more ambivalent attitude toward their nations' old elites.

The new right in both countries admired the social and cultural traditions upheld by these elites and believed in the necessity of social hierarchy. Yet the new right felt that the old regime must be reformed or replaced (if only for its own good) in order to protect the more important long-term interests of the nation. Classic theorists on the nature of elites, such as Gaetano Mosca, Robert Michels, and Vilfredo Pareto agree with the idea of "the ineluctable fact of inequality," an idea shared by members of the new right civilian militarists discussed here.[55] Michels' "iron law of oligarchy" was not necessarily a static concept for explaining the social differentiation that civilian militarists tended to accept. Pareto, for example, argued that a "governing elite is always in a state of slow and continuous transformation" as it sought to adapt to changing conditions. Indeed, a given elite could only have become an elite according to these theorists if it possessed—at least originally—some quality that gave it initial success and allowed it to legitimize rationally its predominant role in the host society. In Mosca's words, "members of a ruling minority regularly have some attribute, real or apparent, which is highly esteemed and very influential in the society in which they live."[56]

New right civilian militarists in both Britain and Germany, of course, not only accepted this fact but sought to marshal it for the more effective pursuit of national expansion abroad by arguing that they were the new class most able to guide their nations' destinies. Their basic quarrel with the traditional landed elites concerned, in Mosca's terms, the ruling "attributes" that would justify social hierarchy in the coming century. Would society remain divided into classes with governing power divided between landed elites and the upper-middle classes, or would, as the geopoliticians and other civilian militarists increasingly desired, a meritocracy dedicated to national power ultimately replace aristocracy? Could "high politics" remain in the hands of the fifty to one hundred individuals (who themselves came from an aristocracy that Gladstone labeled the "upper ten thousand") during an era which Mackinder and others saw as being defined by the pressure put upon governments to become more efficient and rational? As the historians of imperialism R. Robinson and J. Gallagher put it, foreign policy before World War One was "still made at the house parties, not by the man in the street or the man in the Stock Exchange."[57]

The move from a social hierarchy based on birth to one based on wealth and merit was of course gradual and incomplete. Such a model is in fact simply an ideal type, a heuristic device useful for explaining certain trends in social organization that have to be accounted for during this geopolitical age. The geopolitical world view represented a threat to the old order only in that it demanded certain reforms in government and society for the sake of a more efficient conduct of international struggles to come. Yet reform would be hard given the fact that heretofore "Reference to rank and hierarchy had been the foundation of European life."[58] The geopolitician could, in the end, countenance rank and hierarchy only so long as they contributed to, or at least did not hinder, the task of mobilizing society for the interminable struggles (geographically defined) to come. Those who could so organize society that it would be efficient in maintaining a successful foreign policy would, of course, have to be on top of the new social hierarchy.

As Arno Mayer points out, the old regime did not simply collapse in the face of a vigorous bourgeoisie, as it theoretically should have done according to Marxist theory. The old elites did attempt to adjust to some of the realities of the new quality and tempo of interstate competition that Mackinder and other civilian militarists were trying to publicize. The formal imperialism of the last quarter of the century showed a desire among European elites to peg out claims for the future on maps, thereby positioning themselves for the new international system. Yet, with "the remobilization of the old order [largely in reaction to the threats to that order mentioned earlier], Social Darwinism became the dominant worldview of Europe's ruling and governing classes."[59] In a world perceived as marked by the constant and growing competition between nations for space, Social Darwinism seemed a realistic philosophy to civilian militarists and others. Geopoliticians added their own twist to this "prevailing view of the world order [held by governing elites, military circles, and imperial organizations] which stressed struggle, change, competition, the use of force, and the organization of national resources to enhance state power."[60]

In sum, Britain's mission in this Social Darwinist atmosphere became one of defending an already dominant but overextended position as well as the balance of power system itself. Germany, meanwhile, sought to expand outside of its continental base in order to remain a great power in an enlarged world power system. In Britain the geopolitical question focused on how to defend the British Empire in the coming century, while in Germany the geopolitical question turned on how to expand successfully so as to become one of the charmed members of a necessarily small (by geographic logic) club of great world empires in the approaching century. As Lichteim writes, in Germany:

People have to believe in something, and the ruling classes of a decrepit ... empire were only too glad to hitch their wagon to the star of an ultra-modern movement which proclaimed the imminent demise of democracy and the nation state, in the name of geopolitics and the need for larger trans-national or transcontinental agglomerations.[61]

The race for efficiency at home and pursuit of geopolitical aims abroad was, obviously, not universally admired among the ruling elites of middle-sized European states. The very forces represented by Americanization that promised to define the nature of international competition in the twentieth century—such as industrial vitality and social leveling—were antithetical to even the most adaptive of landed elites. W. T. Stead, for example, argued that the majority of average Europeans favored Americanization and all that this symbolized in the way of increased wealth, social leveling, and efficiency. He believed that "It is otherwise with the sovereigns and nobles, who represent feudalism and the Old World monarchical and aristocratic ideas which have as their European centre the Courts of Berlin and Vienna."[62]

The civilian militarist project of remobilizing and reforming the old governing elite could, as we shall see in Mackinder's Britain or Haushofer's Germany, go only so far before that elite would crack under the strains of World

War One and begin to heed the call of the irrational thereafter. Geopoliticians could not help but be aware of the "general leveling of traditional hierarchies," when the "plurality of spaces, the philosophy of perspectivism, the affirmation of positive and negative spaces, the restructuring of forms, and the contracting of social distance assaulted a variety of hierarchical orderings."[63] Challenges against the old governing régimes both at home and abroad were ultimately too overwhelming for the elites to adapt to. The new right civilian militarist *cri de coeur* over Europe's competitive unpreparedness helped, ironically, to spur the disastrous overreaction of European governments to the crises of 1914. Mayer even goes so far as to comment that "The inner spring of Europe's general crisis was the overreaction of old elites to overperceived danger to their overprivileged positions."[64]

The end of the "long nineteenth century" in 1914 marked the last time that even vestiges of the old régimes in Europe would try to manipulate balance of power diplomacy in the classical manner. The war that elites initiated in 1914 turned into a total war that they could not stop at their will, as they should have been able to do according to the tenets of the old balance of power system. The refusal of geopoliticians to acknowledge a gap between domestic and foreign policy seemed to be confirmed by the experience of war. In sum, the Metternichian ideal of a managed balance of power competition between the European great powers (one that would limit competition for the sake of domestic peace at home) appeared quaint by the 1890s and dead by 1918 to the geopolitically informed.

The rise of expert professionals in the period before World War One indicated a new way of justifying social hierarchy at home and power politics abroad. As Harold Perkin notes, "The twentieth century is not, *pace* Franklin D. Roosevelt, the century of the common man but of the uncommon and increasingly professional expert."[65] The geopoliticians were in their own right models of the professional expert attempting to persuade state and society about the usefulness of their expertise. The message of the professional class at the end of the nineteenth century was that the internecine strife between the working class, middle class, and the aristocracy could be adjudicated and tamed by a neutral, rational class of experts whose main aims were the attainment of social efficiency and social harmony at home.

Yet the real versus the imagined benefits of the services of the professional class was not always clear for, as Perkin argues, "That ... the service [of the new expert class] is neither essential nor efficient is no obstacle in principle. It only needs to be thought so by those providing and receiving it."[66] The politics of national efficiency espoused by Mackinder and later civilian militarists sought to sublimate old class conflicts in favor of the higher goal of protecting the nation's interests in the rigorously competitive climate of the twentieth century. Scientific rhetoric was a necessary component to persuading state and society of the merits of expert guidance in matters foreign and domestic.

A new elite and its requisite social hierarchy would seem justifiable to geopoliticians since, according to W. T. Stead:

The future belongs not to brawn but to brains, and the nation which acquires both, as we unfortunately are not doing at the moment, will inevitably [succeed]. It may be said that it is no use looking for the conversion of our governing classes.[67]

The civilian militarist, therefore, even before 1914, felt it incumbent upon himself to re-imagine hierarchies among nations and classes. The crisis of classical liberalism in the face of neo-mercantilist policies, imperialism, and a decidedly un-cosmopolitan nationalism was reflected in a gradual turning to the right of the middle and professional classes.

Civilian militarists before the war, as part of the new professional class, sought to do away with party and class strife at home in order to act strongly abroad. As British Navy League pamphlet declaimed, "be neither Conservatives nor Liberals, but something greater and better, be Englishmen."[68] The British journalist Garvin wrote, for example, that "The twentieth-century ... is going to be dominated in politics as in trade by the widest and strongest combinations of the most efficient individuals."[69] Meritocracy would allow professionals such as the geopoliticians to implement social imperialist policies at home to achieve such "combinations" in order to pursue geopolitics abroad. Social imperialism itself was, as one observer puts it, "designed to draw all classes together in defense of the nation and empire and aimed to prove to the least well-to-do classes that its interests were inseparable from those of the nation."[70]

Eric Hobsbawm asserts, apropos of the intellectual atmosphere in which geopolitical thought arose, that:

> every historian is struck by the fact that the revolutionary transformation of the scientific world view in these years forms part of a more general, and dramatic, abandonment of established and often long accepted values, truths and ways of looking at the world and structuring it conceptually.[71]

According to this theory, the Newtonian world of three dimensions and mechanical causation was giving way to an Einsteinian world of popularized relativism and simultaneity. European imperial expansion, coupled with such changes in technology symbolized by the railroad, telephone, bicycle, submarine cable, automobile, and the airplane, helped usher in this new world. One effect of this view on those in positions of power was that the world, now all but mapped and parceled out by Europeans, could now witness how quick the ramifications of decisions taken in a nation's capital were on far away areas. The imperial historian and theorist J. R. Seeley highlighted the consequences of bringing in large areas of the non-European world into a single world system when he argued that "in the modern world distance has very much lost its effect ... there are signs of a time when states will be vaster than they have hitherto been."[72]

The geopoliticians proved to be sensitive to possible implications of such changes and, therefore, sought to have their nations prepared to protect their spatial domains in a world closing to new opportunities for geographic expansion. Mackinder's fundamental worry, for example, concerned the development of a vast continental European state based on parts of Eastern Europe and Russia that now seemed possible because of the railroad and telegraph which could annihilate the effect of distance on the transport of men and materiel. Similar views pervaded the thought of German and American geopoliticians. A world that had seemed infinitely open to untrammeled expansion for half a millennium now seemed, by the end of the nineteenth century, closed and threatening.

New geopolitical maps could portray the entire world in a visually convincing and holistic fashion, showing and interpreting political and economic interconnections between regions that would not have been possible before the advent of the steamship, train, submarine cable, or telegraph. If it is true (as Donald Lowe believes) that "the field of perception determines the content of knowledge," then the geopoliticians depended on the revolution in European conception of time and space (caused by the new inventions) which made the world seem "closed" and time non-absolute. The British Prime Minister Salisbury indirectly alluded to this new sense of simultaneity in everyday experience when he commented on how the telegraph "combined together almost at one moment ... the opinions of the whole intelligent world with respect to everything that is passing at that time upon the face of the globe."[73] The civilian militarists believed, therefore, that they had to be very precise and scientific in developing foreign policy strategies for the state, since mistakes would be costly and rebound quickly and negatively on the home territory in a spatially closed world system. As decision-making became more complicated for the middle-sized European state from the 1890s on, the quickening pace of communication itself made "perception of the present ... more disconnected, begging for explanation and interpretation."[74]

As an example of how this process affected foreign affairs, one can see in the example of Germany a self-fulfilling perception that time and space were literally running out for its hopes to secure an imperial place in the world system of the new century. This perception thus goaded Germany into crudely spatializing its foreign, and even domestic, policy before World War One. In Britain, Seeley's belief that "the process of state-building has been governed by strict conditions of space" indicated to him and to others at this critical juncture that Britain risked being overshadowed by such giants as Russia and America. What Stephen Kern says concerning the science fiction writers of this time might be applied with equal force to nascent geopoliticians, namely that they:

> reached out for the future as if it were a piece of overripe fruit ... Their stories came into vogue on a grand scale, indicating that, the future was becoming as real to their generation as the past had been for readers of the Gothic novel and historical romance.[75]

Geopoliticians presented their own visual narratives about the zero-sum contest for space with clear beginnings and endings. These beginnings and endings told of how states expand because they are vigorous and geographically informed and decline because they become less vigorous and geographically misinformed. The importance of these visual narratives lies in the fact that:

> While images and representations of nature cannot influence or change nature unless an action taken is based on a correct understanding of its structure, images about nature or the human world can change human reality, irrespective of their truth value, as soon as they are translated into actions and behavior and gain power over the minds of men.[76]

These geopolitically-based visual narratives indicated that geographical opportunities existed for Britain to defend her world empire and for Germany to enter the club of world empires. Geopoliticians hoped to facilitate the "annexation of the space of others, [the] outward movement of people and goods, and the expansive ideology of imperialism [that] was a spatial expression of the active appropriation of the future."[77] While a great part of the nineteenth century saw European energies and interests diverted outside of Europe for purposes of economic and political expansion, the twentieth century was foreseen by the geopoliticians to be an era in which European competitive energies' would turn back on the home continent itself.

Russian and American attitudes toward the future during this period were, on the whole, optimistic compared to those of Germany and Britain. The railroad and its potential for linking up the resources—both human and non-human—of the vast Russian empire for military purposes had intrigued geopoliticians like Mackinder as well as Russian statesmen. The Russian Minister of Finance Count Witte, for example, had discussed the benefits of the trans-Siberian railroad in a memo to Alexander III in 1892, informing him of the promise it offered in making available the wealth of Siberia, in revolutionizing world trade by opening the Chinese market, and in outflanking the British empire in India.[78] A fundamental axiom of geopolitical thought was that through intensified internal development, it would only be a matter of time before Russia began to dwarf Britain and Germany in power potential. American optimism was summed up by Theodore Roosevelt's promise to intervene in Europe to restore the balance of power there if the need arose.[79] That such non-European powers as Russia, the U.S., and Japan felt confident of continued expansion in the future (while European powers such as Britain and Germany were, at best, ambivalent about their future prospects) underscored the waning European vision of Faustian possibilities for expansion that Spengler described as:

> the expansion of the Copernican world picture into that aspect of stellar space that we possess today; the development of Columbus's discovery into a world wide command of the earth's surface by the West ... the passion of our civilization for swift transit, the conquest of the air, the exploration of the Polar regions and the climbing of almost impossible mountain peaks.[80]

Economics and Geopolitics

Civilian militarists were well aware of the interconnections between economics and politics before World War One. Mackinder, as we shall see, was an ardent supporter of Chamberlain's tariff reform campaign, while Haushofer believed that the scientifically justified attainment of *Lebensraum* for Germany would support his autarkic economic philosophy quite suitably. As the balance of power system with its emphasis on limited war waged by middle-sized European states gave way, in geopoliticians' minds, to a geopolitical age of total war between transcontinental states, economic calculations and assumptions became ever more important in the thinking of these theorists. As the boundaries between war and peace grew weaker as states constantly prepared for war even in times of formal peace, so too did the boundaries separating economics and politics become attenuated. Europe increasingly opted, by the end of the nineteenth century, for neo-mercantilist economic policies. France and Germany led the way in this regard, followed by Russia and the U.S., until even responsible political voices could be heard calling for an end to unrestricted free trade in Britain.[81]

The second industrial revolution in industries such as electricity and steel helped to cause a crisis of overproduction which led to the Great Depression. Between 1873 and 1896, the free trade system and international order associated with British power began to come under vociferous attack. It has been said for instance that "Darwin not Cobden became the prophet for the world's economic order" during this period.[82] Big industries, fighting and competing over scarce markets, sought salvation in protectionism and recourse in monopolies and cartels as preferred forms of organization. Civilian militarists such as Mackinder took note of these new economic realities by realizing that this depression, in David Calleo's words, "significantly affected not only domestic politics but also relations among states."[83]

In a period that Joseph Chamberlain was to call an "age of aggregation" in politics and economics, civilian militarists in Britain and Germany advocated a more efficient division of labor at home. Social imperial policies such as the "scientific management" of various activities (including the geopoliticization of foreign policy thinking) was itself a "child of the Great Depression."[84] It was thought that only by near ruthless self-exploitation of the limited resources at home in Britain and Germany could such states compete with the huge agglomerations of power represented by Russia and the U.S. Intensification of social efficiency movements at home—a kind of internal imperialism—came to substitute for expansion abroad as the outer world was systematically divided up between the great powers. The forces that were let loose by the dual revolution of political liberalism and free market economics in the nineteenth century, in other words, did not upset the classic postulates of the balance of power system so long as these potentially destructive forces could be exported abroad in the form of imperial economic and political expansion. But by 1914 the world was already formally divided up between the expansionist powers.

As the nation itself in the neo-mercantilist era took on some of the attributes of a corporate entity, competition between nations took on a totalistic quality not seen before when the non-European world still seemed passively open to Europe's expansive energies. As Hajo Holborn remarks:

> Previously merchants or travelers could cross all political frontiers without special permits and passports except in Russia; but militarization laid the groundwork for treating the national societies as independent, isolated entities. In the contracting geographical conditions of the age of modern capitalism the national states, for reasons of defense, grew more like medieval cities.[85]

Competition between states in the coming age of geopolitics appeared to civilian militarists as more and more of a zero-sum game, one in contrast with the harmonization of interests and reciprocal compensation associated with the old balance of power politics. The neo-mercantilism fostered by the late nineteenth-century depression provided useful support for geopolitical theories. As Fritz Fischer asserts on the subject of German war aims, it appeared to many observers within Germany and abroad during this time that:

> The economic competition reinforced the idea ... that in the twentieth century only 'world states' of continental proportions like the U.S. and Russia, or those with overseas empires like Britain and France, could hope to play leading roles in world affairs.[86]

With the rest of the world divided up by such large imperial powers as France and Britain, many in Germany came to believe that only the reorganization of central Europe into a self-sufficient *Mitteleuropa* could provide the necessary geographic base for participation in the new world power system.

The Anglo-German Duel

As we have seen, geopoliticians as diverse as Mackinder, Haushofer, and Spykman were greatly influenced by the nature of the competition between Britain and Germany before World War One. These geopoliticians tended to reach the conclusion that, as the German historian Michael Geyer puts it, "If Britain was the model for Europe in the nineteenth century, Germany played the same role for the twentieth."[87] Britain's liberal tradition, free market economics, and empire were both feared and admired by many Germans in the nineteenth century. From the late nineteenth century on, however, many in Britain became conscious of Germany as both a model of efficiency and organization and as a threat to Britain's position as the premier world power. Civilian militarists such as Mackinder and Haushofer found inspiration for their geopolitical ideas from the competition between their two countries. As has been noted about this phenomenon, "The conceptions which are developed by one society about another in fact usually say more about the society which develops those conceptions than about the one which is their object."[88]

Geopoliticians were intrigued not only by economic and foreign policy conflicts between the two powers, but they were intrigued as well by the cultural and
social ramifications of this conflict. If it can be said, in the words of Paul
Kennedy, that one "fundamental tendency of global politics in the late nineteenth
century [centered on] the collapse of Britain's position as the Number One world
power," this collapse could be ascribed to the social efficiency and organizational acumen of German society and culture by many civilian militarists of the
time.[89] Mackinder, as well as such other prominent British civilian militarists as
Lord Alfred Milner, fervently believed that domestic reform based on the
German model was necessary in order to pursue the fundamental goal of maintaining the British Empire through the twentieth century. British influence abroad
would be guaranteed, in other words, only if the social hierarchy at home was re-
imagined in geopolitical terms. In pursuit of this visionary activity, the geopoliticians held much in common with the science fiction writers of the day who were
also simultaneously enamored and appalled by the coming century.

Norman Angell summed up such sentiment when he stated that "The whole
tendency at present is to make comparison with Germany to the disadvantage of
ourself [England] and of other European countries."[90] Proto-geopolitical arguments about how to protect the British Empire in the new competitive conditions
were found in the writings of such popular imperial theorists as Charles Dilke,
James Froude, John Ruskin, and J. R. Seeley.[91] All believed in the empire as
being good for Britain as well as being in the best interests of the colonies but,
most importantly, all believed with Seeley that the empire provided a spatial
hedge against future threats from Britain's rivals.

New right elements in Britain, such as the Navy League (formed in 1894),
the Imperial Maritime League (1907), the National Service League (1902), and
the Tariff Reform League (1903) all, like their German counterparts, had a tendency to disparage parliamentary politics as irrelevant, inefficient, or "almost
universally bad" according to the imperial statesman Milner.[92] Such organizations stressed the need for some kind of national and cultural rejuvenation at
home in order to strengthen Britain's ability to defend its empire. As Strachey
wrote to Lord Roberts, the head of the National Service League, "We have got to
prepare not merely new Dreadnoughts but a new and more serious type of man
and woman or we shall go under."[93]

Mackinder was thus acting and reacting to a collection of voices advocating
piecemeal reforms of the Empire. The geopolitical task would be to build on the
work of such unsystematic reformers as Joseph Chamberlain (described by some
contemporaries as a "civilian Boulanger") by pushing a unified reform package
based on the seemingly established facts and foundations of geographic study.
For at a time in Britain when, during the crucial transitional phase entered into
by the 1890s, "the process of [threat] assessment was not unified but divided into
a series of debates over the different forms of national power," the geopolitician
stepped in to offer his services to the state in order to unify national strategy and
put it on sound, rational, and scientific, foundations.[94] However, the danger
remained that, as Brian Porter puts it, "the only way Britain could adequately

safeguard her vital national interests against external changes was by undermining those same interests from inside."[95] Excessive fear of threats from abroad would eventually pose for (especially Anglo-American) geopoliticians the problem of having to advocate domestic policies that could only transform their societies into the very militarized Spartas that they claimed to disdain.

While Britain managed to find an ideological rationale in liberal capitalism for her predominant power in the heyday of her success, Germany never managed to cloak her drive toward European hegemony in so attractive a rationale. While, in Eyre Crowe's words, Britain managed "to harmonize [its national policy] with the general desires and ideals common to all mankind,"[96] Germany failed to convince the world after the advent of its *Weltpolitik* that such harmonization could be had under German auspices. German commentators on the *Deutsche Sendung*, or German mission, tended to define a European—or even a world order—under German leadership in negative terms. As one recent commentator observes, Germany represented "the national incarnation of rebellion against the bourgeois Anglo-French epoch of materialism, individualism, and imperialism."[97] Intellectuals such as Thomas Mann would characterize the divide between the two rival missions as a struggle between Anglo-French civilization versus German *Kultur*.

The *Deutschefrage*, or German question, which so dominated European history from 1870-1945 was based in part on the desire of leading representatives of the German elite to overcome what was believed to be an exclusively Anglo-Saxon world order; an order oppressive in no small part because of its geographical scope. David Calleo stresses the continuity in German history, as when he argues that "In foreign policy, the similarities between imperial and Nazi Germany are manifest. Hitler shared the same geopolitical analysis, the same certainty about conflict among nations, the same craving and rationale for hegemony over Europe."[98] Although such an emphasis on continuity is overstated in this form, this argument does attest to the manner in which geopolitics could aid and abet German, as well as British, "missions" in the scramble for transcontinental power and influence in twentieth century conditions. The German new right gave vent to this desire as represented in such organizations as the German Colonial Society, the two navy leagues, the Imperial Maritime League, the *Wehrverein*, and the Pan-German League, which all sought to strengthen Germany militarily before World War One. The German historian and civilian militarist Erich Marks outlined the rationale for the forced supersession of the British liberal order and the balance of power system for which it stood when he wrote that:

> The idea of increased state autonomy, the idea of power, has replaced it. It is this idea that inspires and guides leading men everywhere. Quite apart from Russia, where this spirit has never disappeared, we find this same motivating force in Roosevelt and Chamberlain, as well as in Bismarck and Kaiser Wilhelm II.[99]

Notes

1. On the subject of professionalization as it pertains to this subject, see H. Perkin, *The Rise of Professional Society: England Since 1880* (New York: Routledge, 1989) and M. Larson, *The Rise of Professionalism: A Sociological Analysis* (Berkeley: U. of Calif. Press, 1977).

2. My use of the "competitive dynamic" concept is taken from E. L. Jones, *The European Miracle: Environments, Economies, and Geopolitics in the History of Europe and Asia* (Cambridge: Cambridge U. Press, 1981).

3. For a positive look at Metternich from a self-styled geopolitician, cf. Henry Kissinger, *A World Restored: Metternich, Castlereagh, and the Problems of Peace, 1812-22* (Boston, Mass.: Houghton Mifflin, 1957).

4. Brian Hudson, "The New Geography and the New Imperialism: 1870-1918," *Antipode* 9 (1971): 13.

5. Arnold Holt-Jensen, *Geography: History and Concepts* (Totowa, NJ: Barnes & Noble Books, 1988), 2-3.

6. Edward Gulick, *Europe's Classical Balance of Power* (Ithaca: Cornell U. Press, 1955), 24.

7. Gulick, *Balance of Power*, 297.

8. "The diplomats of the different powers had much in common. Their backgrounds were generally aristocratic. They were often related by marriage. They had a common political outlook. They even spoke the same language: French was the more or less official medium of diplomatic communications. These common characteristics lubricated the machinery of diplomacy. The basis of diplomatic cooperation, however, was a common Europe, the common commitment of tranquility and therefore to equilibrium that the managed balance of power system expressed." Michael Mandelbaum, *The Fate of Nations: The Search for National Security in the Nineteenth and Twentieth Centuries* (New York: Cambridge U. Press, 1988), 25.

9. Gulick, *Balance of Power*, 30.

10. Robert Gilpin, *War and Change in World Politics* (New York: Cambridge U. Press, 1981), 29.

11. Friedrich von Bernhardi, *Germany and the Next War*, trans. Allen H. Powles (New York: Longman, Green and Co., 1914), 20.

12. A. W. DePorte, *Europe Between the Superpowers: The Enduring Balance* (New Haven: Yale U. Press, 1979), 1.

13. A. J. P. Taylor, *The Struggle for the Mastery of Europe: 1848-1918* (London: Oxford U. Pres, 1971), xxi.

14. John Herz, "The Rise and Demise of the Territorial State," *World Politics* IX (1957), 482.

15. Quoted in Mandelbaum, *Fate*, 8-9.

16. Ludwig Dehio, *Germany and World Politics in the Twentieth Century*, trans. Dieter Pevsner (New York: W. W. Norton & Co. Inc., 1959), 135.

17. On the subject of the formation of ideologies, see P. L. Berger and T. Luckman, *The Social Construction of Reality: A Treatise on the Sociology of Knowledge* (Garden City, New York: Anchor Press, 1967).

18. A. F. K. Organski, *World Politics* (New York: Alfred Knopf, 1968), 355.

19. Organski, *World Politics*, 293.

20. Taylor, *Struggle for the Mastery*, xx.

21. Mandelbaum, *Fate*, 33.

22. Geoffrey Barraclough, *An Introduction to Contemporary History* (Harmondsworth: Penguin, 1967).

23. Gulick, *Balance of Power*, 307.

24. George Lichteim, *Europe in the Twentieth Century* (New York: Praeger, 1972), 7.

25. Lichteim, *Europe*, 13.

26. Gilpin, *War*, 226.

27. F. H. Hinsley, *Power and the Pursuit of Peace: Theory and Practice in the History of Relations Between States* (Cambridge: Cambridge U. Press, 1963), 5.

28. P. R. Viotti and M. V. Kauppi, *International Relations Theory: Realism, Pluralism, Globalism* (New York: Macmillan Publishing Co., 1987), 557.

29. E. H. Carr, *The Twenty Years' Crisis: An Introduction to the Study of International Relations* (New York: Harper & Row, Inc., 1964), 13.

30. Michael Mandelbaum, *The Nuclear Revolution: International Politics Before and After Hiroshima* (Cambridge: Cambridge U. Press, 1981), 88.

31. On the notion that Darwin's thought was as conducive toward the development of a "peace biology" (that supported cooperation over competition in international relations) as it was to the development of a Social Darwinist interpretation, see Paul Crook, *Darwinism, War and History: The Debate Over the Biology of War from the "Origin of Species" to the First World War* (Cambridge: Cambridge U. Press, 1994).

32. Lichteim, *Europe*, 7.

33. Gulick, *Balance of Power*, 68.

34. M. Geyer, "The Militarization of Europe, 1914-1945," in *The Militarization of the Western World* ed. J. Gillis (New Brunswick, NJ: Rutgers U. Press, 1989), 80.

35. Organski, *World Politics*, 364. Here Organski also notes that "In some respects the international order has striking similarities with that of a national society; it is legitimated by an ideology and rooted in the power differential of the groups that compose it."

36. John Keegan, *The Mask of Command* (New York: Viking, 1987), 11.

37. Mandelbaum, *The Fate of Nations*, 5.

38. Hinsley, *Power*, 282.

39. Mandelbaum, *The Nuclear Revolution*, 80.

40. A. L. Friedberg, *The Weary Titan: Britain and the Experience of Relative Decline: 1895-1905* (Princeton: Princeton U. Press, 1988), 10.

41. Friedberg, *Weary Titan*, 282.

42. Friedberg, *Weary Titan*, 290.

43. Kenneth Waltz, *Theory of International Relations* (Reading, Mass.: Addison-Wesley Publishing Co., 1979), 6.

44. S. Woolgar, *Science: The Very Idea* (New York: Tavistock Publications and Ellis Howard Ltd., 1988), 25.

45. Maurice Pearton, *The Knowledgeable State: Diplomacy, War, and Technology Since 1830* (London: Burnett Books, 1982).

46. A. F. K. Organski, *World Politics* (New York: Knopf, 1961), 38.

47. Gulick, *Balance of Power*, 27-28.

48. I. F. Clarke, *Voices Prophesying War: 1763-1984* (London: Oxford U. Press, 1966), 99-100.

49. Taylor, *Struggle*, xxvi.

50. Heinz Gollwitzer, *Europe in the Age of Imperialism: 1880-1914* (New York: Harcourt, Brace & World, 1969), 154.

51. L. K. D. Kristof, "The Origins and Evolution of Geopolitics," *Journal of Conflict Resolution* 4 (1960): 45.

52. J. A. Tyner, "Persuasive Cartography," *Journal of Geography* (1982): 144.

53. On the relationship between geopolitics and realism, see William Fox, "Geopolitics and International Relations," in *On Geopolitics: Classical and Nuclear* (Dordrecht: Martinus Nijhoff Publishers, 1985), eds. C. E. Zoppo and C. Zorgbibe.

54. Carr, *Twenty Years'*, 18.

55. Louis Dumont, *Homo Hierarchicus: The Caste System and Its Implications*, trans. L. Dumont and B. Gulati (Chicago: U. of Chicago Press, 1980), 12.

56. Quoted in Michael Curtis, *The Great Political Theories:* Vol. 2 (New York: Avon Books, 1981), 335.

57. Quoted in Mandelbaum, *The Fate of Nations*, 168.

58. Stephen Kern, *The Culture of Time and Space: 1880-1918* (Cambridge, Mass.: Harvard U. Press, 1983), 208.

59. Arno Mayer, *The Persistence of the Old Regime: Europe to the Great War* (New York: Pantheon, 1981), 282.

60. P. Kennedy, *The Rise and Fall of the Great Powers* (New York: Random House, 1987), 196.

61. Lichteim, *Europe*, 11.

62. W. T. Stead, *The Americanization of the World, or The Trends of the Twentieth Century* (London: H. Markly, 1901), 162.

63. Kern, *Culture*, 315.

64. Mayer, *Persistence*, 304.

65. Harold Perkin, *The Rise of Professional Society: England Since 1880* (London: Routledge, 1989), 2.

66. Perkin, *Professional*, 360.

67. Stead, *Americanization*, 388.

68. Quoted in P. Kennedy and A. Nicholls, eds., *Nationalist and Racialist Movements in Britain and Germany before 1914* (London: Macmillan, 1981), 77.

69. Kennedy and Nicholls, *Nationalist and Racialist*, 32.

70. Quoted in Bernard Semmel, *Imperialism and Social Reform* (New York: Anchor Books, 1968), 24.

71. Eric Hobsbawm, *The Age of Empire: 1875-1914* (NY: Pantheon, 1987), 256.

72. J. R. Seeley, *The Expansion of England: Two Courses of Lectures* (London: Macmillan and Co., 1895), 344.

73. Quoted in Kern, *Culture*, 68.

74. Donald Lowe, *The History of Bourgeois Perception* (1983), 38.

75. Kern, *Culture*, 94.

76. N. Oren, ed., *Images and Reality in International Politics* (New York: St. Martin's Press, 1984), 59.

77. Kern, *Culture*, 92.

78. Barraclough, *Introduction*, 61.

79. A. K. Henrikson, "America's Changing Place in the World: From 'Periphery' to 'Centre'?" in *Centre and Periphery: Spatial Variation in Politic*, ed. J. Gottmann (Beverly Hills: Sage Publications, 1980), 81.

80. Kern, *Culture*, 139.

81. Barraclough, *Introduction*, 60.

82. David Calleo, *The German Problem Reconsidered: Germany and the World Order, 1870 to the Present* (New York: Cambridge U. Press, 1978), 17.

83. Calleo, *German Problem*, 12.

84. Hobsbawm, *Age*, 44.

85. Hajo Holborn, *The Political Collapse of Europe* (New York: Alfred Knopf, 1951), 65.

86. Mandelbaum, *The Fate of Nations*, 46.

87. John Gillis, ed., *The Militarization of the Western World*, 98.

88. Kennedy and Nicholls, *Nationalist and Racialist*, 140.

89. Paul Kennedy, *The Rise of Anglo-German Antagonism: 1860-1914* (London: George Allen & Unwin, 1980), 307.

90. Quoted in Kennedy and Nicholls, *Nationalist and Racialist*, 131.

91. Paul Kennedy, *The Realities Behind Diplomacy: Background Influences on British External Policy: 1865-1980* (London: George Allen & Unwin, 1981), 30.

92. Quoted in Kennedy, *The Rise of Anglo-German Antagonism*, 372.

93. Kennedy, *Rise*, 372.

94. Friedberg, *Weary Titan*, 279.

95. Brian Porter, *Britain, Europe, and the World*, 56.

96. The full text of Eyre Crowe's memorandum on German foreign policy is contained in G. P. Gooch and H. Temperly, eds., *British Documents on the Origins of the War, 1889-1914* (New York: Johnson Reprint Corp., 1928), III.

97. Modris Eksteins, *Rites of Spring: The Great War and the Birth of the Modern Age* (Boston: Houghton Mifflin, Co., 1989), 328.

98. Quoted in Calleo, *German Problem*, 119.

99. Fritz Fischer, *World Power or Decline: The Controversy Over Germany's Aims in the First World War*, trans. L. L. Farrar (New York: W. W. Norton & Co., Inc. 1974), 58.

Chapter 3:
Mackinder's Geopolitical Program

It was outlook which makes your name [Halford Mackinder] world famous to-day as the first who fully enlisted geography as an aid to statecraft and strategy. You previsioned what today has won fashion as geo-politics. Unlike less worthy successors you have always been mindful of the responsibilities owed by science to democracy and to have furthered democracy's cause in your writing and in service to your country. You were the first to provide us with a global concept of the world.
                                        –J. G. Winant, American ambassador to Britain

The European phase of history is passing away.
                                                              –H. Mackinder

The historian Paul Kennedy in the *Rise and Decline of the Great Powers* focuses on the relationship between economic change and military power. In passing, however, he makes a comparison between the relative economic and military decline of Great Britain with that being experienced today, in his view, by the U.S. What Kennedy (and others concerned with the same topic) rarely discuss is the cultural context in which such processes of relative decline take place.[1] Much is to be gained in elucidating the cultural context by studying this perceived decay of Britain's position. Halford J. Mackinder—geographer, teacher, administrator, imperial theorist, politician, advisor to statesmen—was a vocal and central participant in the debate revolving around Edwardian-era fears of economic, cultural, and imperial decline.

Even today, there is a line of interpretation in which Mackinder's theories of empire are often extracted from the *fin de siècle* cultural milieu in which they were born and presented as timelessly objective and applicable. The geographers E. W. Gilbert and W. H. Parker believe, for example, that Mackinder's theories

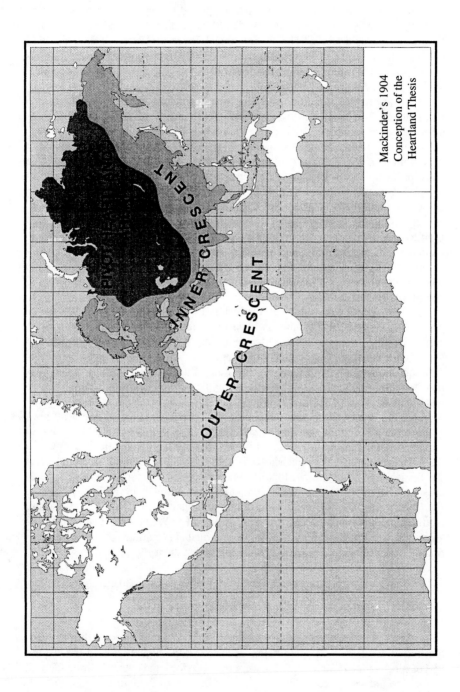

Mackinder's 1904
Conception of the
Heartland Thesis

"deserve to be re-read as they can aptly be applied to our own times," while W. H. Parker observes elsewhere that "It can be argued ... that the 1904 statement [concerning Mackinder's "The Geographical Pivot of History"] is a work of genius independent of the nationality of its author, free from the preoccupations of its time and from the stigmata of geopolitical propaganda ... [it is] conceived wholly from a detached standpoint."[2]

Contrary to this tradition of seeing Mackinder and his ideas as merely one more step on the road to mirroring the eternal reality of international relations through his geopolitics, I will argue here that Mackinder's "new geography" sought to rationalize heightened imperial competition and the old diplomacy that went with it in the late nineteenth century.[3] Mackinder did not just advance the basic propositions of what we call geopolitics. Embedded within his geopolitics is a *geo-domestic* vision of British society as well. Contrary to Mackinder's own avowed commitment to a certain kind of *Realpolitik*, he was at heart, I will argue, a romantic aesthete in his longing for order and harmony in world geo-politics and British geo-domestic politics. He perceived himself as a "landscape gardener" of civilization," not just as a narrowly focused foreign policy com-mentator. He was hopeful that "King Demos" would be contained at home through a philosophy of organic conservatism while enemies abroad were to be contained *via* geopolitics.

As one geographer points out, the history of geography can be construed "as the record of how certain humans have projected their own self-images on to earth, calling their projection 'geography.'"[4] Second, I will argue that Mackinder's unique "projection"—the imposition of a particular power-politics view on the world—contributed to, and was influenced by, the turn of the cen-tury "revolution in perception" discussed by the cultural historians Donald Lowe and Stephen Kern.[5] Third, Mackinder should be recognized as a pessimistic prophet for recognizing and lamenting the overshadowing of the European nation-state by continental power centers. This pessimism led Mackinder to admire certain aspects of German military and civilian culture, just as much as the Nazi sympathizer Karl Haushofer is alleged to have admired Mackinder and the British imperial tradition. Finally, Mackinder can be seen as an early prede-cessor of today's defense intellectual, too often thought of as being born *ex nihilo* only after World War Two in think-tanks such as the RAND Corporation. Both Mackinder—and the defense intellectuals after World War Two—used the authority of scientific-cum-academic professionalism to argue for the subordina-tion of foreign policy to rigid and axiomatic realist theory.

The Academic Entrepreneur: The Education of a Civilian Militarist

Although Mackinder's career spanned the two world wars of this century, his formative years were spent being educated in the high Victorian era. At the age of nineteen in 1880 Mackinder went up to Oxford and entered Christ Church College to pursue a science degree. Having been born in Gainsborough to middle class parents (his father was a doctor), Mackinder must be understood sociologically as belonging to a group that "came from middle—and professional—class backgrounds in northern provincial areas, making their way by scholarships, ... [and whose] ambitions for reform carried with them a strong sense of moral purpose."[6] Mackinder's ambitions were first expressed academically, as he succeeded in achieving a first class honors degree in 1883. He received training in the natural sciences and was greatly interested in Darwin's evolutionary theory. Mackinder's academic career was quite varied, as he took exams in such subjects as animal morphology, physics, chemistry, physiology, and botany. Mackinder also found time to read for the bar and to start studying for a degree in history, deciding that he needed to see "how the theory of evolution would appear in human development."[7]

Mackinder was busy in important activities outside of the laboratory and classroom. Foreshadowing a later important professional interest in military affairs, Mackinder became a member of the Oxford University Rifle Volunteers and of a *Kriegspiel* club founded originally by the military historian Spencer Wilkinson. He also found the time at Oxford to serve successively as Secretary, Treasurer, and President of the Oxford Union while maintaining his membership in the Junior Scientific Club. In the second half of the nineteenth century, under the guiding hand of dons like Benjamin Jowett who were quite interested in imperial affairs, Oxford University was being gradually transformed from being a producer of clerics into a modern university specializing in the training of a governing elite ready to rule over one-fifth of the globe and one-quarter of its population.[8] Even though Mackinder did not spend his time preparing for an examination in Greats, the sense of a governing mission (supposed to be imbibed by a study of the Greek and Roman classics) certainly influenced the way he viewed geography and imperial affairs.

Mackinder embarked on a long teaching career by teaming up with Michael Sadler in the Oxford University Extension movement for the first time in 1885. The mission of the movement was in fact a "crusade to bring knowledge to the working man" by having a series of lecturers tour around the country talking about their areas of academic expertise.[9] Mackinder participated by lecturing on geography, a subject he had long held an intellectual love for as an "outlook" subject that assumed, in his interpretation, the wholeness of the world and the inter-relatedness of all its processes. The lecturing circuit was useful to Mackinder in allowing him an opportunity to spread and hone his ideas concerning the coherence and integrity of geography as a discipline around the country. His ability to connect with an audience could have been predicted, given that he was "recognized as one of the best lecturers of his day at Oxford."[10] Mackinder believed that Britain could no longer rely on the skill of the capable amateur for running an empire in the twentieth century. He argued that, "When we teach the millions, however, we are not training scientific investigators, but the practical striving citizen of an empire which has to hold its place according to the universal law of survival through efficiency and effort."[11] Mackinder did not see the democracies of the nineteenth and twentieth centuries as being on the same level with the democracy of Athens and the creative city-state of Florence during the Renaissance. His view of modern democracy in Britain and elsewhere is summed up in his statement that "those who were the slaves of antiquity and the villeins of the Dark Ages are now become rulers holding lot in the Empire."[12]

At the time that Mackinder was beginning his participation in the Oxford extension movement (1885) there were forty-five professors of geography on the continent, yet not one full-time geography instructor in a British University.[13] The professionalization of geography was proceeding apace in Germany (due to the university reforms of the Napoleonic era and the influence of the great geographers Humboldt and Ritter) and in France, where the debacle of the Franco-Prussian War brought home the relevance of applied geography.[14]

The Royal Geographical Society was made aware of the young Mackinder's extension lectures, and soon another member of the society named Henry Bates asked Mackinder to write down his ideas on the "new geography." After becoming a member of the RGS in 1886, Mackinder found himself delivering an important address in January 1887 to the society entitled, "The Scope and Methods of Geography." The importance of the paper was immense for both Mackinder's career and the future of professional geography in Britain. Up until this time, "Geography itself appeared vague and diffuse, part belonging to history, part to commerce, part to geology."[15] The method of teaching geography in Britain during this period was to split the subject up into physical geography (dominated by the geologists) and political geography (which often was considered subsidiary to history and which emphasized the rote learning of the names of capitals and countries). It is fair to say that during this time geography in Britain was torn asunder by the rival professional disciplines of history and geology and, therefore, that geography had little prestige as a discipline, let alone as a science.

The historian of geographical ideas, Preston E. James, asserts that the professionalization of geography required three things in the nineteenth century.[16] First, it needed a working paradigm to define research problems; second, it needed to find an established niche within national university systems in which it could award advanced degrees to its converts; and, third, it required the availability of jobs (primarily at the primary and secondary levels of education). The RGS in the late nineteenth century was transforming itself from being a glorified gentlemen's club for casual travelers, military men, and explorers into the main instigator of geography's professionalization as a scientific discipline aspiring to the authority of science. The new sentiments expressed toward geography at the time of Mackinder's "Scope and Methods" paper is best summed up by the Marquis of Lorne, a former Governor-General of Canada and author of a book on imperial federation, who argued in his 1886 presidential address to the RGS that:

> to the Statesman the study of the science [of geography] may mean the avoidance of many blunders, the results of which have been only too manifest in our history. Territories which are mere names to the imagination, are easily given away to become the footholds of rivals ... . The science cannot be looked at

with indifference by those who direct the advance of commerce, for they in each fresh advance may find the path to new sources of wealth.[17]

Mackinder's response to the disunity of geography, therefore, was well received when he delivered his paper "On the Scope and Methods of Geography." As he delivered the address to the RGS, one old "Admiral Erasmus Onnabey ... sat in the front row muttering 'damn cheek, damn cheek,'" a statement perhaps testifying to the radical manner in which the young Mackinder attempted to solve certain difficult definitional problems surrounding the professional study of geography in front of a rather conservative audience.[18] At the age of twenty-six, Mackinder was attempting to give professional geography direction in Britain. He did this by showing geography's capability for being all things to all kinds of pragmatic students of the subject. His paper sought to sell geography as a practical discipline as much as it attempted to demonstrate geography's cognitive autonomy *vis à vis* history and geology. Mackinder, for instance, commented that "I believe that on lines such as I have sketched a geography may be worked out which will satisfy at once the practical requirements of the statesman and the merchant, the theoretical requirements of the historian and scientist, and the intellectual requirements of the teacher."[19]

In trying to answer the rhetorical question he posed to his audience at the beginning of the paper (concerning whether geography could be rendered into a discipline instead of a mere body of disparate information), Mackinder had recourse to formulaic solutions to problems heretofore seen as philosophically immune to solution. In seeking to resolve the conflict between the geologists (who thought a geography independent of their subject superfluous) and geographers, for instance, Mackinder managed to cut through this particular Gordian knot by stating that "the geologist looks at the present that he may interpret the past; the geographer looks at the past that he may interpret the present."[20] This axiomatic way of treating difficult problems—and the portentous manner in which such axioms were delivered—were useful to Mackinder in imposing order on the philosophical chaos surrounding the boundaries of the discipline. Mackinder later hoped such a method would impose order on the quickly deteriorating flux of international politics he saw before 1914.

The RGS was pleased both by Mackinder's definition of geography (geography being ultimately defined as "the science whose main function is to trace the interaction of man in society and so much of his environment as varies locally"), and by the unfettered visionary idealism that he brought to the subject (about which he said, "one of the greatest of all gaps lies between the natural sciences and the study of humanity. It is the duty of the geographer to build one bridge over an abyss which in the opinion of many is upsetting the equilibrium of our culture").[21]

The favorable response with which the paper was greeted was concretely shown when the RGS supported Mackinder's candidacy for the post of reader in geography at Oxford in 1887. This was the first full-time university level teaching post in geography at a British university.[22] Mackinder remained a reader in geography at Oxford until 1905, before which time he was instrumental in setting up a school of geography at Oxford in 1899 that he would become director of. These academic posts served as springboards into other academic endeavors (Principal of Reading College, 1893-1904; Lecturer at, and Director of, the London School of Economics, 1894-1925; Oxford University extension lecturer until 1892). With less success he attempted to use these posts as a springboard into politics.

When he ran for Parliament in 1900, Mackinder's career revealed a pattern which showed him to be an "academic entrepreneur."[23] This entrepreneurship was exhibited in the help he gave toward shaping geography into an autonomous discipline, toward establishing and selling the discipline in the new universities (i.e., the LSE and Reading), and through his own use of geography as a vehicle by which he could enter the world of politics and imperial decision-making circles. Just after he joined the RGS and delivered his "Scope and Methods" paper, Mackinder became widely regarded as a "whiz kid" by the old guard at the society.[24] Mackinder's reputation, along with his penchant for applying Darwinian metaphors to human societies and to the realm of power-politics, went hand-in-hand with the fact of his not being "by nature the quiet scholar like J. R. Green but a man of affairs, able to seize an idea and present it forcefully, to attract the attention of those who walk the corridors of power not only in universities but in the State."[25] By the time he stood for Parliament in 1900 Mackinder was clearly desirous of shifting the focus of his career from academia to politics and the cause of imperial unity. This desire might be related to the fact that colleagues of his in the Oxford school of geography were openly criticizing Mackinder's pro-imperial views. This in turn demonstrated the controversy surrounding Mackinder's attempt to transcend the conceptual divide between disinterested scholarship and geographical advocacy.

Mackinder believed that scholarship must inform the handling of public affairs because he believed that scientific rigor was required to run an empire in the conditions of the twentieth century. Under this view, Britain could no longer tolerate a public uninformed and apathetic about Britain's imperial mission or a governing elite out of touch with the scientific aspects of modern governance. This view is embodied in Mackinder's idea that "'thinking in maps' has become an important part of the mental activity of our people," now that the "conquest of space by speed has ... reduced the relative significance of near and easily apprehended things."[26] As so often in Mackinder's career, Germany was the model by which Britain was to be compared. Britain would have to emulate Germany's supposed ability to educate its citizens to think in maps and to seize the opportunities offered by technology to conquer space and time. As he put it, the "way of the capable amateur" was strongly opposed by the German "triumph of organization ... of the strategical, the ways and means mentality."[27]

The "New Geography" and Imperialism

The second phase of Mackinder's career—lasting from 1900, when he first ran for Parliament, to 1914, when he published *The Modern British State*—was marked by his attempt to use his geographic expertise for political purposes. Using geography as a platform on which to stand professionally, Mackinder was able to have his ideas on imperial unity, social reform, world-politics, and tariff reform heard in a number of important circles. In 1901 he joined the Victoria League, which was designed to promote enthusiasm for the British Empire. From 1902-1908, he was a member of the Co-Efficient Society. This organization advocated efficiency and expertise in domestic policy and in the running of the empire abroad. During this busy time, Mackinder also began representing in 1902 the Victoria League on the Visual Instruction Committee of the Colonial Office. The goal of this committee was to foster imperial unity through lectures on different parts of the empire. Of most importance for his career in public life, however, was his decision in 1903 to join Joseph Chamberlain's crusade for imperial preference and economic protectionism by participating in the Tariff Reform League. All this public activity culminated, by 1908, in Mackinder being offered a four-year stipend by the arch-imperialist journalist and administrator, Alfred Milner, for the purpose of gaining a seat in Parliament and spreading the gospel of imperial economic integration.

Mackinder's writing from this period is concerned with the issue of applying geography to the leading economic, imperial, and social problems of the day. As early as 1895, in a piece entitled "Modern Geography, German and English," two important themes were raised that would reappear constantly in his work. The first theme had to do with the limited options open to even the most talented of statesmen. This was so, according to Mackinder, since "Temporary effects contrary to nature may be within human possibilities, but in the long-run nature reasserts her supremacy."[28] Therefore, geographic awareness was necessary. The second theme in this paper of long-term importance for Mackinder's mature thinking on geopolitics was the emphasis placed on the inferiority of British geography *vis à vis* German geography. The latter was assumed to be superior "on the synthetic and philosophical, and therefore on the educational, side of our subject."[29] Mackinder also attributed to the Germans superiority in military efficiency and in the judicious use of neo-mercantilist economic policies.[30] As Mackinder would often state in speeches given in the House of Commons, "What we have to do in order to meet them [the Germans] is to think in similar terms."[31]

Mackinder's most famous piece of writing in this period of his career (and, truly, of his whole life) is his "The Geographical Pivot of History," delivered in the form of a lecture at the RGS in 1904. Here the new geography, outlined in part by Mackinder himself in 1887, showed itself most starkly as being aided by (and aiding) the so-called new imperialism. This imperialism was itself, of course, a process initially defined by the Berlin Colonial Conference (1884-1885) and the subsequent scramble for Africa. If it is true to say that "The geographical societies in European capitals ... were straight formal laboratories of imperialism," then it would be also fair to say that on this occasion Mackinder performed the geographical experiment of the century.[32]

The contents of the paper were very much influenced by events of the time. Mackinder was struck by the phenomenon of Russia as a land power being able to move masses of men and materiel across the vastness of Siberia *via* the Trans-Siberian railroad in order to fight the Japanese during the Russo-Japanese war. This represented to him an example (albeit only a nascent one, given the subsequent Russian failures during this war) of a twentieth century land power's ability to negate the traditional benefits accruing to seapowers. At the same time, Mackinder saw the similarity between the modern mobility given to the Russians through the use of the Trans-Siberian railway and the traditional kind of mobility given to the British through the use of their navy in transporting a whole army to South Africa to fight in the Anglo-Boer War. This fact, when connected with the burgeoning international rivalries of the early 1900s (as expressed, for example, in the Anglo-German naval arms race, the Anglo-Boer War, and the Russo-Japanese war) all suggested to Mackinder two decisive events which would necessitate a corresponding revolution of thinking on international relations.

First, Mackinder put forth the view that "soon after the year 1900" the passing of the four-hundred year old Columbian epoch was at hand.[33] At the beginning of this Columbian epoch the thalassocratic powers (such as Britain, Spain, and France) were able to outflank this land-mass and to shift the world balance of power away from the nomadic, horse-riding warriors dominating this area in their favor. But, at the beginning of the twentieth century, the world balance of power was shifting once again, because, in Mackinder's view, "transcontinental railways are transmuting the conditions of land-power, and nowhere can they have such effect as in the closed heart-land of Euro-Asia."[34] Practically, the pivot area was defined as "that vast area of Euro-Asia which is inaccessible to ships, but in antiquity lay open to the horse-riding nomads, and is today about to be covered with a network of railways."[35] This was a dangerous prospect, since a true "world empire"—escaping the known bounds of the old balance of power system—would now have to be realistically countenanced for the first time. Given that continental resources could now be fully exploited (thanks to rapid technological advances in transport, communications, and industry) and used for fleet-building by the occupier of the pivot area, such a world empire would merely have to expand westward from Eurasia in order to occupy appropriate seaports to project a first-class naval power.

Rather than interpreting this "geopolitical statement of the century" as being either a timeless and objective formulation or as an example of simple imperialist rhetoric, one can instead see it as an attempt to ground discussion of national security matters in the language of science. Thus the concepts embodied in terms like "control" and "causation" in geopolitical discourse offered to their users a way of avoiding the vagaries of history or culture when it came to estimating the relative strengths of nations. The British imperial adventure was, in Mackinder's thinking, defensive, since "It is for the maintenance of our position in the world ... that we have been driven to increase our Empire."[36] Such imperialism was further *depoliticized* by assuming the "neutral fact" of the "eternal struggle for existence as it stands at the opening of the twentieth century."[37] This belief in the idea of "expand or perish" was not unique to Mackinder, being shared as it was by such other diverse figures as Friedrich Ratzel in Germany (who believed that the state was like a biological organism that must either expand or decline) and the conservative statesman Lord Salisbury in Britain (whose "dying nations" speech postulated in its own way the theory that states are healthy only if they are steadily expanding).

What makes Mackinder unique and interesting in this context was the apparent scientific manner in which his discussion of imperialism was depoliticized. Although the age did not lack for explanations or rationalizations of imperialism, Mackinder went beyond the shibboleths of these arguments (many based on simple national pride) to argue that international relations could be mastered through impartial interpretation of an unchanging geography's interaction with the culture and the technology of competing nations. In the pivot paper, Mackinder thought he had found a "formula which shall express certain aspects ... of geographical causation in history" and that such a formula should have a practical value as setting into perspective some of the competing forces in current international politics."[38] The formula was general enough to appear being universally true, being applicable as it was to past, present, and future world political situations. The "geographical constant" in the formula was the apparently permanent fact of the pivot area, passively waiting to have its vast continental natural (human and mineral) resources mobilized by whatever efficient governmental apparatus found itself in control of such a vital area. The great variable in this formula was the nature of the governmental organization overseeing (at any one particular period) the pivot land area, since "the geographical quantities in the calculation are more measurable and more nearly constant than the human."[39] But since "nature in large measure controls," according to Mackinder, British maintenance of its far-flung empire would always depend on the need to constantly contain the "heartland pivot power." In the long-run it did not matter whether this area was administered and organized by Russians, Germans, or even the Chinese—the threats emanating from this area were inevitable given the "geographical realities" of world politics.

The reasoning used in Mackinder's pivot paper would inform his thinking on foreign policy for the rest of his life and deeply influence German and American realist approaches to the subject. Mackinder assumed the primacy of competition over cooperation as a causative force in international relations.[40] He considered nature to be "ruthless" and believed that Britain "must build a power able to contend on equal terms with other powers, or step into the rank of states which exist on sufferance."[41] Mackinder rationalized the need for Britain to adopt the non-democratic methods of its competitors (especially Imperial Germany) for defensive reasons. Intellectuals such as Bertrand Russell—along with assorted nuclear strategists after World War Two who would advocate (at one time or another) the "logic" of a pre-emptive nuclear strike against Stalin's Russia—used the "pre-emptive strike" logic first developed in its modern form by the geopoliticians. This logic is embodied in Mackinder's comment to the effect that "when competing countries seek to monopolize markets by means of customs tariffs, even democracies are compelled to annex empires."[42] (The same arguments would be advanced in the U.S. after World War Two to justify defensive expansionism against an autarkic Soviet Empire.)[43] This type of defensive expansionism is best summed up in Mackinder's argument that "We no longer colonise in vacant lands; each nation hastens to peg out its claim to its neighbour's vineyard before it is too late."[44] Thus, the geopolitical world view justified the return to Europe of competitive energies that heretofore had been exported out of Europe, a justification helping to pave the way to World War One.

Mackinder—as befitted his move away from academic geography to the pursuit of politics from a geopolitical point of view—demonstrated a lifetime interest in spreading the gospel of geopolitical realities in venues as diverse as school textbooks, speeches before Parliament, lectures to bankers, letters to the newspapers, and articles in such journals as the *National Review*. Representative writings embodying the core concepts behind Mackinder's proto-national security discourse include, beside the "Geographical Pivot of History," lectures printed in the *Journal of the Institute of Bankers* on "the Great Trade Routes" (1900), the geography textbook *Britain and the British Seas* (1902), an article on "Geographical Education" (1903), a description of "Man-Power as a Measure of National and Imperial Strength" (1905), "The Teaching of Geography from an Imperial Point of View" (1911), and the civics textbook *The Modern British State* (1914).

In this period, Mackinder sought through his writing to influence current debates concerning imperial policy and social reform, both of which were deemed necessary for what the Fabian Sidney Webb called the "breeding of an ... imperial race."[45] For example, before Mackinder made the crucial decision to leave the imperialist wing of the Liberal Party in 1903 (after being convinced by Leo Amery to join Joseph Chamberlain's Tariff Reform League), he accepted matter-of-factly in "The Great Trade Routes" that Britain's policy of free trade would help the "invisible trade" represented by financial services and the like in London, but that it would cause Britain's increasingly out-moded industry to decline relative to that of government-protected foreign manufacturers.

By 1905, however, Mackinder had thought through the implications of an unfettered free trade for Britain and concluded in the article "Man Power as a Measure of National and Imperial Strength" that autarkic economic policies were needed (much as Haushofer and his Nazi colleagues later decided). In 1904 Mackinder prophesied in his "pivot" paper that the twentieth century would witness the rise of vast continental superstates, and that the only way a geographically smaller power such as Britain could maintain its present status was to pursue a national policy of efficiency. For Mackinder, national efficiency symbolized a whole geo-domestic policy that was designed to go hand in hand with his geopolitics. This meant policies leading to a more effective sharing of human and material resources within a closely federated empire; an empire that would be guarded from threats to its productive base by tariffs from foreign producers. By this reasoning, "The right policy has for its conscious object to attain the greatest sum of man-power in all its complexity—physical, intellectual, and moral."[46] Geographical "trends and facts" therefore seemed objectively to force the hand of the responsible statesman to pursue a policy of "defensive imperialism," given the alternative of being strangled in the twentieth century by behemoth super-states. "Man power"—and all that went into maximizing it— underlay the geo-domestic component of geopolitics. Mackinder's thinking on economic change was as static as his thought on the eternal need to contain the heartland. His geopolitics never allowed for the possibility that national security concerns might be subordinate to economics as an agent of historical change.

Although political recognition of these themes could be found in the mainstream politics of the day (as in the public voice given to them by Joseph Chamberlain), they also had much in common with the Social Darwinist philosophies of the same time. Popularizers of Social Darwinism such as Benjamin Kidd also used the concepts of social efficiency and social organicism that are so familiar in Mackinder's own writings. Mackinder was in accord, for example, with many of the ideas expressed in Kidd's much reprinted *Social Evolution*. This work was indicative of the large literature at the time that sought to apply Darwin's insights concerning natural selection (or, in Herbert Spencer's words, "survival of the fittest") toward the understanding of contemporary human societies.[47] Kidd's thesis in this representative work of the genre was that:

In the silent and strenuous rivalry in which every section of the race is of necessity continually engaged, permanent success appears to be invariably associated with the ethical and moral conditions favourable to the maintenance of a high standard of social efficiency, and with those conditions only.[48]

Further, for Kidd and other Social Darwinists, it was axiomatic that "States are cradled and nurtured in continuous war, and grow up by a kind of natural selection... ."[49] Greta Jones, an acute observer of British Social Darwinism, has shown how this philosophy provided a secularized (i.e., non-religious) basis upon which Kidd, Mackinder, and other like-minded commentators on society could construct their particular visions of a new social and international hierarchy. Social Darwinist themes were useful to Mackinder in so far as they gave him help in imagining a more efficient British social order. The health of the British geo-social order was, in turn, to be measured by its ability to withstand the strains of foreign military and commercial competition.

The growing professionalization of geography in Britain helped to disseminate these ideas. The 1902 Education Act assured, finally, a place for geography in the secondary school curriculum, providing university-certified geographers with jobs and a more professional status. It also allowed geography to become a handmaiden to empire by giving geographers like Mackinder a chance to veil political prescriptions, values, and opinions behind the language of a state-sanctioned discipline. A new geopolitical vocabulary (dominated by words such as "control, result, determine, natural, law, and inevitable") could be presented through the medium of the textbook for the education of the next imperial generation.[50] Mackinder believed that the teacher was an "Imperial representative" and that "in this work of [imperial] consolidation the part of the teacher must be as great as that of the statesman."[51] The statesman in Mackinder's ideal geo-domestic-cum-geopolitical program would be occupied with the task of containing the "inherently" expansive nature of the heartland-based power, while the teacher on the homefront would be responsible for rationalizing this foreign policy in geographic terms to the empire's school-children.[52] Since Mackinder conceived of geography as "a scientific study and a discipline," the old, moral, and subjective nineteenth century debates on the subject of British imperialism would be neutralized by the vocabulary and "lessons" of geography and geopolitics.[53]

As one who thought in broad terms, Mackinder did not recognize a clear boundary between domestic and foreign policies. The division between the two was transcended by his larger organic view of men, societies, and states. His philosophy of power, after all, was broadly based, given that he believed that the "actual balance of political power at any given time is ... the product ... of geographical conditions ... and ... of the relative number, vitality, equipment and organization of competing peoples."[54] Given that geography in his view now favored continental states such as Germany over island nations such as Britain, Mackinder saw ruthless improvement in Britain's internal organization and politics as the only way to compensate for its geographical flaws. He was occasionally wistful about the "scientific policies which are possible in countries in which parties matter little" when it came to creating and implementing domestic policies designed to make the state compete better economically and politically in the new global balance of power.[55] His organic ideology (which stressed the rights of the community and the state over those of individuals) was based on the assumption that education was to be the vehicle by which the increasingly powerful middle and professional classes were to imbibe the politics of social efficiency and state power at home while being convinced of the need for "defensive expansionism" and protectionism. He and other like-minded grand strategists believed in Spencer Wilkinson's conclusion:

> We are not concerned so much with the happiness or welfare of individuals—though we believe that on the whole it will certainly follow on the national welfare—and still less with that of particular social classes, but with the betterment of the race and the greater efficiency of the State.[56]

Mackinder was, therefore, not alone in his views on a geo-domestic program. Popular writers such as H. G. Wells in the *New Machiavellians*, for instance, discussed the need for experts to replace amateur governance, while general interest publications such as the *Spectator* gave vent to the opinion that "there is a universal outcry for efficiency in all departments of society, in all aspects of life ... Give us Efficiency or we die."[57] Mackinder's *dirigiste* philosophy of politics—international and domestic—could not help but be controversial to those who paid close attention. Beatrice Webb had occasion to remark, for example, in a diary entry of 1918 that although Mackinder:

still talks in continents and waterways, in mass movements and momentums
... he has become uncomfortably aware of another kind of mass movement, of
another type of momentum—the uprising of the manual workers within each
modern state ... it is an uncomfortable shadow fully across his admirable maps
of the rise and fall of empires.[58]

According to Mackinder, society was an organic "going concern" that "may
be compared with a running machine."[59] Mackinder's belief that domestic affairs
had to be engineered to meet an overarching geopolitical program enabled fas-
cist fellow travelers such as Haushofer to adopt easily the vocabulary of geopolitics to a German context. That this concern led Mackinder to admire imperial
Germany was defended by him on the basis that such admiration allowed him to
see the need to connect international geopolitics to a domestic geopolitics in
Britain focused on efficiency. There is some irony in this view, given the con-
ventional wisdom that it was Karl Haushofer and his acolytes in Germany from
the 1920s to the fall of the Third Reich who admired and imitated Mackinder's
philosophy and methods. In actuality, although Mackinder gained nothing in the
way of scholarship from Haushofer *per se*, he was greatly inspired by pre-World
War One imperial Germany as a whole. Mackinder admired what he perceived
to be Germany's social efficiency, tariff policy, limits on the power of the working classes, and its military ethos. These were all values he believed to be necessary for any state that aspired to world power status in the twentieth century. As
he pointedly stated in a speech to the House of Commons in 1912, "I do not wor-
ship King Demos."[60] Indeed, part of Mackinder's geo-domestic vision incorporated elements of a proposed "racial contract" by which the unity of the English
race would overcome "mere" democratic and class divisions in the race to attain
national efficiency. As he said in his most mature statement of his philosophy,
the British goal should be to "displace class organization, and all its battle-cries
and merely palliative remedies, by substituting an organic ideal, that of the balanced life of provinces and of the lesser communities."[61]

While deeply admiring specific aspects of Wilhelmine German society and
culture, Mackinder conceived of himself as a British patriot who valued traditional British freedoms and despised governmental centralization and bureaucra-
tization—both of which he associated with the worst aspects of the German state.
Mackinder had a mystical sense of British superiority, even though he recognized that Germany was gradually surpassing Britain in the very measures of
greatness that he deemed to be of highest importance. He once said that "the
English race, the English blood, is valuable as carrying a certain character. That
character is, it seems to me, something physical and therefore not wholly trans-
ferable to except with the blood."[62]

Mackinder saw himself, as he put it, as a "landscape gardener of civilization,
with his organic remedies" for certain flaws in the British body politic.[63] The
organic remedies, of course, could be found in a close study of the positive
aspects of imperial Germany. In the middle of World War One, Mackinder
declared in the House of Commons that:

if your democracies are to hold their own against Germany ... against [any]
scheming autocracies and bureaucracies, then, in sheer self-defence, it is essential that we should equip the Governments of those democracies with some of
those powers ... absolutely essential now if democracies are not to be crushed
by the autocracies.[64]

This defensive appropriation of the enemy's worst features was to unite
civilian militarists in the West through the two world wars and the Cold War. As
the possibility for external expansion came to an end as a viable way to keep
ahead of Germany after 1900 (given the nearly complete formal division of the
world between the great powers), internal "self-exploitation" would now have to
begin such that Britain's "human capital" would be more "fit" and productive
than Germany's on a man-per-man basis (still another example of geo-domestic
policy in action). The only guarantee for Britain being able to contend with
Germany on an equal footing in the twentieth century was for Britain to develop
a coterie of expert advisers, not unlike the expert advisers that would arise after
World War Two in America to deal with a new heartland power, the Soviet
Union. For Mackinder, it was nothing less than a duty "to supply a thinking staff,
a *general staff for civil affairs*, which will prevent our drifting into a dangerous
position [emphasis mine]."[65]

The Post-Columbian Era and the Rise of the
Defense Intellectual

The year 1903 was decisive for Mackinder since he decided to leave the
Liberal party and join Chamberlain's tariff reform campaign. It was also decisive, however, since he decided at this time to resign his appointment at Reading
and to end his university extension work. This change marked Mackinder's
desire to delve into the political world so as to gain a chance at a Cabinet post in
a future conservative government. The historian Bernard Semmel claims that this
was a mistake, since the Cabinet post Mackinder would have surely received in
1906 (the year of the Liberal party's triumph) was forfeited due to his shift on
the issue of free trade.[66] He had moved from being "the outstanding theorist
among the Liberal Imperialists," to being a leading theoretician of conservatives
who would be effectively out of power until 1922, when David Lloyd George's
coalition government finally collapsed.[67]

In 1902, he joined the Coefficient Club, a club that had as its main goal the
engineering of "a new party, comprising both Liberal Imperialists and 'progressive' Unionists." The Club was to serve as a "Brains Trust or General Staff" that
would develop policies of national efficiency both at home and abroad to make
Britain fit for the rigors of the twentieth century.[68] Such efficiency was deemed
all the more necessary given the effect of the Anglo-Boer war on the nation's
psyche. As G. R. Searle says of the impact of this conflict:

the 'cold war' atmosphere thus generated [by the Boer War] prevented a return
of self-assurance and complacency and emphasized the pressing importance of

carrying through reforms that would strengthen the 'scientific' basis of British society and administration and increase the Empire's readiness for a possible war.[69]

The Coefficient Club arose in this atmosphere with the idea of waking up the nation to the need for social reform at home (as in the fostering of the "imperial race" idea) and consolidation of the empire abroad. To accomplish this task, the Coefficient "think tank" relied on twelve experts representing various fields to come up with relevant ideas on the subject of social and imperial reform. Such experts included Mackinder (specializing in geography), Sydney Webb (municipal affairs), J. B. S. Haldane (law), Sir Edward Grey (foreign affairs), Leo Amery (the army), Clinton Dawkins (banking), Bertrand Russell (philosophy and science), Pember Reeves (colonial affairs), W. A. S. Hewins (economics), Leo Maxse (journalism), Carlyon Bellairs (the navy), and H. G. Wells (literature).

Chamberlain's 1903 Birmingham speech calling for tariff reform not only divided the nation, but it also divided the elite Coefficient Club, making it ineffective after 1903 (although it existed formally until 1909). This Edwardian "think tank" therefore never reached its full potential as an advisory body. Its efforts were first seriously hindered by the polarization caused by the issue of tariff reform in 1903. More deeply, there existed an "incompatibility between the national efficiency school of thought ... [and] liberal values."[70] A representative example of a topic chosen for discussion by the Coefficient Club was "militarism and the growth of civilization in the Empire." Mackinder and Amery tended to take the same side on most issues, being the likely members of the club responsible for including in the minutes of a particular meeting the idea that "The true spirit of military efficiency was that shown in Drake's game of bowls or in Moltke's famous 'Kriegmobil.'"[71] That the analogy to war games was made is significant in so far as Mackinder used the words "struggle" and "contest" in his geopolitical theorizing, while (as shown in the autobiographical fragments extant at the Oxford School of Geography) he even made the comparison between the game of chess and life, saying that "Most people play only one game of chess in life."[72]

Though the individuals making up the Coefficient Club decisively split over the issue of tariff reform, the group had some impact on governmental policy-making.[73] During the period from 1900-1914, when Mackinder actively proselytized in behalf of imperial unity and tariff reform, British foreign policy was undergoing dramatic change. Moving from the "splendid isolation" of pre-Anglo-Boer War days to the commitment to Europe represented by the *Entente Cordiale* with France in 1904 and the understanding with Russia in 1907, Britain seemed stumbling *via* the old diplomacy down the path suggested by Mackinder's logic concerning the need to contain the continental power most capable of organizing the heartland's abundant resources, Imperial Germany. Mackinder himself was directly connected to such national figures as Foreign Secretary Sir Edward Grey, J. B. S. Haldane (Minister of War), and Spencer Wilkinson (the popular author)—who were all concerned with the formulation of imperial defense policy.[74]

During the period stretching from 1900-1914, Mackinder's participation in the Coefficient "think tank," his work for the Tariff Reform League and the Colonial Office, and his interest in gaining a foothold in Parliament all testify to his ambition to be heard by the nation's leaders. But he was aware of the need to maintain a foothold in academe, as signified by his acceptance of the Directorship of the London School of Economics, which was offered to him by Sydney Webb in 1903. The atmosphere at the Oxford School of Geography was too rarefied for Mackinder, while the L. S. E. proved ideal for his needs in that its ethos was dominated by the concern for solving the social and political problems of the day.

The idea of vaulting into imperial politics by using the authority of geography as a prestigious basis on which to offer advice on the pressing problems of the day worked for Mackinder in the short-run, but proved harmful to him in the long-term. Mackinder succeeded in articulating a leading concern of Edwardian Britain by raising the issue of, and offering solutions for, the problem of relative national decline. Although the pivot paper did put Mackinder at the center of the public debate on defense after the Anglo-Boer War, his juggling of academic obligations and political demands made his attempt at being an Edwardian academic entrepreneur specializing in imperial problems problematic for his critics.

Mackinder managed, however, to gain a respectful hearing from important imperial decision-makers and a popular audience (Clarendon Press alone sold a half million of Mackinder's books before World War One). Mackinder's contemporary Leo Amery believed, for example, that he had "a more forceful personality and a more powerful brain than either Grey or Haldane," a statement testifying to Mackinder's ability to hold his own intellectually with some of the most important decision-makers of the time. While it has been said that "Geography, perhaps more than other subjects is coloured by and in turn assimilates its surroundings," the same could be said with even more force of geography's subdiscipline, geopolitics.[75] The professionalization of geography—along with the rise of geopolitics as the science concerning the spatial distribution of world power—took place in the quarter century preceding World War One. This was largely because both movements promised to answer the desire to maintain and bolster an increasingly complicated and formalized British empire in an age marked by the decline of the mid-sized nation-state.

An example of the political and cultural "demand-side" helping to explain the power of the Mackinder-shaped professional geography and geopolitics of the time is represented by Mackinder's relationship to a fellow Oxonian, Lord Curzon (Viceroy of India from 1895-1902 and Foreign Minister from 1919-22). Curzon—along with many British imperialists before and after him—was obsessed with the Russian threat to India and, more generally, Russia's threat to the European balance of power. Although Japanese victories against Russia at Mukden and Tsushima showed that the Russian threat was perhaps overrated, Mackinder's warning in the pivot paper concerning the heartland power and its potential was taken seriously by Curzon, who commented favorably on the pivot paper. Curzon had noted previously that "Russia's future is much more what we choose to make it than what she can make it herself."[76] This implied that Britain had a choice to either follow the logic of geopolitics (and contain Russia militarily from bases in the Middle East and India) or to allow the otherwise inevitable expansion of Russian power.

Mackinder's formula of power—"he who controls Eastern Europe controls the heartland; he who controls the heartland controls the World Island; he who controls the World Island controls the World"—provided Curzon and other leading imperial decision-makers of the day with a potentially authoritative basis on which foreign policy could be made, especially since this verbal formulation seemed to be built upon the very structure of the earth.[77] Therefore, Curzon could be emboldened in his belief that Britain could shape Russia's future through the Containment policy suggested by the heartland thesis. The heartland formula or thesis thus attempted to transform the foreign policy debate of the time from a discussion fraught with subjective interpretation and values into a technical debate on the specific means needed to counter the geographically determined threat.

The imposition of even a modicum of rationality on the rapidly changing and chaotic international scene was welcomed in a Britain made increasingly aware of its relative industrial and military decline, especially as compared to the growing powers of Germany and the U.S.A. In this atmosphere, Mackinder's career as an academic entrepreneur could have easily led into the career of an action-intellectual with a Cabinet post. Although Mackinder's support of tariff reform conformed with his neo-mercantilist world view, it had serious short-term political consequences, as when the Liberals (a party Mackinder had abandoned on the tariff issue) came into power in 1906.

The action-intellectual in Mackinder was nevertheless given outlets for expression beginning the same year, when the new head of the War Office asked Mackinder to organize and teach courses in geography, law, accounting, economic theory, statistics, and transportational studies for army officers.[78] Academic theory was (albeit indirectly and tentatively) to be tested in practice as the modern state in Britain and elsewhere sought to meet the perceived needs for increased efficiency. The academic entrepreneur phase of Mackinder's career (lasting, roughly, from 1900 and 1914) would end in the test of the heartland theory itself when Mackinder was sent as High Commissioner to South Russia in 1919 to obstruct the Bolshevik cause.

Given that the basic facts concerning Mackinder's career during the Edwardian and early Georgian period are known, how are we to interpret them in their context? Important portions of the extant literature on Mackinder tend to assume the ahistorical nature of Mackinder's geopolitical formulae and then to either defend or deny the applicability of such formulae to past and current world politics.[79] However, the very same formulae, when examined as historical artifacts, yield much in the way of explanation concerning the genesis of the "defense intellectual" in our century.[80] Roman Kolkowicz, an observer of the phenomenon of the defense intellectual, remarks that "Probably the most significant involvement of intellectuals in affairs of state has come about in this century when the growing needs of the authorities transformed 'clerks' into 'laymen' and 'intellectuals' into 'experts.'"[81]

This general statement can only come to life with the provision of historical examples and interpretation. It is fair to say that Mackinder was the first well-known academic in our century to self-consciously develop theories concerning world politics based on geographical constants and to argue by deduction from these theories what specific policies (foreign and domestic) were necessary to meet assumed "political-cum-geographical realities." Although Mackinder was not concerned with the development and application of specific weapons systems, he was crucial in creating the vocabulary (e.g., the neologisms "man-power," "heartland," and "geopolitics") and theoretical structure (as in the thesis that the heartland must be contained) upon which—in modified form, of course— such later weapons would be justified.[82]

As Bernard Semmel has argued, the reason that our understanding of the phenomenon of the defense intellectual is limited to the post-1945 period has to do with the fact that:

> Much has been written about the leading roles taken in imperial organizations by individual aristocrats, generals, admirals, governors, colonial officers and civil servants, traders and ship owners. In contrast, insufficient weight has hitherto been given to the consent of the educated middle class—the intelligentsia—and to their active participation in the imperialist movement.[83]

Mackinder certainly belonged to this intelligentsia and felt it his duty to educate people and make them aware of the challenges of an increasingly complex, competitive, and scientifically oriented world. Mackinder's idealism in spreading knowledge first found an outlet in his participation in the university extension project and, later, in his crusade to help foster the development of an "imperial race" by pursuing the policies of social imperialism, which included among its goals the instilling of a basic geographic education in all that race's members.[84] Mackinder's scientized rationalization for imperialism and his particular domestic policies were well suited to a new age in which, as described by Heinz Gollwitzer, "there was the idea that learning too must be placed at the service of the nation; thus the theoretician could provide solutions which, in their end effect, were eminently practical."[85]

Mackinder conceived of the natural world being divided into four categories: the hydrosphere, the lithosphere, the atmosphere, and the psychosphere. Since the first three of these categories fit under Mackinder's overarching conception of nature (which for him is a controlling and predatory force in the form of geography), only the psychosphere—that part of the world subject to the influence of man's free will—was ultimately beyond prediction. But the chaos of unpredictability would be blunted by Mackinder's attempt to subject the vagaries of world politics to the constraining parameters of a theory that offered its adherents a way out of the political chaos that some feared would dominate the coming century. Mackinder's geo-domestic and geopolitical views (and the way in which they are interpreted) are important because, as Gollwitzer remarks about such theories, "the opinions men form about facts are often more decisive than the facts themselves."[86]

From Academic Theorist to Action Intellectual: Mackinder and the Litmus Test of Bolshevism

Although Mackinder finally attained his goal of becoming a member of Parliament (in the Camlachie district) in 1910, the years 1919-20 were to be the most decisive of his career. Since the turn of the century, and especially after arriving at a mature world view by 1904 (with the publication of his pivot paper and his turn toward tariff reform), Mackinder was anxious not only to influence the course of British foreign policy, but to guide it directly from the inside of a future Unionist government. The ideology associated with free trade continued to be adhered to strongly by the majority of the governing elites, thereby making Mackinder's rendezvous with power in office a near impossible event, given his firm neo-mercantilist views on economic issues.

In 1919, Mackinder published *Democratic Ideals and Reality*, the second most important work of geographical advocacy in his career after the pivot paper. Unlike American geographers (notably Isaiah Bowman), British geographers were underrepresented in the British delegation at the Versailles peace conference. Although Milner urged that Mackinder be represented on the Saar Basin Delimitation Committee, the closest Mackinder got to the conference was through the indirect influence he hoped his geopolitical ideas would have on the peacemakers. *Democratic Ideals and Reality* was thus a book of advocacy and applied geography; Mackinder's constantly reiterated theme was that "we must base our proposed League on realities."[87]

In 1919 Mackinder felt as confident as he did in 1904 concerning the validity of his pivot thesis. As he states at the outset of his 1919 work, "I feel that the war has established, and not shaken, my former points of view."[88] Mackinder's updated theory on the geographic basis of world power went roughly as follows: 1) the assumption can be made that nations grow unequally in power; 2) society is a going concern, comparable in its internal dynamic to a machine; 3) such geo-social going concerns now interact with one another, for the first time in history, in a well-mapped world and in a closed-space system; 4) by inference, conditions 1), 2), and 3) yield the conclusion that great power conflict was inevitable, given the unequal growth of polities in a post-Columbian environment.

However, the heartland concept still dominated Mackinder's thinking, especially given the fluid political situation obtaining in Eastern Europe after the chaos of World War One and the Bolshevik Revolution. Observation of the events of the recent war led Mackinder to posit a dichotomy between democracy (marked by its obsession with ethics) and societies (like that of the recently defeated Hohenzollern empire) that emphasized the tactics of managerialism and Machiavellianism in the pursuit of power for its own sake. As Mackinder put it, "The thought of the organizer is essentially strategical, whereas that of the true democrat is ethical."[89] The geopolitician was conceived by Mackinder to be a mechanic of sorts who would make sure geo-domestic policy meshed with geo-political needs.

Mackinder—and other committed British imperialists of his generation—struggled with the contradictions inherent in the notion of an imperial democracy. Mackinder always bemoaned the fact that "Democracy refuses to think strategically unless and until compelled to do so for purposes of defence."[90] Yet a strict and crude authoritarianism was abhorrent to Mackinder, subsuming as it did everything under a narrow-minded, technique-obsessed "ways and means" mentality.[91] For Mackinder, the action intellectual who desired to marry scientifically-grounded theory with political practice, the riddle posed by the dichotomy between democracy and authoritarianism was ultimately unsolvable.

Mackinder began as an academic entrepreneur (largely concerned with the professionalization of geography as a servant to imperialism) and later evolved into an action intellectual (spent putting theory into practice in Parliament, army instruction, and finally in his service as High Commissioner to South Russia). This career can be interpreted, ironically, as constituting a series of discrete attempts to marshal certain authoritarian practices imported from abroad for the betterment of the British Empire, not that of British democracy. Specifically, Mackinder's conception of the new geography was spurred on by the example and threat represented by German geography. Moreover, his 1904 formulation of a pseudo-scientific theory seeking to describe the objective geographical parameters of world power was largely a veiled *cri de coeur* over the possibility that Germany might obtain continental hegemony by way of organizing the resources of the heartland.[92]

Germany, in short, was both the enemy and the model in the 1904 statement and in its 1919 update. For Mackinder, it might be said that:

> She [Germany] was the enemy, the competitor who must be warded off British shores by a tariff, and she was the model, a nation in which the system advocated by Chamberlain was in effective and successful operation. It is not an infrequent occurrence in history that a nation prepares itself to meet its enemies by aping them.[93]

At the root of Mackinder's partial seduction by German geography (and its Ratzelian emphasis on social evolutionism) and German organizational methods (centered around military and social efficiency) was his profound antipathy to the practice of modern democracy as he saw it working in Britain. His emotional and intellectual attachment to British imperialism was, on the other hand, continuous and proudly proclaimed. He thought, for example, that "The British empire will last so long as it is performing a vital service to humanity."[94] This abstract idealization of empire as a servant of humanity was a far cry from his denigration of democracy as practiced by the mother country. Mackinder concluded in his updated 1919 statement of the heartland thesis that even the most advanced democracies produced "half-educated people" susceptible to manipulation by demagogues and yellow journalism. Again, Mackinder showed himself to be more of a romantic than a realist in failing to see the worst of the German system and the best of the Anglo-American.

Democratic Ideals and Reality was thus, among other things, a call for the governing elites of the victorious powers at Versailles to contain the volatile, Bolshevik-influenced masses at home and to contain the Bolshevik power that now appeared most capable of organizing the heartland area.[95] As Mackinder argued, "the management of men, high and low, is more difficult and more important under the conditions of modern reality than it ever was."[96] Mackinder's geopolitical formulae and equations, his social imperialism, and his unshakeable belief in the moral worth of the imperial venture were all constituent parts of a philosophy of service in the *noblesse oblige* tradition. Mackinder's domestic and foreign geopolitics assumed the existence of a coherent elite that could implement necessary policies by persuading "geo-domesticated" masses into active acceptance of the long-term merits of these policies.

His 1919 appointment to the office of High Commissioner to South Russia by his friend and fellow Royal Geographical Society member, Lord Curzon (who then headed the Foreign office) gave Mackinder his most important chance to see his geographically informed political program put to the test. Curzon had read both the pivot paper and *Democratic Ideals and Reality* and was impressed enough to give Mackinder the important post of High Commissioner on 23 October 1919 (under the auspices of the national unity coalition, governing from 1916-22), in order to give assistance to General Denikin, who was at that time leading the "white" counter-revolutionary forces against the Bolsheviks. Curzon expressed his personal impression of the importance of the mission when he wrote, in a letter to Mackinder dated 2 December 1919 that:

> This [Mackinder's report on the mission] will be of the greatest value to the government not only for enabling them to understand the present situation, but in helping them to form alone a policy for the future, when the military contributions to General Denikin's army have for reasons with which you are familiar come to an end.[97]

Both Mackinder and Curzon were wary of the expected negative public opinion the mission would cause were it made public. The possibility of granting sufficient and continuous aid to Denikin was hindered at the start by two problems. As Mackinder wrote in his "Report on the Situation in South Russia" on the HMS *Centaur* off Marseilles in the aftermath of his mission (21 January 1920), the two difficulties that hindered implementation of any serious anti-Bolshevik strategy included "the possible jealousy of France, and the ... hostility of certain classes of our own electorate."[98] Here Mackinder expressed his own fear that a true geopolitics had no hopes of being implemented without the preexistence of a coherent geo-domestic policy that would neutralize such disabling "hostility."

To save Britain and its imperial interests from the Bolshevik ideological and military threat, Curzon and Mackinder desired that the geopolitical program outlined in the latter's 1904 statement (and modified in its 1919 form) be followed.

The task would be to divide up Eastern Europe to such an extent that no one dominant governmental apparatus could arise to organize the heartland's resources. Mackinder asked rhetorically in *Democratic Ideals and Reality*, "What if the Great Continent, the whole world-Island or a large part of it, were at some future time to become a single and united base of sea-power?"[99] The year 1919 represented a golden opportunity for Mackinder to put academic geopolitical logic into practice in support of his beloved British Empire.

Even if from the very beginning both Mackinder and Curzon saw such a plan to be inimical to the wishes of the democratic electorate in the mother country, both the action intellectual and the imperialist foreign minister were determined to protect the British Empire according to the logic of geopolitics. Mackinder had always disdained the traditional methods employed by the British government in protecting its interests abroad, characterizing them at one point as "the way of the capable amateur."[100] By mid-December of 1919 Mackinder, armed with scientific theories based in large part on the prestige of a newly professionalized British geography, made his way to southern Russia by way of Eastern Europe determined to show geography's relevance to imperial policy.

Before meeting Denikin on 10 January 1920, Mackinder stopped in Warsaw, Bucharest, and Sofia in order to forge a general anti-Bolshevik alliance. His conversations with the Polish general Pilsudski led Mackinder to believe in the possibility of creating a pan-Eastern European anti-Bolshevik alliance, whose two most important leaders would be Denikin and Pilsudski. Agreement was finally reached with Denikin on the acceptance in principle of the proposed alliance. According to Mackinder's plan, Denikin was to accept arbitration on the issue of the Russo-Polish border. Mackinder also planned an unexpected enlargement of the Versailles settlement in Eastern Europe that would see the creation of such new states in the areas of Daghestan, Azerbaijan, Armenia, Georgia, South Russia, the Ukraine, and White Russia.

Mackinder's stay in southern Russia convinced him that the only way his geopolitical schema could be applied to the heartland area was to see the "new Russian Czardom of the Proletariat" annihilated.[101] As he wrote in his official report to the government, "the only final remedy is to kill Bolshevism at the source."[102] Although in May 1919 Denikin's army had reached as far north as Orel (250 miles south of Moscow), this was to be the maximum extent of his advance. By January 1920 Denikin's military position and the condition of his army were so bad that Mackinder could do nothing more in southern Russia. Thus, he left for London on 16 January of the same year. Mackinder was left to try and convince the coalition government headed by Lloyd George on the merits of aiding the anti-Bolshevik cause.

Mackinder's official report argued that the following immediate steps be taken: 1) Britain should not agree to peace with the Bolsheviks; 2) Britain should recognize General Denikin as the legitimate representative of the Russian government; and 3), that the Baltic states, the Poles under Pilsudski, and Georgia and Azerbaijan under Denikin should all come together in a formal coalition against the Bolsheviks.[103] The objective geopolitical logic of the situation suggested to Mackinder that unless the British intervened, the heartland would fall under the sway of the Russian revolutionary government, thereby threatening the hard-won gains not only of the western Allies in the recent world war, but also those of the British Empire. Mackinder wrote in his report, for example, that "It is only by strong immediate measures, taken before the thawing of the Volga ice [in 1920], that the advance of Bolshevism, sweeping forward like a prairie fire, can be limited, and kept away from India and Lower Asia, pending the advance from Poland and Odessa."[104] Geopolitics in practice therefore meant not only the formation of defensive barriers against the heartland power, but the formation of ideological *cordon sanitaires* around it as well.

The geo-domestic side of Mackinder's geopolitics is made quite clear when he reflects in his report that:

> In regard to the other difficulty, the hostility of our own working classes, I feel that the time has come when the truth should be carried home to them. They must be made to realise that, whatever the communistic ideals originally characteristic of Bolshevism, there is today a growing threat from Moscow of a state of affairs which will render this world very unsafe for democracies.[105]

Mackinder and other geopoliticians thus distrusted democracies and their ability to fend off alien idealogies without the guiding hand of geopolitical logic. As early as 1904 Mackinder had been arguing for what was essentially a policy of geo-Containment against the power that dominated the Eurasian continent (the heartland), and now in 1920 he was, in essence, espousing what would one day be called the "domino theory" that so preoccupied American defense intellectuals and strategists in the Korean and Vietnam wars. Mackinder's political prescriptions were based on, and presupposed, the objectivity of British professional geography. In *Democratic Ideals and Reality*, Mackinder argued that:

> human society is still related to the facts of geography not as they are, but in no small measure as they have been approached in the course of history. It is only with an effort that we can yet realize them in the true, the complete, and therefore detached, perspective of the twentieth century.[106]

The Aftermath of 1919, or, The Politics of Geopolitical Interpretation

On the surface, Mackinder's failure to convince the government to follow his advice on Eastern Europe and Russia symbolizes his larger failure to gain the power and influence that he and his contemporaries thought was his due. Mackinder's extension lecture colleague, Michael Sadler, asked rhetorically after Mackinder's death, "[given the latter's] ability, strength, courage he has not been placed as he should have been—Why?"[107] It always seemed that Mackinder was going against the grain of mainstream democratic British political opinion, as when he became a fervent exponent of tariff reform in 1903 and when he advo-

cated an anti-Bolshevik foreign policy at a time in 1920, when Britons were tired
of war and many were at least sympathetic to the change in Russian governments.

Mackinder's geopolitics and geo-domestic social imperialism were fundamentally antithetical and threatening to the basic tenets of Britain's liberal culture. There was a fundamental contradiction, in other words, between the
individualistic values espoused by liberalism and the organic collectivism
favored by the geopoliticians. The liberalism developed over a century by such
figures as Bentham, Mill, Cobden, and Bright emphasized individualism, free
markets, and a minimum of central government. Mackinder's thinking on foreign
and domestic affairs assumed, in contradiction to basic tenets of dominant liberal
theory, the need for corporatism (since unfettered individualism was seen as hin-
dering national efficiency), protected markets, and a strong central government
that could "manage men" effectively at home and abroad for purposes of imperial unity and balance of power politics.

For Mackinder, the assumptions upon which his geopolitical theory rested
were not merely the expression of philosophical preference, but rather scientific
axioms grounded in empirical correspondence with reality. His advocacy of consensus and decisive action at home and abroad—in contrast to the inherent confusion and compromise that characterized truly democratic politics—is reflected
in the very methodology that led him to his geopolitical discoveries. As he says
of this methodology:

> If you can so state the facts after investigation in the scientific spirit that they
> are practically unchallengeable, and if you can compare the alternatives of pol-
> icy in the same detached spirit, then you have accomplished 9/10s of the road
> toward unanimity.[108]

Politics—be they geopolitics abroad or geo-social imperial politics at home—
therefore did not have to be the messy affair Mackinder and the other imperialist
critics saw them in actuality to be in pre-World War One Britain.

Mackinder's agenda—indeed, even most of his geopolitics and geo-domestic thought—was ultimately defanged and co-opted by the very same liberal
culture that he avowedly sought to defend. Ironically, Mackinder, who throughout his career conceived of himself as a master realist discerning the underlying
geographical basis of world politics, held a naive view of what the majority of
his countrymen were thinking. For Mackinder, these fellow citizens were the
"half-educated" requiring direction and management from experts such as himself who were capable of discerning Britain's "true" long-term interests. The
problem was that the elite and the "half-educated" that Mackinder sought to
influence with his heartland theory were, with a few important exceptions, incapable of sympathizing with his vision. What the elites—in an era of mass
politics—wanted in Mackinder's Britain (as well as in Haushofer's Germany and
Spykman's America) was a tamed geopolitics that could be used selectively and
rhetorically to sell short-term and self-serving policies in a new pseudo-scientific
vocabulary.

The formal program of imperialism advocated by personages as diverse as Mackinder, Milner, Curzon, and Roseberry never achieved the status of a popular cause as its advocates desired. Instead, the more the banner of a formal, sophisticated, and rationally planned imperialism was raised, the more the notion of an "imperial democracy" came to seem a simple oxymoron to the British public, not to mention a threat to an elite who could no longer enjoy the fruits of such an imperialism on the cheap. The liberal elite's response to Mackinder's geopolitics after the experience of World War One is summed up by H. A. L Fisher's comment on Mackinder's report and recommendations to the Cabinet on the situation in southern Russia. As this historian and Liberal member of Parliament wrote concerning his views on the report: "Cabinet on Russia—Mackinder's absurd report. As I had to leave early I let the PM know in writing that I disagree with it."[109] The subtleties and arcana of geopolitics simply did not lend themselves to being translated into the increasingly democratic political discourse of popular British liberal culture or into the short-term cost-benefit calculus of the establishment. As for non-elite segment of the British public, reaction to geopolitical thinking was symbolized by Mackinder's loss of his Camlachie seat to a Labor party candidate in the general election of 1922. This result was to be expected given Mackinder's fear of holding a public meeting in Glasgow after the announcement of his anti-Bolshevik mission to Russia.

Although it can be said that Mackinder was successful in disseminating his message during the academic entrepreneur stage of his career, he was at best only partially successful in implementing his theories in practice as an action-intellectual in Russia. The utter incomprehension of H. A. L. Fisher and others like him toward Mackinder and his beliefs was due in part to the fact that Mackinder was overly committed to a static conception of geopolitics that discounted the importance of ideology and economics. Mackinder was indeed one of the first to base a whole system of thought on "a new sense of world unity that became ever sharper in the decades that followed as the railroad, telephone, bicycle, automobile, airplane, and cinema revolutionized the sense of distance."[110]

Geopolitics imposed order on what seemed to be a chaotic falling away from the comprehensible verities of a Newtonian universe. The most dynamic and productive part of Mackinder's intellectual life (encompassing the period from 1890 to 1919) overlaps with a period that the historians Stephen Kern and Donald Lowe categorize as being marked by a revolution in perception, a period constituting "a cultural revolution of the broadest scope ... one that involved essential structures of human experience and basic forms of human expression" and described by the other historian simply as "a perceptual revolution of 1905-1915."[111] The important consequence of this revolution with regard to Mackinder is the fact that "with the speeding-up of communication, perception of the present became more disconnected, begging for explanation or interpretation."[112] Mackinder, therefore, is best understood as an action intellectual who discerned the import of this "cultural revolution" in perception and cognition and sought to interpret this revolution (through the framework of geopolitics) for the benefit of empire abroad and a geo-domestically realized harmony at home.

Mackinder was an acute observer of the changed texture and perception of life brought about by technological breakthroughs, and sought to base his careers as both an academic entrepreneur and as an action-intellectual on his ability to interpret such changes for the benefit of the British Empire. While Alfred Thayer Mahan was writing about a world already on the wane when he emphasized the importance of a big navy in *The Influence of Seapower on History*, Mackinder thought he was predicting the future by showing how the Columbian era of seapower was inexorably giving way to an era dominated by landpower (although both geo-strategic thinkers shared a deep distrust of democracy).[113] But his focus on land power led him to lose focus on the power of capitalism to reframe the whole concept of international competition itself. He was unable to envision the formation after World War Two of a geoeconomic consensus politics in which, as Edward Luttwak puts it, "the logic of conflict is transformed by the grammar of commerce." While in the era stretching from 1870-1945 one could still craft a plausible argument that the territorial size of a state mattered (at least in *Realpolitik*, if not in moral, terms), after 1945 capitalism would transmute the very conditions which made territory so geopolitically valuable in the first place. We currently live in an era, for example, in which multinational firms on the cutting edge of globalization do not so much identify with territorial states as they do with the values of efficiency and the pursuit of cheaper labor costs. However, in an era marked by an epochal cognitive shift in perception, Mackinder was at the forefront of the effort to impose intellectual coherency on all the unsettling changes occurring in the twilight of what Arno Mayer has called the "persisting old regime." That Mackinder faced much resistance reflects the *vis inertiae* of a liberal political culture that was, except for its most perceptive elements, out of sync with the great changes in technological and scientific developments that had taken place up to 1914. This liberal culture was also, when pressed, bound to resist the profoundly illiberal domestic component of an overreaching geopolitical program.

The cultural barriers preventing the effective transmission of the geopolitical message were not permanent. Indeed, the culture to which Mackinder was speaking was itself changing, especially as the old liberal elite and its shibboleths came under increasing attack in the aftermath of the difficult Anglo-Boer War. Yet Bernard Semmel's question regarding British defense policy of this era (and that after World War One) remains: "Could a liberal and democratic public opinion be made to understand the harsh necessities of the world-wide struggle for power?"[114] The genealogy of geopolitics would suggest a positive response to this question, if public opinion could be made fearful enough of foreign threats. Two world wars and a "revolution in perception" later, Mackinder allowed himself to feel that his geopolitical prognostications were justified, as when he asked rhetorically in a speech after being awarded a medal from the American Geographical Association (presented by the American Ambassador to Britain, J.

G. Winant, in 1944), "Is not the cause of our two world wars fundamentally geographical?"[115]

Despite all of Mackinder's efforts to spread the geopolitical gospel in Britain, geopolitics instead (in the words of the geographer Isaiah Bowman) "migrated ... to America."[116] Though Mackinder always had to work hard in getting a hearing in Britain, his message was heard with enthusiasm by conservative geographers, statesmen, and, later, defense intellectuals in Germany and the United States. The reception of Mackinder's ideas was ultimately blunted in Britain by certain aspects of its culture. Martin Wiener, in his *English Culture and the Decline of the Industrial Spirit*, points out that efficiency and coherent long-term planning (both concerns of Mackinder) were "values that were not as encouraged in British society as they were, for example, in America."[117]

The cult of the educated amateur and practical man in British culture represented a "conflict of social values ... [which] were expressed in the two widespread and contrasting cultural symbols of Workshop and Garden."[118] Mackinder and his imperialist brethren saw the need to strengthen the workshop mentality in British life since they believed that Britain's imperial future would continue to depend on the strength of its old industrial base. Such attitudes, however, offended a particular segment of elite defenders of the garden metaphor for the British way of life. Such people believed that the true soul of authentic British life resided in the British countryside and not in London and Manchester, which represented for them the utter philistinism of industrial culture. The impact this had on Mackinder and his ideas was anything but negligible in his home country, since the "established elite regarded him as an uncouth, provincial outsider. He was 'coarse-grained' to Beatrice Webb, 'brutal' to Bertrand Russell, and apparently a 'philistine' to Balfour [who was Mackinder's supposed compatriot in the conservative party]."[119]

Eric Hobsbawm reminds us in *The Age of Empire* that this era "was not only an economic and political but a cultural phenomenon."[120] An examination of Mackinder's various careers—first as a leader in the professionalization of geography, then as an academic entrepreneur, and finally as an action intellectual *manqué*—attests to the cogency of Hobsbawm's remark. The phenomenon of European imperialism, and, in this case, British imperialism in particular, show the importance of bourgeois liberal culture as a crucial mediator between imperialists and the imperialized.

W. H. Parker posits that a "river is a geographical fact, but the culture of the people approaching it will determine whether it is to be a barrier or a means of communication, a water supply or a source of power."[121] Mackinder's geopolitical interpretation of "geographical reality" offered not only policy recommendations for Britain's conduct of external affairs, but a policy of geo-social imperialism at home as well. That this interpretation ultimately found only limited support within British governing circles attests to the limits placed upon a purely power-politics view of the world by a liberal democratic culture increasingly bent on facing up to the contradictions and economic costs inherent in the idea of an imperial democracy.

The manner in which Mackinder attempted to have his ideas heard and acted upon by the imperial decision-makers of his day set an important precedent for what would later be called the defense intellectual, a precedent that sought to depoliticize and objectify the debate on imperialism through the use of the language and the authority of science. The fact that Mackinder anticipated what a majority of policy-makers in the Western world were at least tacitly assuming after World War Two to be true merely underscores the truth of the idea that:

> The problems which scientists recognize, the methods they use, the types of theories they regard as satisfactory in general or adequate in particular, the ideas and models they use in solving them, are those of men and women whose life, even in the present, is only partly confined within the laboratory or study.[122]

Halford Mackinder was certainly an archetypal and important representative of what T. W. Heyck has labeled the "emergence of the 'intellectuals'" taking place in Britain and elsewhere at this time.[123] Mackinder's legacy lies not so much in the official policy he tried to influence, but rather in his ability to prepare the way for a popular acceptance of a geopolitical view of the world.

Notes

1. Concerning the cultural context of international relations, I am particularly influenced by Akira Iriye's "Culture and Power: International Relations as Intercultural Relations," SHAFR presidential address given at San Francisco, 29 December 1978.

2. E. W. Gilbert and W. H. Parker, "Mackinder's 'Democratic Ideals and Reality' After Fifty Years," *Geographical Journal* 135 (1969): 229; W. H. Parker, *Mackinder: Geography as an Aid to Statecraft* (Oxford: Clarendon Press, 1982), 161.

3. On other attempts to place Mackinder in an imperial context, see B. Hudson, "The New Geography and the New Imperialism: 1870-1918," *Antipode* 9 (1977) and G. Kearns, "Closed Space and Political Practice: Frederick Jackson Turner and Halford Mackinder," *Environment and Planning D: Society and Space* 1 (1984).

4. D. R. Stoddart, ed., *Geography, Ideology, and Social Concern* (Totowa: Barnes and Noble, 1981), 90.

5. I am referring to Donald Lowe's *History of Bourgeois Perception* (Chicago: The U. of C. Press, 1982) and Stephen Kern's *The Culture of Time and Space* (Cambridge, MA: Harvard U. Press, 1983).

6. Brian Blouet, *Halford Mackinder: A Biography* (College Station: Texas A & M University Press, 1987), 22.

7. Blouet, *Halford Mackinder*, 26.

8. Richard Symonds, *Oxford and Empire* (New York: St. Martin's Press, 1986), 10 and *passim*.

9. Blouet, *Halford Mackinder*, 28.

10. Blouet, *Halford Mackinder*, 100.

11. Halford Mackinder, "The Teaching of Geography from an Imperial Point of View," *Geographical Teacher* 6 (1911): 83.

12. Halford Mackinder, "Higher Education," in *The Nation's Need: Chapters on Education*, ed. Spencer Wilkinson (London: Archibald Constable and Company, Ltd., 1903), 233.

13. Symonds, *Oxford*, 141.

14. Eugen Weber, in *Peasants into Frenchman*, stresses the importance of education in the making of the modern French nation as defined by its geography. Symonds notes as well, in *Oxford and Empire* (p. 142), that "if the [British] Empire was to develop any cohesion, then education must play a vital role in bringing citizens of many parts of the world to some understanding of the Imperial ideal."

15. Stoddart, *Geography, Ideology*, 197.

16. Preston E. James, *All Possible Worlds: A History of Geographical Ideas* (New York: The Odyssey Press, 1972), xi.

17. Quoted in Blouet, *Halford Mackinder*, 36.

18. Quoted in Blouet, *Halford Mackinder*, 40.

19. Halford Mackinder, "On the Scope and Methods of Geography" reprinted in Mackinder, *Democratic Ideals and Reality* (New York: Holt, 1962), 239.

20. Mackinder, "Scope," 218.

21. Mackinder, "Scope," 214 and 217.

22. On the nuances regarding the establishment of the post of reader of geography at Oxford, see D. R. Stoddart, *On Geography* (New York: Basil Blackwell, 1986), 124-125.

23. The term "academic entrepreneur" to describe this aspect of Mackinder's career is also used by D. R. Stoddart, *On Geography*, 73.

24. T. W. Freeman, *A History of Modern British Geography* (London: Longmans, 1980), 82.

25. Freeman, *History*, 42.

26. Mackinder, "The Teaching of Geography From an Imperial Point of View," 84. Mackinder also saw the geography as a latter-day "queen of the sciences." In his view, "The geographer takes from the astronomer, the physicist, chemist, geologist, biologist, historian, economist, and strategist certain results of their special studies, combines them into his own vision of a dynamic system, builds up his natural regions and finally groups these into his world conception."

27. Mackinder, *Democratic Ideals and Reality*, 143-148.

28. Mackinder, "Modern Geography, German and English," *Geographical Journal* 6 (1895): 367-79.

29. Mackinder, "The Teaching of Geography From an Imperial Point of View," 367.

30. As Gollwitzer points out, apropos of Mackinder and others, in *Europe in the Age of Imperialism* (p. 102), "the founding and strengthening of the Hohenzollern Reich, and the Prussian-German army, made a strong impression on a great many Englishmen and was one of the reasons they began to pursue an imperialist course in power politics and military policy."

31. *Hansard's Parliamentary Debates*, Fifth Series, House of Commons, 10 January 1916.

32. Heinz Gollwitzer, *Europe in the Age of Imperialism* (London: Thames and Hudson Ltd., 1969), 161.

33. It should be remembered that Mackinder was aware of how this passing of the four-hundred-year-old Columbian epoch (an epoch dominated by Europe) coincided with the rise of the U.S. and Japan and non-European world powers (as demonstrated conclusively by the victory of the U.S. in the Spanish-American War of 1898 and by the Japanese victory over Russia in the Russo-Japanese War of 1904-5). It should also be noted that Mackinder's thinking on the Columbian epoch occurred at a time of public

reflection on Columbus and the Columbian legacy (as manifested most obviously in Chicago's Columbian Exposition of 1893).

34. Mackinder, "The Geographical Pivot of History," reprinted in *Democratic Ideal and Reality*, 259.

35. Mackinder, "Geographical," 265.

36. Mackinder, "The Great Trade Routes," *Journal of the Institute of Bankers* 21 (1900): 155.

37. Mackinder, *Britain and the British Seas* (Oxford: Clarendon Press, 1902), 343.

38. Mackinder, "Geographical," 242.

39. Mackinder, "Geographical," 263.

40. On the fact that this competition was not universally read into the nature of things, see L. Clark, *Social Darwinism in France* (U. of Alabama Press, 1984), 3.

41. Mackinder, "Man-Power as a Measure of National and Imperial Strength," *National and English Review* 14 (1905): 143. He already wondered in his work whether "it may be that the balance of geographical advantages has already inclined against England, and that she is maintaining her position by inertia." Mackinder, "The Physical Basis of Political Geography," *Scottish Geographical Magazine* 6 (1890): 80.

42. Mackinder, *Britain and the British Seas*, 342.

43. J. L. Gaddis comments that Containment (as a doctrine justifying defensive expansionism) offers a "line of reasoning reminiscent of Halford Mackinder's geopolitics." Gaddis, *Strategies of Containment* (New York: Oxford U. Press, 1982), 57.

44. Mackinder, "The Music of the Spheres," *Proceedings of the Royal Philosophical Society of Glasgow* 63 (1937): 177.

45. Sydney Webb, "Twentieth Century Politics," lecture to the Fabian Society, November 8th, 1901 (Oxford School of Geography).

46. Webb, "Twentieth Century Politics," 142.

47. Much of the Anglo-American literature on this topic is discussed in Richard Hofstadter's *Social Darwinism in American Thought* (Boston: Beacon Press, 1992).

48. Benjamin Kidd, *Social Evolution* (New York: Grosset & Dunlap, 1898), viii.

49. Kidd, *Social Evolution*, 45.

50. Geoffrey Parker, *Western Geopolitical Thought in the Twentieth Century* (New York: St. Martin's Press, 1985), 42.

51. Mackinder, "The teaching of Geography From an Imperial Point of View," *Geographical Teacher* 6 (1911), 79.

52. Clarendon Press sold 1.4 million copies of the geographer A. J. Herbertson's textbooks while George Philips sold one-half million copies of Mackinder's works before World War One (Symonds, 145). Herbertson was a colleague of Mackinder's at Oxford who believed that "The country which first gives this [geographical] training to its statesmen will have an immeasurable advantage in its struggle for existence" (Symonds, 144).

53. Predictably, this version of geography was not accepted without questioning in Britain. Many liberals thus opposed teaching geography in universities because it was thought to promote militarism. The response was attributable in no small part to the visceral association made by many between the device of the map and the scientific, thorough approach to war maintained by the German General Staff and the militarism it stood for. See Symonds, 145.

54. Mackinder, "Geographical Pivot of History," 263.

55. *Hansard's Parliamentary Debates*, Fifth Series, House of Commons, 23 February 1910.

56. Wilkinson, *The Nation's Need*, 250.

57. Quoted in G. R. Searle, *The Quest For National Efficiency* (Berkeley: U. of California Press, 1971), 81.

58. Quoted in G. Kearns, "Halford John Mackinder," *Geographers: Biobibliographical Studies*, vol. 9. Edited by T. W. Freeman (London and New York: Mansell Publishing, 1985), 79.

59. Mackinder, *Democratic Ideals and Reality*, 8.

60. *Hansard's Parliamentary Debates*, House of Commons, 19 February 1912.

61. Mackinder, *Democratic Ideals and Reality*, 241-2.

62. Mackinder, "The English Tradition and the Empire," *United Empire* 16 (1925): 3.

63. Mackinder, *Democratic Ideals and Reality*, 196.

64. *Hansard's Parliamentary Debates*, Fifth Series, House of Commons, 16 May 1917. In the same speech, he also asserted that "democracy is in no position to cope with the wiles, calculations, and organizations of autocracy and bureaucracies."

65. *Hansard's Parliamentary Debates*.

66. Bernard Semmel, *Imperialism and Social Reform* (New York: Anchor Books, 1968), 166.

67. Semmel, *Imperialism*, 61.

68. G. R. Searle, *The Quest for National Efficiency* (Berkeley: U. of Calif. Press, 1971), 145.

69. Searle, *Quest*, 143.

70. Searle, *Quest*, 256.

71. One must say "likely" since the minutes of the Coefficient club's meetings never attribute individual names to the printed views discussed during the meetings (on file at the Oxford School of Geography). Since Amery was the club's expert on military affairs, and since Mackinder was also interested in such affairs and was close to Amery intellectually, such an attribution of views seems appropriate and probable. There was even a morbid tendency to "think the unthinkable" in early Coefficient club meetings, as when Russell quit the club after Amery suggested sending the bulk of Britain's population over to Canada in case of a war with the United States.

72. Mackinder Papers, Autobiographical Fragments, Oxford School of Geography.

73. These individuals could be labeled variously as Roseberyites (liberal imperialist followers of the former P. M.), Milnerites (conservative imperialist followers of the former High Commissioner to South Africa), and Fabians (followers of the socialist reformers Sydney and Beatrice Webb).

74. Wilkinson was in the audience when Mackinder delivered his Pivot paper at the RGS in 1904, and could easily have informed his brother-in-law Eyre Crowe (an official at the Foreign Office responsible for the famous 1907 memorandum on German aims and intentions in foreign policy) of its contents.

75. Parker, *Western Geopolitical Theory*, 49.

76. Quoted in Blouet, *Halford Mackinder*, 113.

77. Mackinder, *Democratic Ideals and Reality*, 150.

78. Mackinder mentions in the autobiographical fragments he left after his death that "About fifty Captains and Majors passed through them [the courses], some of whom are now Generals. In this connection I visited most of the Army & Navy centres of Education from the Staff College at Camerley, and the War College at Portsmouth to Osborne and the Duke of York's school. I lectured to many hundred Officers" (Mackinder Papers, Oxford School of Geography).

79. Representative of this category of work are E. W. Gilbert, *Sir Halford Mackinder 1861-1947: An Appreciation of His Life and Work* (London: Bell, 1961)and G. Parker, *Mackinder: Geography as an Aid to Statecraft* (Oxford: Clarendon Press, 1982).

80. Thus Fred Kaplan, in *Wizards of Armageddon* (New York: Simon & Schuster, 1983) begins his story after World War Two, tacitly assuming the necessity of correlating the advent of nuclear weapons with the advent of the "defense intellectual" who arose to develop rational strategies for their use.

81. Roman Kolkowicz, "The Strange Career of the Defence Intellectuals," *Orbis* (1987): 179.

82. Mackinder's influence on the German geographer Karl Haushofer and his journal *Zeitschrift für Geopolitik* is well-known (Haushofer called Mackinder's pivot thesis "the greatest of all geographical world views" [Quoted in Blouet, *Halford Mackinder*, 78]). His indirect influence on Hitler is subject to debate, but Hugh Trevor-Roper sums up the popular view when he writes: "That Hess was a channel whereby Haushofer's geopolitical ideas were conveyed to Hitler's mind, there to be transformed into the doctrine of Eastern *Lebensraum*, seems to me almost certain" (quoted in W. H. Parker, *Mackinder*, 182). Less studied is the connection between geopolitics as first formulated by Mackinder and the American Containment policy first articulated by George Kennan. After *Newsweek* in February 1941 made the grandiose claim that Nazi grand strategy was based on Mackinder's ideas, "Geopolitics became an American fad" (Blouet, *Halford Mackinder*, 191). The publication history of *Democratic Ideas and Reality* (1919) illustrates this since the book was specifically reissued for American readers in 1942 with two prefaces by Americans, while a Penguin paperback edition appeared in 1944. Mackinder's ideas also found their way to an American audience *via* the works of the American geographers Nicholas Spykman, Hans Weigert, and R. Strausz-Hupé.

83. Gollwitzer, *Europe*, 110.

84. As defined by Bernard Semmel in *Imperialism and Social Reform*, social imperialism "was designed to draw all classes together in defence of the nation and empire and aimed to prove to the least well-to-do class that its interests were inseparable from those of the nation" (p. 24).

85. Gollwitzer, *Europe*, 110.

86. Gollwitzer, *Europe*, 74.

87. Mackinder, *Democratic Ideals and Reality*, 208.

88. Mackinder, *Democratic Ideals and Reality*, preface.

89. Mackinder, *Democratic Ideals and Reality*, 15.

90. Mackinder, *Democratic Ideals and Reality*, 23.

91. Mackinder, *Democratic Ideals and Reality*, 143. He still maintained that "The rapid German growth was a triumph of organization ... of the strategical, the 'ways and means' mentality."

92. A possibility that did not seem to Mackinder far from reality since the events of 1904-05 showed how weak the political and military structure of imperial Russia really was, given its poor performance in war against Japan and its paralysis in the face of revolution.

93. Semmel, *Imperialism*, 118.

94. Mackinder, "The English Tradition and the Empire: Some Thoughts on Lord Milner's Credo and the Imperial Committees," *United Empire* 16 (1925): 5.

95. Mackinder thus gave intellectual credence to the early Containment policy aimed at Bolshevik Russia and described by Arno Mayer, *The Politics and Diplomacy of Peacemaking* (New York: Knopf, 1967).

96. Mackinder, *Democratic Ideals and Reality*, 10.

97. The full text of Curzon's instructions to Mackinder can be found at the Public Record Office, London, or in E. L. Woodward and R. Butler, eds., *Documents on British Foreign Policy, 1919-39*, First Series, vol. 3, HMSO 1949, 672-678, 681.

98. Mackinder's report on the situation in south Russia, printed in Woodward and Butler, eds., *Documents on British Foreign Policy, 1919-1939*, 768-787.

99. Mackinder, *Democratic Ideals and Reality*, 170.

100. Mackinder, *Democratic Ideals and Reality*, 148.

101. Quoted in Blouet, *Halford Mackinder*, 174.

102. Mackinder's report.

103. Mackinder's report.

104. Mackinder's report.

105. Mackinder's report.

106. Mackinder, *Democratic Ideals and Reality*, 30.

107. Quoted in Blouet, *Halford Mackinder*, 188.

108. Mackinder, "The English Tradition and the Empire," 73.

109. Quoted in Blouet, *Halford Mackinder*, 176.

110. Stephen Kern, *The Culture of Time and Space* (Cambridge, Mass.: Harvard U. Press, 1983), 213.

111. Kern, *Culture*, 5. Donald Lowe elaborates on this thesis in his *History of Bourgeois Perception* by arguing that "Recent scholarship reveals that communications media, hierarchy of sensing, and epistemic order change in time. Hence the perceptual field constituted by them differs from period to period. There is a history of perception" (p. 2). Further (p. 7), "the communications media in each period, whether oral, chirographic, typographic, or electronic, emphasize different senses or combinations of them, to support a different hierarchical organization of sensing. And change in the culture of communications media ultimately leads to change in the hierarchy of sensing."

112. Kern, *Culture*, 30.

113. Unfortunately, Mahan's thoughts about domestic affairs are as ignored as Mackinder's. Along with Mackinder, he questioned the ability of a democracy to meet the threats posed by its less scrupulous adversaries. He wondered "Whether a democratic government will have the foresight, the keen sensitiveness to national position and credit, the willingness to insure its prosperity by adequate outpouring of money in times of peace, all which are necessary for military preparation, is yet an open question. Popular governments are not generally favourable to military expenditure, however necessary, and there are signs that England tends to drop behind." A. T. Mahan, *The Influence of Sea Power on History: 1660-1805* (Englewood Cliffs, NJ: Prentice Hall Inc., 1980), 56.

114. Bernard Semmel, *Liberalism and Naval Strategy* (Boston: Allen & Unwin, 1986), 179.

115. Speech at the American Embassy in London by the American Ambassador, printed in the *Geographical Journal* 103 (1944): 131.

116. The enthusiastic reception that geopolitics was to receive after World War Two through the intellectual auspices of such emigré scholar-geographers as Nicholas Spykman is well shown in Ambassador Winant's speech on the occasion of the award of the A. G. S. Medal to Mackinder. In effect taking symbolic guardianship of the flame of geopolitical thought on behalf of the U.S., Winant said (in regard to Mackinder) that "It was outlook which makes your name world famous to-day as the first who fully enlisted geography as an aid to statecraft and strategy. You previsioned what has won fashion a geo-politics. Unlike less worthy successors you have always been mindful of the responsibilities owed by science to democracy and to have furthered democracy's cause in your

geography as an aid to statecraft and strategy. You previsioned what has won fashion a geo-politics. Unlike less worthy successors you have always been mindful of the responsibilities owed by science to democracy and to have furthered democracy's cause in your writing and in service to your country. You were the first to provide us with a global concept of the world ... " (*Geographical Journal* 103, p. 131).

117. Martin Wiener, *English Culture and the Decline of the Industrial Spirit* (Cambridge: Cambridge U. Press, 1981), 15.

118. Wiener, *English Culture*, 6.

119. Blouet, *Halford Mackinder*, 137.

120. Eric Hobsbawm, *The Age of Empire* (New York: Pantheon, 1987), 76.

121. W. H. Parker, 121.

122. Hobsbawm, *Age*, 251.

123. T. W. Heyck, in *The Transformation of Intellectual Life in Victorian England* (1987) dates the rise of the intellectuals from 1870-1900. These intellectuals "were a self-conscious, distinct group with common attitudes of superiority, aloofness and detachment" (Heyck, *Transformation*, 9).

Chapter 4:
Haushofer and the Pursuit of German Geopolitics

> The politics of a state is in its geography.
>
> –Napoleon

> For my father was that lot ordained.
> It once lay in the power of his will
> To thrust the demon back into prison.
> But my father broke the seal.
> He sensed not the breath of evil.
> He set the demon free to roam throughout the world.
>
> –Albrecht Haushofer, *Sonnets from Moabite Prison*

Karl Haushofer believed in the Latin adage *fas est hob doceri*—it is necessary to learn from one's enemies. After serving as an officer in the German army during World War One, Haushofer began his career as a geopolitician intent on using the insights gained from the study of Mackinder's writings. He took these writings to embody the greatest of all geopolitical views. German conservatives such as Haushofer and the soldier Heinz Guderian serve as examples of influential Germans who spent much time in the interwar years struggling with the question of why Germany lost the Great War. While Guderian and other forward-looking German soldiers were seeking inspiration from British theorists of armored warfare such as Liddell Hart and J. F. C. Fuller, Haushofer found particular inspiration in Mackinder's "pivot paper" of 1904, which viewed Eastern Europe and western Russia as potentially providing the strongest basis for world power in the twentieth century. Hart, Fuller, and Mackinder all bemoaned the fact that their own leaders did not take their ideas seriously.

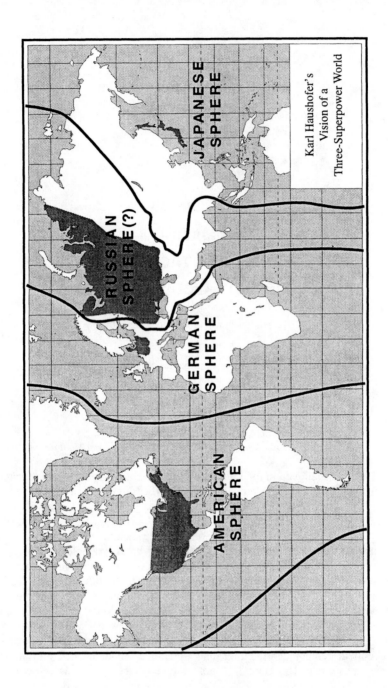

Karl Haushofer's
Vision of a
Three-Superpower World

Never did they imagine that Germans such as Haushofer and Guderian would be their most enthusiastic students.

During the time of Germany's greatest military successes in World War Two, foreign observers were struck, among other things, by Germany's blitzkrieg tactics and the country's seeming reliance on Haushofer's geopolitics. A small cottage industry devoted to explicating the nefarious influence the geopolitician Haushofer was thought to have on Hitler developed in America shortly after the outbreak of war. This work was exemplified by a *Reader's Digest* article of July 1941 titled "The Thousand Scientists Behind Hitler" that argued: "Dr. Haushofer and his men dominate Hitler's thinking," and that Hitler's military campaigns could not start "until Haushofer was ready."[1] Contemporary observers who knew Germany better and treated the phenomenon of Nazism in a scholarly way took a more nuanced approach to Haushofer's influence, seeing him as someone helping to shape the popular cartographic consciousness. Siegfried Neumann, for example, argued for the paramount influence of Hitler in Nazi Germany by claiming that "The Haushofer school made a whole generation think spatially" (while arguing for the necessity of America to do likewise).[2] Haushofer and the other geopoliticians under review took as their task the need to make their nations think in terms of continents.

The image contemporary observers had of World War Two (and that persists to a great extent today) tends to take for granted the importance geopolitically inspired maps played in that conflict. The image of Hitler and the "numerous portrayals of military leaders bent over maps in Nazi publications" attest to the importance of maps as symbols that shape their users' image of reality for good and for bad.[3] Nazi propaganda films such as *Sieg im Westen* (*Victory in the West*, 1940) exploited maps to make Nazi military victories seem inevitable and just. Propaganda maps could be used for immediate military advantage as well. Maps portraying the hopelessness of the allied position at Dunkirk were dropped on British soldiers there in 1940 just as the Nazis were about to expel the them from the continent. Propaganda publications in book form (such as the *War in Maps* volume that was distributed through the German Library of Information in New York in 1941) sought to develop *spatial* arguments for the inevitability (and justifiability) of German victories up to that point. The *War in Maps* volume was soothingly prefaced with the assertion that "Together the text and the maps solve many problems difficult to understand from official communiques and newspaper dispatches. Certain formerly incomprehensible phases of the war are suddenly revealed as *simple problems* in geopolitics."[4]

Haushofer's influence appeared to his contemporaries so great that even Father Edmund Walsh (a professor at Georgetown University)—assigned to interrogate Haushofer after the war for possible war crimes violations—admitted that the German *Geopolitiker* had influenced the lectures he gave at the General Staff School at Ft. Leavenworth, Kansas and at the Georgetown School of Foreign Affairs. Even in 1955 when the RAND Corporation produced a study on the Haushofer-influenced publication *Zeitschrift für Geopolitik*, the view of Haushofer as an evil mastermind continued to prevail. In the language of the

RAND study, "Haushofer hammered away at this concept [geopolitics] until, chiefly as a result of his efforts, it became a household word throughout Germany."[5] The U.S. government took the threat of Haushofer and German geopolitics seriously enough to hire the respected American geographer Derwent Whittlesey during the war to analyze German geopolitical literature.[6]

While Haushofer became widely known outside of Germany during World War Two, he was already well known as an author and academic in Germany during the 1920s and 1930s. Publishing some 500 items during the course of his career, he became best known inside of Germany for his most popular book *Weltpolitik von Heute* (1934) which went on to sell over 100,000 copies. All told, Haushofer's writings went through more editions than any other books in Germany save those of Hitler and Alfred Rosenberg in the interwar period. Advertisements of his book compared Haushofer to the great *Denker* tradition represented by Machiavelli, Kant, and Darwin.[7] By 1932, one year before the Nazi *Machtergreifung*, geopolitics was accepted as an examination subject in German universities.

Even though his publishing output in Germany and his recognition outside of Germany during World War Two were impressive, the most common interpretation of Haushofer as the master influence behind Hitler's conception of *Lebensraum* is wrong.[8] For years after World War Two, many observers took for granted the one-time existence of a geopolitical institute led by Haushofer in Munich that was said to have heavily influenced Nazi views on foreign policy. In fact, no such institute ever existed, and any of the influence Haushofer originally had with Hitler began to wane drastically after the Munich Conference when Haushofer expressed reservations about the rapid and openly aggressive course of expansion being embarked upon by Hitler.[9] The clearest illustration of their differences would come when Hitler invaded the Soviet Union in direct opposition to Haushofer's long-standing view on the necessity of cooperation between Germany and the U.S.S.R. The attempt to find a genetic link between Haushofer's ideas and Hitler's actions in misconceived. A better question concerns how Haushofer succeeded in mobilizing Germany's "spatial awareness" on a popular level. He certainly gave legitimacy to the idea that Germany's leading problem between 1870 and 1945 was its "lack" of territory, rather than its lack of democracy. Haushofer's adherence to geopolitics—seemingly validated in the West by Mackinder's many writings—helped neutralize claims that he was simply a non-scientific propagandist. Indeed, the very structure of geopolitical discourse, as we have seen, was naturally conducive to a profoundly anti-democratic politics and the growth of an elite coterie of defense intellectuals.

What stands out about Haushofer is his fear (one shared by Mackinder) that middle-sized nation states like Germany were being gradually dwarfed in significance by larger continental states such as the United States and Russia. Indeed, contrary to the particular demonization of Haushofer by his contemporary and present-day critics as a *Blut und Boden* believing Nazi, Haushofer actually shared more in common in terms of his geopolitical methodology and conclusions with like-minded organic conservatives in Britain and America. All such conservatives were pessimistic about the future of middle-sized nation states, for all saw possession of space as the highest marker of international status for nations. Such conservatives also saw Western capitalism as a socially dangerous form of economic organization. Most importantly, the geopolitically-minded among them took advantage of the propaganda possibilities inherent in maps to argue for the scientific inevitability of their conclusions. Their apparently pragmatic and scientifically based realism would live on to influence the school of postwar American realists who, like their geopolitical forebears, tended to downplay the power of ideas and ideals.

Haushofer's Career

Born in 1869 and living until 1946, Haushofer's life aptly overlaps with Germany's rise to great power status during the very same geopolitical age it helped to define. From the Franco-Prussian War of 1870-71 to the end of World War Two in 1945, Germany's military prowess and determination to expand spatially—along with its near success in doing so—impressed upon the language of international politics the largely unquestioned axiom that the more physical space a nation controlled, the greater would be its power and prestige.

Haushofer's early career as a military man (charged as he was with defending the recently created boundaries of the Second Reich) could only have reinforced this axiom in his mind. After graduating from the Royal Maximilian Gymnasium in Bavaria in 1887, Haushofer joined the regiment of Prince-Regent Luitpold of Bavaria, in which unit he became a non-commissioned officer in 1888. Eventually, Haushofer was deemed "outstandingly suited for the teaching profession" by his teachers at the Bavarian war academy where he studied for three years (1895-98). In 1896 he married Martha Meyer-Dross who, being Jewish, would lead to Haushofer being placed under increasing suspicion during World War Two. By 1899 Haushofer won assignment to the Bavarian General Staff. His career as a teacher began in 1904 when he started teaching modern military history at the Bavarian War Academy.

An important turning point in his life came in 1908 when he was sent as a Bavarian military observer to the Far East. There he visited Japan, India, Korea, and China until his travels ended in 1910. This experience strongly turned Haushofer's intellectual interests in the direction of studying the relation between geography and world politics, as evidenced by the publication of his first work *Dai Nihon* in 1913. In this same year he began doctoral work in geography at the University of Munich. His study was interrupted by the outbreak of World War One and his subsequent service in the German army. During this time he commanded units of the Bavarian contingent in the German army on both the Western and Eastern fronts until 1918. His wartime letters attest to the final shaping of a conservative world view that would later be articulated with great constancy in the 1920s and 1930s.[10]

After the war, Haushofer left the Bavarian army in 1919 with the rank of major-general and returned to the academic life in Munich that he had left in

1914. After finishing his doctorate, Haushofer stayed on at Munich as a *Privatdozent* (lecturer) in geography where he first met Rudolf Hess, a favorite student who would later serve as his patron after the National Socialists came to power (at least until Hess flew to Scotland 1941). In 1921, Haushofer was made *Honorarprofessor* (extraordinary professor) at the University of Munich, a position he would maintain to the end of World War Two.

Haushofer first began to enter in the political life of his country in 1923 when he participated in secret negotiations with the U.S.S.R. These negotiations would eventuate in the signing of the Rapallo Treaty and in the end of Germany's diplomatic isolation. A favorite theme of Haushofer's concerned the inevitable struggle between the "have" powers represented by Britain, France, and the U.S. and the "have not" powers represented by Germany, the U.S.S.R., Italy, and Japan. The "have" powers possessed disproportionate space while "have not" powers such as Germany and the U.S.S.R. would have to work together to gain their "fair share" of territory. Haushofer was a great believer in the "spatial dialectic" theory of history whereby progress is attained *via* the struggle of political entities over territory. World history becomes, in this view, but a footnote on the *a priori* logic of geopolitics.

This theme dominated Haushofer's contributions to the *Zeitschrift für Geopolitik*, the journal which he helped to edit from 1924-1931. During this time the journal published writings that attacked the Versailles Treaty much in the same way that Hitler did; that is, as a brutal *Diktat* having no moral legitimacy. The journal therefore played a role in legitimizing resistance to the Versailles system by helping to foment a climate of opinion conducive to Hitler's campaign for power. In 1924, Haushofer was introduced to Hitler by Hess in the Landsberg prison where Hitler was "imprisoned" after the failed Beer Hall Putsch of 1923 (an imprisonment Hitler would later sarcastically refer to as "my university time"). Haushofer would later take pride in the fact that he had given Hitler Ratzel's book, but would deny after the war that he personally influenced *Mein Kampf*, claiming as he did to his interrogator Father Walsh after World War Two that he did not take Hitler's book seriously enough to review in *ZfG*.[11]

Contrary to popular belief, Haushofer's greatest influence crested well before the outbreak of war in 1939. Besides gaining public exposure through his output of books and articles for *ZfG*, Haushofer was a leading member of three important organizations during the interwar period. He co-founded the German Academy in 1926, chaired the *Volksdeutscher Rat* (ethnic German council) from 1933-35 under Hess's auspices, and chaired the *Volksbund für das Deutschtum im Ausland* (People's League for Germans and German Culture Abroad) from 1938-1942. All of these organizations were concerned with the spreading of German cultural influence abroad. Haushofer's participation in the Munich Conference of 1938 represented the apogee of his influence on the Nazi government (even though overseas he would be perceived at the time as becoming ever more influential on Nazi policies). After disagreement with Hitler about the need for immediate further expansion in the wake of the Munich conference, in 1939 Haushofer retired from his university position and turned down an offer to serve as ambassador to Japan. After Hess's flight to Scotland in 1941, Haushofer came under increasing suspicion by the Nazi authorities because of his close ties with his former pupil. His son Albrecht, a geographer in his own right, was executed by the SS on 23 April 1945 for taking part in resistance activity against the Nazi regime. Haushofer and his wife, despondent over the death of their eldest son and the destruction of their vision of Germany as a world power, took their own lives on 10 March 1946.

Precursors to Haushofer and the German Geopolitical Vision

As the term "geopolitics" became part of the *lingua franca* in serious discussions of world events during the course of World War Two, commentators trying to put the term into historical context often went back to ancient Greece as a starting point. The attempt to find a genealogy for applied geopolitics by harking back to figures as diverse as Aristotle, Bodin, Montesquieu, Buckle, Ritter, Kjellèn, and Mackinder as part of a coherent "geopolitical tradition" helped to lend credence and legitimacy to Haushofer's efforts. Haushofer himself was concerned to legitimize his geopolitics with particular reference to the geographer Friedrich Ratzel and the Swedish political scientist Rudolf Kjellèn. Both figures were enormously important for helping to define the geopolitical era in European history (1870-1945) by first using the terms "geopolitics" (coined by Kjellèn) and "*Lebensraum*" (coined by Ratzel) to describe it.

Like Haushofer, Ratzel and Kjellèn cannot be said to be direct forebears of Nazi ideology in any strict teleological sense. All three were ardent German conservatives who believed in the social hierarchy typified by the Second Reich. They also desired to see Germany hegemony over the European continent based on a new world balance of power system rather than on the basis of racial ideology. Although Ratzel introduced *Lebensraum* as a term into modern political discourse, his primary interest lay in formulating the laws behind the territorial growth and decay of political entities. Ratzel's famous seven laws went as follows:

> 1) The space of states increases with the growth of culture; 2) The growth of states follows other symptoms of development: ideas, commercial production, missionary activity; 3) The growth of states proceeds by the amalgamation and absorption of smaller units; 4) The frontier is the [external] organ of the state, and as such it is the [measure] of the growth, the strength, and the [health] of that organism; 5) In its growth the state tends to include politically valuable sections: coast lines, river beds, plains, regions rich in resources; 6) The first impetus for territorial growth comes to the primitive state from without, from a higher organization; 7) The general trend toward amalgamation transmits the tendency of territorial growth from state to state and increases the tendency in the process of transmission.[12]

These laws of growth gave expression to the Social Darwinistic fear felt by Ratzel and other German conservatives that Germany must expand or perish.

98 Chapter 4

The catalyst for this perception was encapsulated in Ratzel's view that the mid-sized European nation-state of the nineteenth century was outmoded. Ratzel's principle concerning the *Primat des Grossraum* is illumined in his comment that:

> The European system of rural but intensively used spaces is retrograde in the face of [contemporary states based on *Grossraum*] because it cannot be [the pattern] of the future: a pattern which today, as it has for millenia, strives unremittingly after ever-larger spaces. The larger states, such as represented by the United States, are the modern expression of a political state in which new developments take place, and which especially benefit from the accomplishment of commerce.[13]

Ratzel and other nationalist Germans worried over the fact that Germany's portion of the figure of an average yearly 620,000 square kilometers annexed per year (from 1875-1914) by European colonial powers was miniscule in comparison to that spatial area amassed by Britain and France during this time. Ratzel's founding of the *Alldeutscher Verband* in 1890 represented an attempt to translate his theory of political geography into political action.

Ratzel died before Haushofer turned from military life to geography. Rudolf Kjellèn, on the other land, lived to 1922, long enough to exchange ideas with Haushofer through correspondence. While Haushofer was at the front during World War One, for example, he found the time to express his admiration for Kjellèn's geopolitical thinking. On 10 October 1917, Haushofer thanked Kjellèn for the latter's *Die Grössmachte der Gegenwart*, a work that, like Ratzel's writings, was concerned with the struggle of great European states to adjust to a post-European balance of power.

This book would go through twenty-two editions between 1914 and 1930 and is judged by Sven Holdar as "probably the most circulated 'geopolitical' work through history."[14] Just as Ratzel provided Haushofer with the concept of *Lebensraum*, Kjellèn provided Haushofer with the term "geopolitics" itself. As a political scientist at Uppsala University, he found that the audience for his ideas was primarily in Germany rather than in his native Sweden. Geopolitics itself was but one of five terms Kjellèn used to divide up the political life conducted by modern states. As for the other terms, "eco-politics" for Kjellèn reflected a state's attitude toward economic organization, "ethno-politics" analyzed a state according to its ethnic make-up, "demo-politics" analyzed a state its population size and distribution, "crato-politics" examined a state for its method of political organization, and "geo-politics" studied the state according to its geographical situation.

Geopolitics was, therefore, never as important for Kjellèn as it would be for Haushofer. Kjellèn simply intended that his categories be used as heuristic tools by political scientists in their attempt to compare and analyze nation-states. Kjellèn, like Ratzel and Haushofer, was conservative and pro-German in his outlook. Like the others, he also saw nationalism as providing the cohesive force holding society together. At the same time, he abhorred the notion of class as divisive and weakening for the body politic.[15] Besides providing Haushofer with the term geopolitics, Kjellèn—perhaps more importantly—provided Haushofer with an idea of a "pan-regional" view of the world that the latter would subsequently develop in detail. As Kjellèn saw it, the U.S. was likely to dominate over the Americas in the future just as Germany and Japan were likely to dominate their respective regional backyards. Kjellèn assumed that Britain and France were in decline (even before World War One) because of the rise of a new world balance of power that was quickly eclipsing the now parochial European balance of power that once so dominated Europe. Underlying Kjellèn's analysis of world politics was his deeply held belief that the liberal and egalitarian values associated with the French Revolution were gradually and inexorably giving way to the hierarchical and nationalistic values associated with Germany in the early twentieth century.

Haushofer can be thought of as important not so much for any truly original idea he might have developed over the course of his career, but rather for his tremendous ability to synthesize and simplify important ideas for general and elite consumption (including Mackinder's warning concerning the vulnerable status of the medium-sized nation-state). Haushofer, as we shall see, combined Ratzel's *Lebensraum* idea with Kjellèn's notion of geopolitics to develop a coherent world view designed to "teach Germany's masters," as he put it, to avoid the mistakes made in the Great War in the inevitable struggles to come. This Haushoferian *Weltanschauung* was also, of course, greatly influenced by Mackinder's heartland concept; a concept which gave Germany a seemingly rational reason for seeking a power base on the European continent rather than overseas (as Tirpitz and the navalists had advocated during the Second Reich). Once the ideas behind *Lebensraum*, geopolitics, and the heartland were carefully melded together by Haushofer, *Geopolitik* as it developed in the twenties and thirties would find fertile ground among a population long exposed to the idea of Germany as the leading power of Europe. This idea of Germany at the head of *Mitteleuropa* (and described in great detail by continentalist-minded civilian militarists such as J. Partsch, F. Naumann, A. Hettner, and A. Penck) incorporated the perpetual German sense of being fated to occupy a dangerous central position in Europe. Geography in this cultural context therefore took on a life of its own by becoming an actor in its own right.

The Organizational Context of Geopolitics in the Interwar Period

The *Zeitschrift für Geopolitik* was but one of six important geographical journals published between 1933-1945.[16] *ZfG* itself was aimed at a general readership (with a circulation of 7,500 copies at its height), being sold at news stands and taking contributions from writers who were not professional geographers. Other writers besides Haushofer contributed to the *ZfG* and other publications associated with geopolitics. Otto Maull, Erich Obst, Hermann Lautensach, Kurt Sapper, F. Termer, and H. Hassinger were all geographers equally concerned with geopolitics in this period. The important research concerns of these and other geographers in Weimar and Nazi Germany included Germany's relations with Japan, Austria, Scandinavia, and Africa. It would be fair to say as well that attention to political geography dominated over physical geography in the German geographical research of this period, a fact that is understandable in the context of Germany's preoccupation with revising the Versailles peace treaty. The Nazis were especially interested in fostering geographical research on Austria and the Soviet Union (*Ostforschung*) in the 1930s.[17] Both of these particular interests were connected with the Nazi foreign policy aims of obtaining *Anschluss* with Austria and planning future territorial expansion at the expense of Eastern Europe and Russia.

Defining what exactly *Geopolitik* meant was difficult for German geographers of this time. Haushofer himself retreated from the opportunity to define geopolitics at various points in his career.[18] F. Hesse assayed a definition in a *ZfG* article that captures the assumption of what geopolitics was for many German geographers of the day by writing that "Das Werden und Vergehen der Geschichte zeigt bei aller Unterschiedlichkeit im einzelnen eine gleiche Erscheinung: Das Wachstum der Menschen an Zahl und dammit zugleich der Große der von ihnen beherrschten Raume" [For all the particularities history shows in its evolution and fading periods, a unique phenomenon stands out: a growth in population naturally leads to a growth in the space that people will rule over].[19] German nationalist geographers from Ratzel to Haushofer built their geographical theories on this fundamental assumption that the larger the population, the larger the territory that population deserved. An attempt to define that potentially amorphous subject of geopolitics was made in 1928 when Haushofer and other editors of *ZfG* declared that:

> Geopolitics is the science of the conditioning of political processes by the earth. It is based on the broad foundations of geography, especially political geography, as the science of political space organisms and their structure. The essence of regions as comprehended from the geographical point of view provides the framework for geopolitics within which the course of political processes must proceed if they are to succeed in the long term. Though political leaders will occasionally reach beyond this frame, the earth dependency will always eventually exert its determining influence.[20]

Interestingly enough, *ZfG* was not totally closed to anti-geopolitical viewpoints before 1933 (after which date, of course, opposing opinions to the attainment of *Lebensraum* could not be countenanced in print under the *Gleichschaltung* policy of the Nazis). Karl Wittfogel, for example, published a critique of geopolitics that interpreted it as a kind of bourgeois substitute for Marxism. Where Marxism assumed class conflict to be the drivewheel of history, Wittfogel saw geopolitics substituting conflict over space for conflict between the classes as the main theme in historical evolution. This point, in fact, would later be partially shared by Nazis who disliked the prominent place given to

Raumpolitik (spatial politics) over and above *Rassenpolitik* (race politics) in *ZfG*.

German geographers were not the only figures in Germany to have some influence in shaping the cartographic consciousness of the German populace. Figures as diverse as Ewald Banse, Oswald Spengler, and Hans Grimm all participated in this effort (really one of mental mobilization) to equate a state's prestige and well-being with its size. A leading theme in Spengler's *Decline of the West*, after all, concerns the idea that a people's identity is bound up in a mystical way with the "organic" connection it has to a particular territory. While the geographer Ratzel might have introduced *Lebensraum* into the official German political vocabulary, it was the novelist Hans Grimm whose *Volk Ohne Raum* helped to popularize the notion of *Lebensraum*. This novel deals with the protagonist Cornelius Freebott's search for land in British-run South Africa. After being rudely rebuffed there by the anti-German British, Freebott returns to Germany realizing that farmland and *room for expansion can only be obtained in Europe itself*. The implication of the novel was that the overseas colonization strategy pursued by Britain and France would have to be matched by a German attempt to colonize Eastern Europe. This tale underscores the two defining halves of the geopolitical age. During the first half (1870-1914), territorial expansion was—to a great extent—coterminous with the colonial enterprise conducted outside of Europe. During the second half of this era (1914-1945), the territorial aspirations of countries such as Germany focused on Europe itself. *Volk ohne raum* first appeared in 1926. By 1933, 265,000 copies of the novel had been sold. Another signal that geopolitical logic was reaching the popular imagination is found in the fact that Ewald Banse's *Germany Prepares for War* appeared in 1934 and caused a public outcry abroad for its advocacy of forcible German expansion based on the immutable facts of geography.

Official Nazi reaction to geopolitics was—contrary to what one might expect—quite mixed. On the one hand, the Nazis found the geopoliticians' emphasis on *Lebensraum* useful. On the other hand, the Nazis were uncomfortable with the relatively independent course taken by *ZfG* and individual geopoliticians. The *Gleichschaltung* that was sweeping other German institutions in the wake of the Nazi rise to power eventually affected German geography as well. In 1934, geographical teachers from the primary level to the university level were re-organized and re-oriented under Nazi auspices. Nazi concern over geopoliticians' penchant for emphasizing spatial over racial politics came to a head in 1935 at a meeting held at Bad Sarow. The *Arbeitsgemeinschaft für Geopolitik* (Geopolitical Study Group) was pressured after this meeting to put *Rassendenken* (race-thinking) on an equal plane with *Raumdenken* (space-thinking). When spatial ideology threatened to achieve primacy over racial ideology, Nazi authorities were prepared to force a reversal of priorities in German geopolitics. By 1941 the ultimate dominance of Nazi ideology over a truly independent geopolitics was shown when the Nazi organization *Deutsche Geographische Gesellschaft* was founded. This organization sought to put all other geographical organizations under one leading Nazi dominated organization.

The effects of this move on German geopolitical thought was most famously demonstrated when the *ZfG* editorial line on the necessity for harmonious Russo-German relations abruptly shifted toward support of the Nazi invasion of Russia in 1941. Previous to this date, German geopoliticians such as Haushofer were persistent advocates of political cooperation between Germany and Russia. After the invasion of Russia, however, an argument was offered by the *ZfG* in defense of the invasion. Since space had "shrunken" since Napoleon's invasion of Russia in 1812 because of technological developments, it was now (mechanically) argued that Hitler's invasion should not be compared to Napoleon's disastrous venture. The rationale given for this weak argument went as follows: "If, for example, the Führer occupied Europe from the English Channel to the Urals, the area would present him with the same problems as were presented Napoleon in a [mere] march to the Rhine" given the relative shrinking of space since the Napoleonic era.[21] This officially supportive statement was repudiated by Haushofer after the war when he stated that Hitler's Russian venture constituted a "deadly sin" against geopolitics.

Geopolitik as a Response to Germany's *Mittelage* : Haushofer's Goals for Germany

After the end of the war, Justice Jackson, working for the prosecution at the Nuremberg Trials, instructed Dr. Walsh, an American expert on geopolitics who later "set out to transform the Georgetown School of Foreign Service into an American version of Hashofer's Institute of Geopolitics,"[22] to deal with Haushofer in the following manner:

> Dr. Walsh will endeavor to have Haushofer prepare a final statement which shall point out the evil consequences of German geopolitics and why it developed the way it did. This admission ... should be far more profitable from an educational point of view than would result from putting Haushofer in the dock as merely one more among the twenty-two already indicted.[23]

The ideas that caused so much fear abroad in regard to German geopolitics dealt with a number of constant themes. Haushofer and his followers always believed in the need for Germany's leaders to see geopolitics as being of practical use. As Haushofer proclaimed in the *ZfG*, "Die Neuordnung des Verhaltnisses eines Volkes zu seinem Boden gehort zu den größten aufgeben, die dem Staatsman gestellt sind [the building of a proper relationship between a people and its territory is among the greatest tasks that belongs to the statesman]."[24] Haushofer would constantly reiterate this theme of, as he put it, the need to "educate our masters," in large part because of his belief that World War One had been lost by Germany's confused grand strategy of seeking to be a great sea power and land power at the same time. Geopolitics, according to Haushofer, should aspire to serve as the "geographical conscience of the state." Contrary to critics' assertions that Haushofer was a geographical determinist, he himself claimed that only "some twenty-five percent" of a state's situation is determined by geopolitical factors. This twenty-five percent could have a decisive effect in international conflict, however.

In order to have a nation reap the benefits of geopolitical knowledge, the German public's cartographic consciousness would have to be raised. As Haushofer exhorted the German public through the *ZfG* in 1936, "Do not be narrow-minded but think in large terms of great spaces, in continents and oceans, and thereby direct your course with that of your Führer."[25] Haushofer and other German geopoliticians wrongly believed that since the geographically informed American Inquiry had aided the "Anglo-Saxon" powers in effecting an anti-German peace treaty after World War One, German geopolitics constituted a kind of defensive cartographic response to the Versailles settlement. For Haushofer believed that geopolitics, "as an exact science ... deserves serious consideration" by Germany's governmental authorities.[26]

Geopolitics should be of interest to Germany's rulers so that Germany would not be outdistanced in the twentieth century by larger land-based territories. As Haushofer put it:

> In a world that tends more and more toward large-space organization such as the British Empire, the United States, and the Soviet Union, a small internally torn and overpopulated continent would be unable to maintain itself in the long run. Only a united Europe had a chance to stand up against the giant powers who today dominate the face of the earth.[27]

Haushofer in much of his writing expressed the same paranoia over Britain that Mackinder expressed over Germany. Where Mackinder perceived that British seapower could no longer compete with great landpowers in the geopolitical era, Haushofer sensed that Germany's territorial basis was too small compared to larger territorial entities.

Haushofer agreed with Mackinder on two important themes in particular. First, he accepted Mackinder's notion that the struggle between land and sea-powers originated with Europe's sea-borne expansion outside of Europe beginning in the fifteenth century.[28] Secondly, he joined with Mackinder in fearing and respecting the landpower represented by the Soviet Union. Haushofer's geopolitical eschatology uniquely differed from Mackinder's, however, in the importance he placed upon the Far East. He thought highly of Japan as a geopolitical model worthy of German emulation for its calculated, patient, and seemingly single-minded pursuit of hegemony in the Far East and for its conservative social hierarchy. He believed that the "Indo-Pacific" region was the ultimate location of a future great war, greater even than the Second World War.

At the core of Haushofer's thinking about world politics was his so-called *Panideen* notions. Haushofer envisioned America, Germany, Japan, and possibly Russia as dominating their respective geographical regions. The *Panideen* he talked about amounted to "supernational all-englobing ideas seeking to manifest themselves in space." America, therefore, would dominate North and South America with its democratic ideals, Germany would dominate Europe and Africa with its own particular world view, and Japan would exercise predominant influence over East Asian affairs. Russia was something of a wild card in this geopolitical vision since Haushofer was not sure whether she would cooperate peacefully in this largely tripartite continentalist division of the world or not. If Russia cooperated, her influence could extend to India (but not Eastern Europe, which was to be reserved for German influence). If Russia chose not to cooperate, Haushofer, like Mackinder, could envision at some unspecified date conflict between Germany and Russia occurring over the heartland.

Never was his advocacy of this conflict as impatient and impulsive as Hitler's, however. It is fair to say that Haushofer largely counted on cooperation with the Russians in his geopolitical schemes, as is evident in his comment that "irrespective of whether they are organized by the Soviets or any other power" good relations with the heartland power would be most beneficial to Germany.[29] No matter how Russia fit into the *Panideen* scheme, each pan-regional grouping was to be autarkic since every central power in each region was to be surrounded by exploitable, colonizable territories. Germany, therefore, would attain economic self-sufficiency in the future by running surrounding areas of Europe and Africa in a way similar to the manner in which he believed the British had run India.

The rationale for seeing the world divided into pan-regions was enunciated in a variety of ways over time. Haushofer, of course, was insistent upon the fact that great powers of European size were no longer adequate in facing up to the new realities of international politics. His ability to strike a chord with many Germans—Nazi and non-Nazi alike—also had something to do with his ability to touch upon the general German anxiety regarding encirclement, or *Einkreisung*. The desire to find ways to break out of this "middle" position was thus eminently exploitable by the German geopoliticians. Haushofer and other German geographers sympathetic to geopolitics were also adept at exploiting the idea of self-determination. Since Germany's *Volksboden* and *Kulturboden* overlapped with the sovereignty claimed by a host of surrounding European states, Haushofer was able to capitalize on another incendiary issue. The larger struggle against the Versailles settlement would have to be waged, in Haushofer's view, not alone but in cooperation with other "have-not" powers of the interwar period such as Russia and Japan (and India and China, if possible). Haushofer also sought to delegitimize certain borders in his quest for rationalizing German geopolitical aims. For Haushofer, "borders are anything but ideal—they are living organisms extending and recoiling like the skin and other protective organs of the human body."[30] Finally, Germany was justified in seeking hegemony in its pan-region of Europe and Africa because of the unjust distribution of population in Europe. Haushofer arrived at a figure of a healthy population-to-land ratio of one hundred people per square kilometer. Germany, having one hundred thirty-three people per square kilometer of territory, was, geopolitically speaking, duty-bound to pursue *Lebensraum*. In his words:

For every nation is primarily concerned with the task of maintaining itself in a hostile environment, and since its very existence depends on the possession of an adequate space, the preservation and protection of that space must determine all its policies.[31]

German geopolitics as understood by Haushofer was, in many ways, quite dualistic. Established seapowers—embodied for Haushofer by Britain and America—would always be in conflict with rising world powers such as Germany and Japan. While Haushofer believed Germany could be flexible in regard to the tactics of expansion (regarding such elements as timing, alliances, and ideological rationales), his attitudes toward the "Anglo-Saxon" powers, as he liked to call them, were anything but flexible. Japan, Russia, and Germany were "the only group of powers able to defend [themselves] ... against the Anglo-Saxon tutelage."[32] As early as 1918 Haushofer expressed his hatred of the capitalist and democratic western states in a rather pungent manner: "Schwindelgewerbe des angelsachsischen Plutokraten—und Gross-Kapitalistenringes, dem wir ... in Grunde doch alles Elend des Europaischen Krieges zu verdanken haben [it is to the cheating Anglo-Saxon plutocrats and capitalist cliques that we have to thank for the misery of the European war]."[33] Britain, France, and now America were all lumped together as "space robbers" who had taken more than their fair share of territory in the epochal geopolitical division of the world; a division that was taking place largely without Germany's participation.

Haushofer and Domestic Geopolitics

In 1943, Haushofer reflected upon what he believed he and his fellow geopoliticians had been fighting for since the end of World War One. Facing official distrust and knowing the war was essentially lost at this point, Haushofer summed up what he and other German geopoliticians had been trying to say for almost two decades:

Aber gerade die treuesten unserer Leser erinnern sich, das in der Z. f. G. viele dieser Bewegungen seit Jahrzenten vorausgesagt worden sind: die Abwehrsuche der ubervolkerin raumbeengten Machte des inneren Halbmonds der Alten Welt, der 'Havenots' gegen die 'Haves'; der Wiederaufstieg Sudostasiens zur Selstbestimmung; die Dynamik und latent Energie des Japanischen Reichs; die kommendend Ubergriffe der Pan-ideen, Panamerikas vor anderen; die Einheit der Indo-pazifischen Raumes trotz dem trennungsversuch von Singapur...[Devoted readers of Z. f. G. remember that the leading movements in world politics for decades have been predicted on these pages. Such movements include: The search for defense of the overpopulated and spatially confined powers of the inner crescent of the old world (a search pitting the spatial 'have-nots' against the spatial 'haves'); the dynamic and latent energy of the Japanese empire; the resurrection of Southeast Asia to self-determination; the coming dominance of the pan-ideas (especially that of Pan-

America); and the unity of the Indo-Pacific space in spite of the divisive example of Singapore].[34]

This summation of German geopolitical views does not incorporate the domestic policy implications of geopolitics, however. In this area Haushofer shared with Mackinder a belief in the usefulness of geosocial policy to describe the purpose of the modern nation-state. Only a united and harmoniously functioning state would be healthy enough to pursue geopolitical goals abroad. Haushofer can therefore be considered a reactionary, but in a traditionalist, rather than in a National Socialist, sense. Haushofer was never a Nazi party member even though his anti-Semitism and expansionary aims coincided at least partially with Nazi ideology.[35]

Haushofer believed that domestic unity was predicated on maintaining the traditional social hierarchy of Imperial Germany, limiting the extent of free-market capitalism, and fighting against the cosmopolitanism associated with urbanization. Haushofer shared with many conservative Germans the view that Jews symbolized the cosmopolitanism, urbanism, and capitalism that threatened the semi-feudal social order of Imperial Germany. He differentiated between assimilated west European Jews (such as his wife) and the so-called *Ost-Juden*, or Jews from Eastern Europe and Russia.[36] He had no official connection with the Holocaust and disagreed, at least privately, with Nazi racial ideology.[37] Haushofer believed that "The more hopeless its position, the more reason for a people to think in terms of the planet without regard to mistaken race prejudice."[38] Haushofer was thus loathe to sacrifice the mantle of scientific legitimacy surrounding geopolitics by appending Nazi racial ideology to his spatial science.

In a larger sense, it might be said that Haushofer sought to match the unchecked capitalist expansion of the Anglo-Saxon powers with German territorial expansion. Because Haushofer associated urbanism with the international capitalism that he saw as threatening to German culture, Haushofer argued that "Urbanization may also be considered as a weakening of space mentality."[39] Capitalism as practiced by the Anglo-Saxon powers was understood by Haushofer to contribute to economic and social decay. He thought this decay could only be held at bay by a renascent Germany that concentrated on territorial expansion, even at the expense of participation in the international capitalist economy. Haushofer, like other German conservatives and Nazis, believed in the inherent superiority of the agrarian lifestyle over the citified lifestyle associated with modernity. In the end, Haushofer's wager on the primacy of space as a measure of power would be proved wrong in the course of two world wars; wars which instead demonstrated the even greater power of "rootless" Anglo-Saxon capitalism to shape international relations and great power hierarchies.

In sum, Haushofer assumed that German geopolitical aims abroad could only be secured on the basis of an applied domestic geopolitics. Geopolitics, as it applied to foreign and domestic affairs, had to be sold not only to the statesman but to the average citizen as well. Thus Haushofer used the radio to gain mass exposure to his ideas in his monthly survey of world politics.[40] The guiding principle of publicizing geopolitics involved getting the German populace to "learn to think in continents." For Haushofer, it was "imperative that even the average citizen have an intelligent understanding of the exigencies of foreign policy."[41] The geopolitical era, among other things, witnessed the growth of mass politics and mass education; facts that necessitated Haushofer's attention to selling geopolitics on a popular level as well as to the statesmen that he so hoped to influence. After the fall of the Kaiser's Second Reich, the kind of conservative political power that Haushofer wished to see rule Germany in the post-World War One era could only do so on the basis of popular approbation. Haushofer was successful in popularizing such terms as "soil mastery," "space struggle," "organic frontiers," "manometers" and making them relevant to conservative political arguments of the day.[42] Haushofer understood the importance of education in the political life of Germany. As he stated, "What seemed most lacking in the resumption of the educational process for the training of German youth after the war was the capability to think in terms of wide space (in continents!)"[43] Besides recognizing the importance of the educational system for spreading the geopolitical gospel, Haushofer was concerned with winning the working class over to the cause of German geopolitics. According to Haushofer, until the geopoliticians arrived, no one took "the trouble to *explain to the German worker that most of his troubles were caused by lack of space* ... instead the worker's attention was diverted to petty quarrels about materialistic interpretations of history [emphasis mine]."[44] In short, Haushofer—along with Mackinder—envisioned geopolitics as an antidote to Marxism as well as to Anglo-Saxon capitalism.

Haushofer's Influence on Hitler

Many students of the relationship between Hitler and Haushofer still adhere to the view expressed by the historian Klaus Hildebrand, who holds that "The circle around the Munich geopolitician Professor Karl Haushofer... seems to be responsible for the idea of *Lebensraum* and its adoption in Hitler's program."[45] Not only was there no discernible "Munich school," there is also no clear evidence to suggest that Haushofer was a leading architect behind Nazi foreign policy. It is true that Haushofer met perhaps ten times with Hitler between 1922 and 1938 and famously provided the latter with copies of Ratzel's *Political Geography* and Clausewitz's *On War* to him during the future dictator's stay in Landsberg prison. Some students of this period suggest as well that he provided Hitler with the *Lebensraum* term which would become a pillar of Nazi ideology.[46] As the Nazi period drew to an end, Haushofer himself reflected over his reputed influence on Hitler in the following manner:

I visited the Führer then in the Landsberg fortress on various occasions. In 1923 and 1924 the prisoner merely thumbed through what he found of geopolitical literature in the fortress. Now certainly I stimulated the people, counselled [them]. In certain parts of *Mein Kampf* there are strong traces of this. But then they popularized my train of thought falsely and for the purposes of propaganda.[47]

The truth concerning Haushofer's influence on Hitler probably lies some-where between the "master architect" thesis and the self-serving humble dis-avowals offered by Haushofer after the Nazi collapse. Both Hitler and Haushofer were useful to one another. Hitler seemed to Haushofer up until 1939 the kind of *Lebensraum*-attaining leader he had been hoping for since the end of World War One.[48] Hitler's desire to reverse the Versailles settlement and his desire to see Germany expand territorially under the guise of exercising the Wilsonian right of self-determination (as in the *Anschluss* with Austria) overlapped with Haushofer's sense of Germany's mission. Hitler appeared to be the leader who might follow geopolitical axioms successfully in transforming Germany from its small European nation-state status into a world power. Hitler and the Nazis bene-fited from cooperation with Haushofer because of the geopolitician's ability to lend the patina of scientific legitimacy to Nazi purposes and propaganda aims. The relationship therefore did not involve mutual influence so much as it sug-gested a convergence of thought on the broader aims of German foreign and domestic policy.

This convergence of thought between the two concerning the belief that Germany was physically too small to compete militarily and economically with its competitors underlines the fact that German geopolitics and Nazi ideology expressed in different ways the assumption that the possession of great space was synonymous with great power status. The geopolitical era (1870-1945) in European history was itself marked, in a sense, by the conflict between two dominating ideologies: the belief in the primacy of capitalism's border-piercing productive powers and the contrasting belief in an autarkic geopolitics that privileged control of space over markets as a measure of national well-being and strength.

The noteworthy thing about the relationship between Hitler's and Haushofer's world views was how they supported the latter ideology and casti-gated the former. The capitalist "Anglo-Saxon" powers were thus seen as anti-thetical to Germany's organic, autarkic integrity. Haushofer shared with Hitler the feeling that Anglo-Saxon capitalist culture was partly responsible for the increasing sense the "Nothing is rooted within us any longer. Everything is superficial, flies away form us. The thinking of our people is becoming restless and hasty. All life is being torn asunder."[49] Although they had much in common in their spatial politics, Hitler's elevation of racial politics onto or even above the plane occupied by his spatial policies seemed to Haushofer self-defeating. Hitler's obsession with what Arno Mayer has termed "Judeo-Bolshevism" would, of course, lead to the invasion of Russia and the consequent two-front war that German geopoliticians had long warned against.

Nevertheless, it is useful to see how the geopolitical era's concerns were expressed in Nazi ideology as well as in Haushofer's geopolitics, if only to see how powerful and pervasive these concerns were in defining the "geopolitical age." The period 1870-1945 was a map-hungry age; an age in which German geopoliticians, educators, and political figures such as Hitler relied on maps as validating tools for their belief in the need for the accumulation of ever more territorial space. Such personages of this era also used maps as consensually accepted markers of relative national status.[50] Just as one can speak of capital accumulation, geopolitical theorists of this age believed in the necessity for the continual accumulation of space as a sign of national power, virtue, and health. In an aside on his study of Nazi war aims, Norman Rich notes the importance of maps in the Nazi era when he writes that "Ethnic maps, linguistic maps, geopolitical maps, maps embodying every variety of claim and speculation decorated Nazi party offices, government buildings and schoolrooms."[51]

Hitler shared in the geopolitical era's obsession with space. R. G. L. Waite, a biographer of Hitler, notes that "All his life, Adolf Hitler had been fascinated with space."[52] One does not have to psychoanalyze Hitler to see why this might be the case. His *Mein Kampf*, *Secret Conversations*, speeches, and *Table-Talk* serve as repositories of his thought that amply testify to his desire to see Germany break out of the outdated European balance of power system and enter a new world balance of power system by leading a unified Europe under German control. Hitler was constant in his belief that "Only if all of Europe is united under a strong central power can there be any security for Europe from now on. Small sovereign states no longer have a right to exist."[53]

Mein Kampf, which Hitler dictated to Haushofer's favorite student Rudolf Hess, was full of geopolitical concerns and jargon. A theme of the book's chapter fourteen (which concentrates on foreign policy) is that "Germany will either be a world power or there will be no Germany."[54] This feeling, of course, was not unique to Hitler and Haushofer alone, but no doubt was also shared by the millions of Germans who supported the Nazis, as well as by statesmen and citizens in Europe's western democracies.[55] Hitler declared in this same chapter, for instance, that "Today we find ourselves in a world of great power states in process of formation, with our own Reich sinking more and more into insignificance."[56] With the rise of the American union, Hitler declared, "a new power of such dimensions has come into being as threatens to upset the whole former power and orders of ranks of the states."[57]

Competing nations in the minds of Hitler and Haushofer were therefore to be compared with Germany almost solely on the basis of *spatial* attributes. Missing from their observations of such countries as Britain, Russia, China, and America was detailed attention to cultural patterns, history, and economic conditions. Hitler simply said of these countries in *Mein Kampf* that "All are spatial formations having ... an area more than ten times greater than the present German Reich."[58] In connection with this all-important comparison, Hitler complained as well about "the absurd area of five hundred thousand square kilometers" that Germany occupied.[59] For Hitler, as for the German geopoliticians in general, the nation's ability to control more and more space was correlated with its hypothesized significance and well-being. Hitler asserted in this regard that "the general power-political strength of the state to no small extent is determined by geo-military considerations."[60] Of interest too in *Mein Kampf* is Hitler's expression of a pre-rational love of a land area identified with a favored culture, a love expressed as well by the organic conservatives Haushofer and

Mackinder. According to Hitler, one could "Never forget that the most sacred right on this earth is a man's right to have earth to till with his own hands, and the most sacred sacrifice that blood that a man sheds for earth."[61] In a world goaded into rapid change between 1870 and 1945 by such forces as modern capitalism, mass democracy, and modern science, European nationalists such as Hitler (and philosophers of a geo-social conservatism such as Haushofer and Mackinder) preferred to view space and its successful control as a marker of stability and order.

Hitler's *Secret Conversations* elaborates in the context of the late 1920s some of the geopolitical themes discussed earlier in *Mein Kampf*. Peacefully awaiting for Europe's unification through the evolution of European democracy and capitalism was viewed with great disfavor by Hitler.[62] Such a unification must be accomplished "naturally" and "organically" through war. At the end of such conflict, one clear leader of Europe would emerge as the most fit to lead. A guiding philosophy for Germany's attempt to unify Europe by force was offered in Hitler's view that:

> Politics is the art of carrying out a people's struggle for its earthly existence. Foreign policy is the art of safeguarding the momentary, necessary living space, in quantity and quality, for a people. Domestic policy is the art of preserving the necessary employment of force for this in the form of its race value and numbers.[63]

This last idea hints at a domestic geopolitical agenda that Hitler to some extent shared with Haushofer and Mackinder. The nation could be made fit for expansion from within only if it succeeded in taming the unruly forces of capitalism, urbanism, and cosmopolitanism.

Haushofer's vision of geopolitics coincided with Hitler's foreign and domestic policies until roughly 1939. In 1934, Haushofer expressed the view in his *Der National-Sozialistische Gedanke in der Welt* that geopolitics and National Socialism were indeed in true harmony in their aims. In the same year he even wrote a letter to a friend in which he said that "Hitler had not forgotten that I was at Landsberg every week."[64] In 1939, however, Haushofer believed that the map of Europe then encompassed as much of the *Deutschtum* as possible for the time being.[65] From this point onward, Haushofer would express public support of Nazi policies but maintain private doubt about them. His last meeting with Hitler on 10 November 1938 (after the Munich conference at which Haushofer had been an advisor) was a stormy one.[66] In essence, Hitler and Haushofer differed about the timing and tactics of expansion and not over the need for expansion itself. Haushofer believed in exercising caution and restraint in pursuing territorial gains, qualities which Hitler was increasingly lacking from 1939 onward. Haushofer still hoped, for example, that German colonization efforts outside of Europe and *Lebensraum* in the East could be achieved by stealth and diplomacy.[67]

Tragically for Haushofer, agreement with Hitler seemed to cover only the most general of aims, such as the idea that Germany must expand territorially in order that it might be recognized among the elite of continentally based super-powers of the twentieth century. The direct response of the Nazis to some of Haushofer's ideas shows how greatly they differed on the means required to reach the goal of an expanded Germany. Nazi criticism of the geopoliticians came as early as 1937 when they called upon the geopoliticians to emphasize the importance of race *vis à vis* space and to downplay the importance of coopera-tion with Bolshevik Russia.[68] The Nazis and Haushofer's geopolitical school were bound to come into conflict with one another given the former's emphasis on a racially based ideology and the latter's strong environmentalism.

In 1941, the Nazis banned Haushofer's *Continental Block* (1941) because of its call for cooperation between the U.S.S.R. and Germany in the same year of Germany's attack on the Soviets. Haushofer's success in influencing the Nazis to cooperate with the Japanese was, in the short term, successful, but a failure in the long-term. In the end, Haushofer would claim after the war that among the Nazis only Rudolf Hess and Otto von Neurath were good students of geopolitics. Hess's flight to Scotland in 1941 and Von Neurath's earlier dismissal by the Nazis as foreign minister suggest how weak the personal connections were between the geopoliticians and Nazis.[69] Haushofer would claim after the war that "From autumn 1938 onward was the Way of Sorrow for German geopolitics."[70] Hitler's aide Martin Bormann gave credence to the notion that geopolitics ulti-mately failed to live up the expectations of the Nazi establishment when he ordered, near the end of the war, that "Haushofer should no longer be given any publicity."[71]

German Geopolitics in an International Context

The question of whether or not Haushofer had significant and direct impact on Hitler and his policies is not, ultimately, the most interesting question to raise about Haushofer and his geopolitics. What is most interesting about Haushofer and German geopolitics is the way in which he and his school articulated extraordinarily well German fears of being outsized in a twentieth century bal-ance of power system no longer focused on Europe. In expertly and articulately expressing this fear in the manner of a classic defense intellectual, Haushofer differed in degree rather than in kind from figures such as Mackinder. This inter-pretation differs from wartime and postwar attempts to hermetically seal "bad" geopolitics from "good" Anglo-American geopolitics or to treat each in isolation as mere apologists for fascism. Both Mackinder and Haushofer shared an aes-thetic belief in the efficacy of the organic metaphor as applied to state and soci-ety. In addition, they saw the need for a fairly rigid social hierarchy while fearing that the classical European balance of power system was becoming rapidly out-moded in the context of the growth of super-states such the U.S. and U.S.S.R.

Formal and informal geopolitical thinking in the period lasting from 1870 to 1945 expressed the hopes and fears of many who were witnessing the world being territorially divided up at rapid rates. In this era of fluid boundaries, geo-politics served a social function (especially in the Germany of post-World War

One years) in providing intellectual order and simplification in a time of immensely disorienting change. This intellectual stability offered by geopolitics as a key to international relations stood in contrast to the unstable and relativizing effects industrialization, modernism, and modern science were having on European societies. Sigmund Neumann during World War Two went so far as to say, in fact, that "Geopolitics must be considered as a reaction against Marxism, or better, as its counterpart, bourgeois Marxism."[72] Both Marxism and geopolitics offered their learned and unlearned believers confident explanations about the determining factors of history and the fate of nations in an era when the very ability to measure "power" was in flux. After all, the function played by dialectical materialism in the Soviet Union was mirrored in the West's reverence for geopolitical theory (especially in the period 1870-1945).

German geopolitics was, contrary to the aspirations of its creators, ultimately an unrealistic realism. By ignoring the role ideas and ideals have on a society, for example, Haushofer missed the truth of the *higher* realism that Mackinder at moments seemed aware of. Haushofer assumed that isolated geopolitical logic could be coldly used by German statesmen to advance Germany's territorial goals without having to take into account such non-material "epiphenomena" as ideas and ideals. Hans Speier, writing to an American audience during World War Two, argued that with German geopolitics, "geography becomes irrelevant: a puppet show with continents as actors unfold in its place."[73] He went on to say that "Today, maps are distributed on posters and slides, in books as propaganda atlases, on post cards, in magazines, newspapers and leaflets, in moving pictures, and on postage stamps."[74] It was ultimately in the area of gaining publicity that German geopolitics scored its greatest gains. By taking advantage of the era's new media for the mobilization of a unified and nationalized cartographic consciousness, German geopolitics gained the attraction (and eventual emulation) of foreign observers while offering the veneer of scientific legitimacy to Nazi goals.

An American student of German geopolitics, Father Walsh, would claim even after the war that roughly seventy-five percent of geopolitics was correct. As he said after the war, "Is there such a thing as legitimate geopolitics? Assuredly yes."[75] In the postwar attempt to paint Haushofer as an aberrational figure in geopolitics, the fear of the Soviet Union would continue to loom behind the attempt to differentiate the "bad" geopolitics associated with Haushofer from the "good" represented by Containment-minded western geopolitics. As Haushofer's interrogator put it, "The unknown geopoliticians behind the iron curtain in eastern Europe are maintaining a deep silence and are succeeding to an extent that must bring a sardonic smile to the ghost of Karl Haushofer."[76]

Notes

1. Quoted in J. H. Paterson, "German Geopolitics Reassessed," *Political Geography Quarterly* 6.2 (1987): 107.

2. Sigmund Neumann, "Fashions in Space," *Foreign Affairs*, 21.2 (1943): 278. Neumann also stated here that "It is on this first level of geopolitics that much can be learnt by an American world which has still not outgrown its grammar school days of scanty geographical instruction."

3. G. Henrik Herb, "Persuasive Cartography in Geopolitik and National Socialism," *Political Geography Quarterly* 8.3 (1989): 297.

4. G. Wirsing, ed., *The War in Maps* (New York: German Library of Information, 1941), preface. On page 6 it is asserted that Germany was again defensively struggling against *Einkreisung*, an "Encirclement [that] is the old, reliable tool of the West in its efforts to keep Central Europe in a state of political impotence."

5. Ewald Schnitzer, *German Geopolitics Revived* (Santa Monica: Rand Corporation, 1954), 2.

6. Derwent Whittlesey's papers are housed at the Harvard University Archives.

7. Edmund A. Walsh, *Total Power* (New York: Doubleday, 1948), 7.

8. For the classic view concerning the genetic link theory between Haushofer and Hitler, see Hugh Trevor-Roper's introduction and preface to *Hitler's Table Talk: 1941-1944* (London: Weidenfeld and Nicolson, 1973). An example of a recent argument against this view is found in H.-A. Jacobsen, "Kampf um Lebensraum: Zur Rolle des Geopolitikers Karl Haushofer im Dritten Reich," *German Studies Review* 4 (1979).

9. On this point, see H. Heske, "Karl Haushofer: His role in German Geopolitics and in Nazi politics," *Political Geography Quarterly* 6.2 (1987).

10. Information on this subject (along with other facts relating to Haushofer's career) is in part based on documents relating to Karl Haushofer in the German Federal Archives in Koblenz.

11. This interrogator was E. A. Walsh whose book (*Total Power*) concerns his impressions of Haushofer after the war.

12. Quoted in Robert Strausz-Hupé, *Geopolitics: The Struggle for Space and Power* (New York: G. P. Putnam, 1941), 30.

13. Quoted in M. Bassin, "Imperialism and the Nation State in Friedrich Ratzel's Political Geography" *Progress in Human Geography* 11 (1987): 480. Ratzel expressed this sentiment in a somewhat different way when he wrote that "Today every European statesman should try to learn something of Asia's and America's space sense so as to realize the smallness of European divisions and the dangers inherent in our ignorance of non-European space ideas. It is important for Europeans to know how the meager political quantities of our continent look from the height of American or Asiatic space concepts. Some day Europe's multitudinous states, viewed by Asiatic standards of political unity, might tempt someone into plans of dangerous boldness." Quoted in Andreas Dorpalen, *The World of General Haushofer: Geopolitics in Action* (New York: Farrar and Rinehart, 1942), 89.

14. Sven Holdar, "The Ideal State and the Power of Geography: The Life-Work of Rudolf Kjellèn," *Political Geography Quarterly* 11. 3 (1992): 321. There was even a Braille edition produced for disabled soldiers after the war.

15. Holdar, *Political*, 309. It is interesting to note in this regard that Kjellèn believed in the superiority of mixed races. A common culture was more important in his view than a common ethnicity. Holdar, *Political*, 313.

16. The *ZfG* published between 1924-1944. It was revived after the war and published from 1951-1968. H. Heske observes of these and other journals published in the Nazi period that "For all academic journals in the Nazi period, the propaganda ministry-association-publisher-editor chain determined the contents" (Heske, 271). This

Anpassung (pressure to conform) was furthered by the the dependence of these journals on government finance.

17. Heske, "Karl Haushofer," 279.

18. Jacobsen, passim.

19. F. Hesse, *Zeitschrift für Geopolitik* 1 (1924): 1.

20. Quoted in Gearóid Ò'Tuathail, *Critical Geopolitics* (Minneapolis: U. of Minnesota Pr., 1996), 46-7.

21. Carl Troll, "Geographic Science in Germany During the Period 1933-1945: A Critique and Justification," trans. by Eric Fischer, *Annals of the Association of American Geographers* 39, no. 1 (1947): 132.

22. Quoted in Ò'Tuathail, 49.

23. Walsh, *Total Power*, 36.

24. K. Haushofer, *Zeitschrift für Geopolitik* 11.4.

25. Walsh, *Total Power*, 45.

26. Quoted in Andreas Dorpalen, ed., *The World of General Haushofer: Geopolitics in Action* (New York: Farrar and Rinehart, 1942), 27.

27. Quoted in Dorpalen, *World*, 142.

28. As Haushofer put it, *Wehr-Geographie* "derives its strongest guiding force from the conflict between oceanism and continentalism which dominates all geography." Quoted in Dorpalen, *World*, 304.

29. Quoted in G. Stoakes, *Hitler and the Quest for World Dominion* (New York: St. Martin's Press, 1986), 151.

30. Quoted in Dorpalen, *World*, 107.

31. Quoted in Dorpalen, *World*, 38.

32. Quoted in Geoffrey Parker, *Western Geopolitical Thought in the Twentieth Century* (New York: St. Martin's Press, 1985), 67.

33. Quoted in D. Diner, "Gundbuch des Planeten: Zur Geopolitk der Karl Haushofer," *Vierteljahreshefte für Zeitgeschichte* 32 (1984): 11. He also spoke at this time of a special hate for "dollar-lusting" America.

34. K. Haushofer, "Zwei Jahrzehnte Geopolitik," *Zeitschrift fur Geopolitik* (1943): 184.

35. D. H. Norton, "Karl Haushofer and the German Academy, 1925-1945," *Central European History 1* (1968): 88. It is true that in 1938 Haushofer admitted keeping party activities secret on Hess's orders "for purposes of camouflage."

36. Mark Bassin notes how Haushofer showed some emotion when asked about the Holocaust in 1946. Bassin, 132.

37. H. A. Jacobsen, "Kampf um Lebensraum: Zur Rolle des Geopolitikers Karl Haushofer im Dritten Reich," *German Studies Reveiw* 4 (1981): 91.

38. Quoted in Dorpalen, *World*, 162.

39. Quoted in Dorpalen, *World*, 207.

40. T. W. Freeman, ed., *Geographers: Biobibliographical Studies:* Volume 12 (London: Mansell, 1988), 101.

41. Quoted in Dorpalen, *World*, 40.

42. Walsh, *Total Power*, 6-7.

43. Walsh, *Total Power*, 345.

44. Quoted in Dorpalen, *World*, 43.

45. Klaus Hildebrand, *The Foreign Policy of the Third Reich*, trans. by Anthony Fothergill (Berkeley: U. of California Press, 1973), 19. From the perspective of popular history, J. Fest holds that "Hitler dictated to him [Hess] parts of his ideological testament *Mein Kampf* and it was no doubt here that the dominating idea of *Lebensraum* found its

way into National Socialist ideology." Fest, *Hitler* (New York: Vintage Books, 1975), 191.

46. Heske, "Karl Haushofer," 270.

47. Quoted in Stoakes, *Hitler*, 156.

48. Jacobsen agrees that until 1939, Haushofer's goals overlapped with Hitler's. Jacobsen, 104.

49. Quoted in Fest, *Hitler*, 207.

50. Concerning the notion of interpretive communities and their role in the validation of "acceptable" knowledge, see Stanley Fish, *Is There a Text in this Class?: The Authority of Interpretive Communities* (Cambridge, Mass.: Harvard U. Press, 1980).

51. Norman Rich, *Hitler's War Aims: Ideology, the Nazi State, and the Course of Expansion*, vol. 1 (London: W. W. Norton & Co., Inc., 1974), xi.

52. R. G. L. Waite, *The Psychopathic God* (New York: Basic Books, Inc., 1977), 78. Hitler had also spoken often of the "grandeur of open spaces" in his "table talk."

53. Quoted in Walsh, *Total Power*, 48.

54. Adolf Hitler, *Mein Kampf*, trans. Ralph Manheim (Boston: Houghton Mifflin Co., 1971), 654.

55. The French were concerned with birthrates, manpower, and borders in a geopolitical sense even though France never produced a leading geopolitician of the stature of Haushofer or Mackinder (indeed, it produced some of its greatest critics).

56. Hitler, *Mein Kampf*, 645.

57. *Hitler's Secret Conversations: 1941-1944* (New York: Octagon Books, 1972), 83.

58. Hitler, *Mein Kampf*, 644.

59. Hitler, like Haushofer, trumpeted the fact that "there are, on average, 136 people to one square kilometer." *Secret Conversations*, 19.

60. Hitler, *Mein Kampf*, 643.

61. Hitler, *Mein Kampf*, 664.

62. *Secret Conversations*, 106. Hitler spoke of the futility in trying to "realize the Pan-European idea through a purely formal unification of European nations, without having to be forced in centuries-long struggles by a European ruling power."

63. *Secret Conversations*, 24.

64. Quoted in Stoakes, *Hitler*, 145.

65. E. Zoppo and C. Zorgbibe, eds., *On Geopolitics: Classical and Nuclear* (Dordrecht: 1985), 70.

66. J. D. Hamilton discusses the meeting well. Hamilton, *Motive for a Mission: The Story Behind Hess's Flight to Britain* (London: Macmillan, 1971), 71.

67. Hamilton, *Motive*, 84.

68. Heske, "Karl Haushofer," 140.

69. Walsh recalls Hess's explanation that, "I flew to England because my astrologers convinced me I was ordained to bring peace. Also, my old professor, Haushofer, had a curious dream. He saw me, the German born in Egypt, striding through the tapestried halls of English castles bringing peace between the two great nations."

70. Walsh, *Total Power*, 351. Walsh believed—even after World War Two—that "German geopolitics had originally—from 1919 to 1932—goals quite similar to American geopolitics."

71. Quoted in Hamilton, *Motive*, 211.

72. Neumann, "Fashions," 287.

73. Hans Speier, "Magic Geography," *Social Research* 8.3 (1941): 327.

74. Speier, "Magic Geography," 340.

75. Walsh, *Total Power*, 49.
76. Walsh, *Total Power*, 279.

Chapter 5:
Nicholas Spykman and the Creation of an American Geopolitics

Whether we view Mackinder's theory as fact or fancy, the entire American concept of Containment is inextricably bound up with his presentation of the Heartland theory before the Royal Geographical Society 60 years ago.
–G. E. Pearcy, Geographer of the State Department, 1964

Geopolitically the [Cold War] struggle, in the first instance, was for control over the Eurasian landmass and, eventually, even for global preponderance. Each side understood that either the successful ejection of the one from the western and eastern fringes of Eurasia or the effective containment of the other would ultimately determine the geostrategic outcome of the contest.
–Z. Brzezinski, 1992

Scholarly and popular awareness of geopolitical thought greatly increased with the beginning of World War Two in America. Geopolitics had long been overshadowed in the interwar period by the forces of isolationism and Wilsonian idealism. This began to change beginning on 23 August 1939 when the nonaggression pact between Nazi Germany and the Soviet Union was signed. Soon thereafter, the *New Statesman and Nation*, a British publication, reintroduced Mackinder into public consciousness in an article arguing that the newly signed pact was part of a larger geopolitical design whose origins lay in Mackinder's works.[1]

Such treatment of Mackinder was prescient in that it foreshadowed subsequent American attempts to link Nazi grand strategy to Haushofer and, ultimately, to Mackinder's original ruminations over the importance of the heartland in international affairs. Robert Strausz-Hupé, for example, spoke for many commentators on the geopolitical tradition when he stated the then

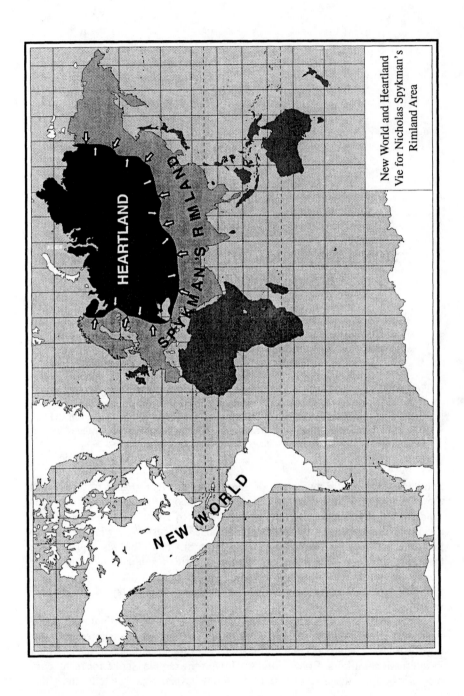

New World and Heartland
Vie for Nicholas Spykman's
Rimland Area

seemingly obvious fact that "For the leaders of Nazi Germany geopolitics is the blueprint for world conquest."[2] The shock of Pearl Harbor and the subsequent American involvement in a truly global war brought forth the need to raise American cartographic consciousness. Such consciousness-raising was deemed a necessary part of the war effort by political geographers and other commentators on geopolitics because of their belief in the need to reorient Americans to the exigencies of a new age in international affairs; a new age that would see the U.S. assume superpower status.[3]

Early Nazi battlefield successes spurred American observers to emulate elements of Nazi strategy for allied purposes. *Life* characterized the popular presentation of the geopolitical world view to an American audience *via* its December 21, 1942 issue with an article entitled "Geopolitics: The Lurid Career of a Scientific System Which a Briton Invented, the Germans Used, and the Americans Need to Study." The writer Frederick Sondern attempted to direct this message to a large audience through the *Reader's Digest* when, in an article titled "Hitler's Scientists: 1,000 Nazi Scientists, Technicians and Spies Are Working Under Dr. Karl Haushofer for the Third Reich," he wrote that "their ideas, their charts, maps, statistics, information and plans have dictated Hitler's moves for the very beginning."[4] It seemed only logical to many to emulate the apparent success of Haushofer and his "school." MGM's motion picture *Plan for Destruction* and Frank Capra's *Why We Fight* series also gave specific attention to Haushofer to illustrate the need for "slashing the tentacles of the geopolitical octopus with a brand of geopolitics of our own."[5] The political scientist Frederick Schuman argued during the first stage of the war, after all, that "*Geopolitik* has indeed become the inescapable frame of reference for all realistic thought and action in the realm of power politics in an age in which technology has made of all the planet one neighborhood, one marketplace, and one battlefield."[6] The phenomenon of Hitler and the course of World War Two would prepare the way for the legitimization of realism as the favored philosophy among postwar American foreign policy-makers. Coverage of European geopolitics and the subsequent growth of an indigenous American geopolitics would help pave the way, then, for the rise to dominance of a realist paradigm of international relations that would have enormous consequences for official and popular views of the Soviet Union after the war's end.

An American Geopolitics?

German *Geopolitik* was alluring and threatening at the same time to its American students and popularizers during the war. Interest in Haushofer's "school"—as measured by the output of books and articles on the subject—reached its peak in 1942 and declined thereafter.[7] Even those academics, military men, and journalists who believed in the efficacy of geopolitics in theory felt compelled to draw a distinction between a strictly German *Geopolitik* on the one hand and a pure Anglo-Saxon geopolitical tradition stemming from Mahan to Mackinder on the other. Mackinder's *Democratic Ideals and Reality* was reissued in 1942 to favorable reviews. Typical of the reception of the return this work occasioned was the comment that "Adam Smith, Thoreau, Karl Marx—to name pioneering thinkers who occur to mind at once—knew the disappointment of having their first editions go begging."[8]

If geopolitics had "migrated from Germany to America" as Isaiah Bowman, the most well-known American geographer of the day put it, the question then became one of how to legitimate a hated tool of the enemy for one's own purposes.[9] The danger of not Americanizing the geopolitical tradition before putting it to use is best illustrated in the case of the geographer G. T. Renner, who caused a stir when he published an article entitled "Maps for a New World" which seemed to acknowledge the geographic legitimacy of Germany's war aims. Using maps which in cold *Realpolitik* fashion rearranged the European map (while countenancing the elimination of Switzerland, among other things), Renner basically argued that "It is entirely possible to have a strong united Germany surrounded by eight other strong European nations any one of which would be tough enough to discourage aggression."[10] Even Walter Lippmann weighed in with a denunciation of Renner for appearing to regard nations as "inanimate objects" fit for manipulation by stronger powers. Indeed, geopoliticians reinforced a "billiard ball" model of international relations with culture and history left out.

Clearly, if there was to be a legitimization of geopolitics in America, it would have to be "humanized" as the émigré scholar Hans Weigert phrased it. Weigert's desire that "We must learn our own geopolitics" came eventually to stand for the larger aim of mobilizing support for a realist view of the world after the apparent failure of Wilsonian idealism.[11] This mobilization would be all the easier if it could be shown that realism in the guidance of America's foreign affairs was based on objective facts, such as the seemingly immutable facts of geography. As Frederick Schuman observed at the time in his article "Let us Learn Our Geopolitics," "The practice of geopolitics, or even of old-fashioned political realism, however, has hitherto proved impossible during peacetime in democracies whose statesmen and voters alike have no grasp of geo-strategic realities."[12] The implication of this and other wartime accounts of geopolitics was that geopolitics was not only a tool of foreign policy, but that it could also legitimate the need for repression on the home front when the state was threatened by other spatially expansive powers.

Haushofer, after all, was not the only geopolitician who saw democracies as being potentially unruly and unfit for the pursuit of "national greatness." Mackinder and the leading American geopolitical thinker Nicholas Spykman, for example, also saw geopolitics as lending objective support for channeling open-ended democratic debates about domestic and foreign affairs toward narrowly realist conclusions. Schuman implicitly argued that the policy-making elites of America might do well to understand the fact that "Those who use it [geopolitics] intelligently are all but certain to prevail over enemies who have no knowledge of its use."[13] This argument could be directed just as easily against domestic idealists as it could be against foreign enemies. Even the editors of *Fortune*

Magazine saw the domestic uses to which an Americanized geopolitics could be put. Stating that the U.S. "has no 'Institute of Geo-Politics' yet," the editors of *Fortune* argued in 1942 that "Business cannot afford to overlook this new science which, borrowing from the experience of some progressive international corporation, is bound to have a tremendous influence on all business operations both now and after the war."[14] Indeed, by June 1942 a Geopolitical Section within the Military Intelligence Service was created to study geography to help planning for war and peace, while in September of that year Henry Luce participated in a meeting on geopolitics attended by other elite figures from the journalistic world.[15] That U.S. business interests also saw the geo-domestic agenda as helpful in offering a plan to rationalize productive capacity on the home front during the war is shown in a *Business Week* editorial which argued the need to "define our long-term needs and objectives, tighten up all our planning organizations, and objectively co-ordinate all our activities."[16]

A large part of the problem American observers had in accepting German *Geopolitik* at face value had to do with the underlying methodological issues surrounding *Geopolitik*. German geopolitics was continually lambasted as a pseudo-science or, at best, a *Zweckwissenschaft* that was opposed to a "pure"— and presumably unapplied—science. Isaiah Bowman, director of the American Geographical Association and an advisor to President Roosevelt, articulated the acceptable view that, in essence, "foreign" geopolitics constituted little more than political ideology while Anglo-American political geography must be untainted by political considerations.[17] Or, as the Yale political scientist and geopolitical thinker Nicholas Spykman defined it, the Germans were "engaged in advocating policy, which is hardly a scientific endeavor."[18] Geopolitics—which had been developed in no small part in response to Germany's territorial ambitions in the era 1870-1945—thus risk being tainted *via* Germany's seeming willingness to use the doctrine for its own ends.

Toward a World Balance of Power System

Henry Luce declared the twentieth century to be an American one. One outcome of the widespread public discussion of geopolitics during World War Two was the attempt to ready the American populace for its responsibilities in a new world balance of power system that could no longer be centered on Europe. Articles discussing geopolitics—accompanied with maps showing the centrality of the U.S. in this new system—were important in getting the message across to America that, in the words of one widely used geography textbook, "The geopolitical center of the Anglo-Saxon peoples has crossed the Atlantic from London to Washington."[19] This message was not confined to books, newspapers, and periodicals. German films such as *Der Feldzug im Polen* (Campaign Against Poland) and *Sieg im Westen* (Victory in the West) used maps to highlight the righteousness of the spatial logic (based on geographical science) underlying Nazi foreign policy. American war films, such as those in Frank Capra's *Why We Fight* series, used maps to opposite effect, showing how Nazi spatial dynamism must be counteracted by a geographically astute free world. One such film, MGM's *Plan for Destruction* focused on Karl Haushofer as the virtual master-mind of Germany's territorial advance whose master plan is to gain control of the heartland and link up with the Japanese before a final showdown with the U.S. The film concludes with the reassuring message that America and its allies have learned the lessons of Haushofer and are thus capable of "slashing the tentacles of the geopolitical octopus with a brand of geopolitics of our own."[20] Indeed, Gearóid Ò'Tuathail shows how Luce organized a media conference in late 1942 on geopolitics as a civilian component to the War Department's establishment of a Geopolitical Section.[21]

The dominant American geopolitical narrative of the time described the passing of the torch of world leadership from Britain to the U.S. based on the "immutable" facts of geography. Such reasoning took for granted the idea that the twentieth century would ultimately be dominated by states of continental proportions given the crude geopolitical correlation of territorial extent with national power. As one commentary on "America's Destiny" summarized, "The only peace we are interested in is a *Pax Americana*, in exactly the same sense as there was once a *Pax Romana* and a *Pax Britannica*."[22]

Spykman and other realist-minded American geopolitical thinkers attempted through their articles and textbooks to explain the new centrality of the U.S. in international affairs in easy-to-understand terms through the use of artfully designed maps and simple geopolitical formulas. While Spykman and other American commentators declared that "The center of world power has left west-ern Europe," Mackinder was already, in his last formulation of the pivot thesis in 1943, imagining Britain as an "aerodome" and France as a "bridgehead" for the expression of American power into the postwar era.[23]

Spykman and the Advocacy of an American Geopolitics: "Geography does not argue; it just is."[24]

Nicholas Spykman was the only American geopolitical thinker equivalent in stature to Mackinder or Haushofer. Spykman, born in the Netherlands in 1893, worked as a journalist in the Middle East before emigrating to the U.S. where he earned in his Ph.D. in political science at the University of California in 1923. After teaching political science and sociology at the University of California from 1923-1925, Spykman went to Yale where he taught until his death in 1943. In 1936, he became the first director of the Yale Institute of International Studies where he was influential in advocating a realist approach to world affairs. During the war years he also taught at the University of Virginia in a school for commis-sioned army officers who were being trained for the administration of occupied territories.

Spykman is chiefly remembered for his interest in the relation between for-eign policy and geography. His most notable works include *American Strategy and World Politics, The Geography of the Peace,* and two articles entitled "Geography and Foreign policy" that appeared in the *American Political Science*

Review. American Strategy, written before Pearl Harbor, won widespread attention partly because of its appearance at a time when there was a demand to see a coherent articulation of America's world role during and after the war. This book received a favorable review on the front page of the *New York Times Book Review* and mostly favorable plaudits elsewhere for its geopolitically framed argument against isolationism. The doyen of American geography, Isaiah Bowman, said of the book that "Every government official responsible for policy should read it once a year."[25] Although Hans Weigert heard the "voice of destructive nihilism in Spykman's work," he also said in his review that:

> In Washington, the voluminous treatise was a bestseller; at Yale it fascinated the students, and in Charlottesville, Spykman's lectures had a deep effect on the thinking of army officers undergoing a thorough training in the field of international relations and geography.[26]

As early as 1938 Spykman had adumbrated themes that would not only play a role in his influential books, but also ideas that would provide scholarly justification for the Containment policy (and its implementation by defense intellectuals) aimed at the Soviet Union after the war. In his "Geography and Foreign Policy" articles, he laid down certain geopolitical axioms that directly attacked Wilsonian idealism. It has been observed that after World War One, there was a production of "textbooks and courses [regarding international affairs] which had nothing to do whatever with any geopolitical realities."[27] Spykman and the British scholar E. H. Carr were among the first scholars to voice criticism of the Anglo-American idealist approach to foreign affairs. For Spykman, war was not an aberration; rather, for him, periods of peace represented "temporary armistices."[28] In an anarchic world of competing states, Spykman believed that the realist must base his view of other nations on the basis of their capabilities rather than on their avowed intentions.

The realities behind international politics in Spykman's thought ultimately derived from what he perceived as geographic reality. Spykman then followed Mackinder and Haushofer in finding his objective foundation for a realistic foreign policy in geography. For Spykman, geography is "the most fundamentally conditioning factor in the formation of national policy because it is the most permanent."[29] Other factors in addition to geography that a correct view of foreign policy must take into account, according to Spykman, were the population density, economy, ethnic make-up, form of government, and the psychology of a particular state. This geo-domestic vision is in accord with that of Mackinder and Haushofer. All three thought that the state should represent the "organic whole" of the people that constituted the ethnic backbone of the nation. The reference to "ethnic makeup" on Spykman's part points out the geopolitician's tendency to biologize the state into a whole whose sum threatened to be less than its parts unless its policy elite could be assured of domestic harmony and unity. Ultimately, however, Spykman reasoned that "If the foreign policy of a state is to be practical, it should be designed not in terms of some dream world but in terms of the reality of international relations, in terms of power politics."[30]

One could, in this account of international relations, understand any state's attitude toward foreign affairs by understanding its geographic position. Spykman believed that "Every Foreign Office, whatever may be the atlas it uses, operates mentally with a different map of the world."[31] States on the map were, in this view, like billiard balls on a pool table, interacting with one another in fairly predictable fashion according to the dictates of geographic necessity. The object of interstate conflict for Spykman could only be the accumulation of more and more *territory*. In Spykman's view:

> It seems possible, then, to view the frontiers of states existing at any given moment as a political-geographic expression of temporary power relationships in a dynamic world in which expansion is a normal by-product of an inevitable struggle for power.[32]

While Mackinder had historicized Europe's balance of power system (situating it between the Columbian voyages and the late nineteenth century when it became outmoded), he and his acolytes failed to foresee that economic development might in time make traditional geopolitical analysis outdated (especially after 1945).

In his most well-known work, *America's Strategy*, Spykman applied the geopolitical principles first laid down in his 1938 articles to America's geopolitical options in World War Two. The book's leading theme concerned the need for the U.S. to abandon its isolationism and to view security in world-wide, rather than regional, terms. As Spykman framed the debate, "In a period of total war the field of struggle coincides with the total earth's surface. Only statesmen who can do their political and strategic thinking in terms of a round earth and a three-dimensional warfare can save their countries from being outmaneuvered."[33] The American public must become *cartographically conscious* of the fact that the world had become a "single field of forces" and that "Hemisphere defense is no defense at all."[34] The isolationist view that America would be safe relying on her own resources while protecting Latin America from encroachment from abroad was therefore deemed to be impossible in the geopolitical era. Americans, henceforth, would have to be as concerned about the Eurasian heartland as Monroe once was about South America.

Mackinder and Haushofer would not have disagreed with Spykman's view that Germany's grand strategy in the war would naturally be to seek dominance over the heartland. In this geopolitical view, the German attainment of such a war aim would allow the Nazis to compete with America on continentally equal terms. Germany's plan boiled down in Spykman's view to "gaining a position [in Europe] similar to that which the United States enjoys in the New World."[35] Interventionism could therefore be sold to the American public on the sound principles of geopolitical self-interest. The fear of one-power domination of Eurasia would continue to lie behind postwar American foreign policy from 1947 through the end of the Cold War. Spykman, along with lesser-known advocates for an American geopolitics, would succeed in lending scientific credence to this position; a position made all the more persuasive through its advocates' reliance on a spatial-verbal rhetoric unique to geopolitics. Choices in foreign and domestic policy would have to be "realistically" narrowed, after all, if one accepted the postulate that if the "Old World can be united or organized in such a manner that large masses of unbalanced power can become available for action across the ocean, the New World will be encircled."[36]

Such recourse to the seemingly objective principles of geopolitics would, Spykman hoped, neutralize what appeared to him as the fractious, unscientific foreign policy debates of the day that hindered the realist statesman in untrammeled pursuit of "national security." Spykman expressed the belief, for example, that the average citizen in a democracy has a preference for "dying on his own soil instead of abroad [which] is a serious handicap to the democratic state."[37] Only an elite armed by the verities of geopolitical wisdom could match threatening nations on their own *Realpolitik* terms. Spykman countenanced the possibility that, in the democratic culture of America, irrelevant passions and emotions would have to be stirred up in order to garner popular support for geopolitically precise interventions abroad that would be needed to rectify occasional imbalances of power. As he argued, "unless public opinion is educated to the strategic advantages of offensive action or inspired by a messianic ideology, the nation will offer the lives of its sons only for national defense."[38] There developed, therefore, an American *domestic* geopolitics in addition to an American foreign geopolitics (just as there had always been a domestic component to the geopolitical traditions associated with Mackinder and Haushofer). In essence, domestic geopolitics took as its core principle the idea that hierarchy and order would have to prevail over unorthodoxy and dissent at home if the nation was to be able to pursue a rational and effective geopolitics abroad. For example, the American nation's organic unity was not as strong as it might be, according to Spykman, given the "ethnic fault lines" caused by "hyphenated Americans."[39] This could only be considered a dangerous thing in a geopolitical era defined as one in which "Belligerents attempt to conquer the enemy state from within by means of fifth columnists."[40]

While *American Strategy* was written just before Pearl Harbor, Spykman's second major work, *Geography of the Peace*, appeared in 1944 when German and Japanese fortunes were clearly on the wane. Spykman in this latter work went beyond attacking isolationism on geopolitical grounds by articulating his "rimland" theory of international relations. Spykman defined the rimland as that sector of the "Eurasian land mass [which] must be viewed as an intermediate region, situated as it is between the heartland and the marginal seas. It functions as a vast buffer zone of conflict between sea power and land power."[41] Where Mackinder had been concerned about control of the Eurasian heartland, Spykman believed that more concern should be shown for control over rimland territories. Spykman's book was therefore full of wartime maps depicting Germany and Japan as jointly attempting to control rimland areas stretching from northwestern Europe to southeastern Asia as necessary first steps toward controlling all of Eurasia. Revising Mackinder's famous dictum, Spykman summed up the core principle of his geo-strategic world view when he wrote: "Who controls the rimland rules Eurasia; who rules Eurasia controls the destinies of the world."[42] Spykman therefore believed that the whole of World War Two should be understood by the American public as a struggle against joint German-Japanese control of the rimland area. In this account, the nature of the enemy regimes was immaterial; what counted was *Realpolitik* attention to whatever political entity controlled or threatened to control Eurasia. As Spykman saw it, "Security must, therefore, be understood in terms of the integrity of control over the land."[43]

Spykman's *Geography of the Peace* was in large part directed toward influencing public opinion on the shape of the peace to come after World War Two. Spykman believed that it was incumbent upon the three superpowers—the U.S., Britain, and the Soviet Union—to cooperate in using their power to guarantee a balance of power along the rimland of Eurasia. While Spykman advocated cooperation between the Anglo-American powers and the Soviets in pursuit of this grand design, Spykman's geopolitical reasoning allowed for other outcomes. Spykman always assumed geography to be "the most fundamental factor in the foreign policy of states because it is the most permanent"; in his view, "Ministers come and go, even dictators die, but mountain ranges stand unperturbed."[44] So while it was to be hoped that cooperation among the three powers would continue after the war, Spykman warned his audience that the Soviet Union's geographic situation might very well forestall such cooperation. "One must remember," he advised, "that Alexander I, Czar of all the Russias, bequeathed to Joseph Stalin, simple member of the communist party, not only his powers but his endless struggle for access to the sea."[45] In the larger tradition of realism that geopolitics was giving apparent scientific sanction to, this advice represented the belief that foreign intentions, ideology, and even culture were ultimately inscrutable while foreign capabilities and geographic realities were to be privileged as objective givens in the formulation of foreign policy. It was natural that Spykman would use direct geopolitical logic in concluding that "it may be that the pressure of Russia outward toward the rimlands will constitute one important aspect of the postwar settlement."[46]

Spykman's influence on his realist compatriots was recognized early on in the Cold War. E. S. Furniss observed that the structure of Spykman's view of international relations "underlies the one which many leading scholars now follow."[47] While not all realists (such as the important international relations scholar Hans Morgenthau) were geopoliticians, all geopoliticians were effective in helping to "naturalize" realism for a wide audience beginning in World War Two through persuasive syntheses of map and text. Spykman's geopolitical theories, however, vied for the attention of this audience with other geopolitical views of America's role in the world. The airman's view of the world (and its accompanying polar azimuthal equidistant projection maps) were introduced through *Life* magazine and many other vehicles of the popular press. A leading advocate of this view, Alexander de Seversky, saw the upper regions of North America and the Soviet Union surrounding the north pole as constituting an "area of decision," control over which would determine the hierarchy of world powers in the near future. In both editions of *New Compass of the World*—an important anthology of wartime (circa 1944) and early postwar (circa 1949) geo-strategic views of the world, a leading theme concerned the idea that "The compass of the world still points north" and that "the North Pole is, in the age of air power, close to the pivot of world strategy, whether one looks at it from Washington, Tokyo, or Berchtesgaden."[48]

Cartographic Consciousness and the Cold War

World War Two represented a high point in popular and scholarly interest in geopolitical literature. This literature, while often nominally directed against German *Geopolitik*, provided a simple and understandable narrative about the realities of world politics. This geopolitical narrative not only played a role in turning American public opinion against isolationism, but also helped in laying the groundwork for gaining public support, or at least acquiescence, for a postwar American globalist foreign policy. Yet one still has to explain the conservative nuclear strategist Colin Gray's remark that "In practice, geopolitical lore permeates our thought (and action) on international relations, but it tends to be unacknowledged."[49]

While the absolute number of scholarly and popular writings concerning geopolitics declined in the aftermath of World War Two (and began to reappear with some frequency in the 1980s), geopolitics continued to underpin government rationales, scholarly studies, and popular analyses of postwar foreign policy issues.[50] A long-time member of the American political science community, W. T. R. Fox, recalls how "Power analysis at Chicago and politico-military studies at Yale and Princeton prepared the ground for 'applied political geography' to be folded into academic study of international relations."[51] Geopolitical reasoning, in other words, continued to surround taken for granted assumptions in the study and implementation of foreign policy even though the term itself had become tainted because of its associations with Nazism.[52] Fox could thus claim that "The importance of the intellectual contribution of specialists in geopolitics is not to be measured by the number of references to the word geopolitics in the wartime and postwar literature of international relations."[53] Stanley Hoffman, another scholar of international relations and a student of American foreign policy, noted in his account of American academic study of international relations that Spykman's work, together with Hans Morgenthau's, brought the kind of realism to foreign affairs thinking in America that E. H. Carr brought to Britain.[54]

The mobilization of the nation's cartographic consciousness began in earnest after the outbreak of World War Two as a reaction against isolationism and German *Geopolitik*. Only after World War Two would this changed consciousness be exploited to lend credence to the worst fears about the menace represented by maps (colored in ominous red) depicting a monolithic Russo-Chinese communism dominating Eurasia. During the war, however, social scientists such as Hans Speier worried that Americans would be susceptible to the visual arguments made in the enemy's propaganda maps. The solution, for Speier and others, was to fight maps with maps:

> propaganda by maps should be fought with other maps rather than words ... verbal denial of the content of a map must overcome the profound distrust of those ideas which contradict the evidence of sense impressions, and in addition, must substitute an enumeration of details for the perception of a whole.[55]

For domestic purposes, the geopolitically-minded could not trust the average citizen to use critical thinking when looking at maps. The danger in this approach was that one might be tempted to emulate the enemy in distorting maps for political purposes while, at the same time, arguing for their objectivity. Certainly, such students of geopolitical analysis as Spykman and the West Point instructor Colonel Beukema expressed during World War Two the feeling that democracies were—by definition—at a disadvantage in waging war by the map. Beukema believed that, from a geopolitical perspective, "this war is driving home into American consciousness the discovery of democracy's structural and functional weaknesses for the waging of a large-scale war."[56] In this account, a geopolitical foreign policy could only be conducted effectively if the homefront were not confused or demoralized by competing geographical interpretations of reality. The organic conception of the geopolitically knowledgeable state, in short, could be threatened by too much individual freedom.

S. Whittemore Boggs, a geographer at the Department of State during World War Two, expressed little faith in the ability of the individual citizen to tell the difference between a good and bad map. Boggs argued in the pages of the State Department *Bulletin* that "In what may be called 'cartohypnosis' or 'hypnotism by cartography,' the map user or the audience exhibits a high degree of suggestibility in respect to stimuli aroused by the map and its explanatory text."[57] The answer to the problem of people being led astray by the wrong kind of maps was for a self-appointed geopolitical elite to teach people to read maps the "right way." The privileged few able to discern the underlying "geographic realities" surrounding the Cold War would have to, as it were, inoculate a fickle and susceptible public to the enemy's "mass hypnotism" and "delusion" *via* cartography.[58]

The shock of Pearl Harbor and the resulting entry of the U.S. into the global battlefield of World War Two provided the crisis that succeeded in galvanizing a popular interest in new ways of conceptualizing America's world role. This interest was taken as an opportunity by geographers and popular writers to enter the national conversation concerning what appropriate cartographic responses were adequate to a radically changed international environment. Robert Strausz-Hupé, in an article titled "It's Smart to be Geopolitical," noted at the time that "The awakening of the American public to global consciousness created a ready market for "systems of global politics."[59] And, as we have seen, many of those writing for this market were concerned to advance à la Spykman an internationalist American cartographic world view lest the American public be swayed by the enemy's cartographic propaganda into a continuing support of isolationism.

Pearl Harbor represented an ideal moment for the advancement—by cartographic means—of such an internationalist world view since, as Isaiah Bowman noted, after "Pearl Harbor we had to think in global terms and we were nationally unprepared for such thinking."[60]

In the 1949 edition of the most widely used textbook on political geography until the late 1950s, the authors Fifield and Pearcy discussed how such cartographic mobilization was being experienced by the average citizen. They noted the fact that "The disposition of American forces on all the inhabited continents of the world has resulted in the appearance of an atlas in many an American home."[61] Representative of the popular effort to participate in this effort to reorient American views of the world was the publication in 1944 of the popular *Look at the World: The Fortune Atlas for World Strategy*. This was, of course, published by the magazine of the same title that had already expressed editorial approval of an American geopolitics and its possible benefits for American business. Although critical of Spykman's *Realpolitik* thinking, Hans Weigert in his article "Maps are Weapons" gave indication that the mobilization of America's spatial awareness was having some effect. He was of the opinion that "What never happened before here, especially not during the First World War, is happening now: the country is becoming increasingly 'space conscious,' is beginning to think in terms of continents and oceans."[62] Weigert in the same article took great satisfaction in the fact that "Today even remote farmhands talk of Dakar. The location of Odessa and Kiev is to the man who happens to live in Vermont often more familiar than the relative location of, for example, Akron and Cincinnati."[63] By the end of 1942, *Life* magazine was reporting that around 1500 courses on geopolitics were being offered in American colleges. The magazine commented that "On campuses all over the country musty old geographers are blossoming out as shiny new geopoliticians."[64]

The effort of Spykman and others to transform America's cartographic self-understanding was helped immensely by the fact that a geographically curious leader was in the White House. Roosevelt had been connected with the American Geographical Society and had known and received advice from Bowman since World War One. In addition to such ties, Roosevelt was prepared to participate, on occasion, in the effort to raise the nation's cartographic consciousness. At Christmas in 1942, Roosevelt symbolically took command of the world when he was given the gift of a large globe (some 50 inches in circumference) that was said to be the largest detailed military globe ever made to that point.[65] A few months later (in February 1943) he explained to an advisor what his rhetorical strategy would entail in an upcoming speech on the war effort. He announced:

> I'm going to ask the American people to take out their maps. I'm going to speak about strange places that many of them never heard of—places that are now the battleground for civilization. I'm going to ask the newspapers to print maps of the whole world. I want to explain to the people something about geography—what our problem is and what the over-all strategy of this war has to be. I want to tell it to them in simple terms of ABC ...[66]

Just as it had once seemed natural to Americans that the U.S. was isolated from the *Sturm und Drang* engulfing the rest of the world at any given time, it was becoming increasingly natural in the war years and beyond to justify the necessity of constant American political and military involvement with the rest of the world on the basis of geopolitical necessity.

Part of this mobilization effort required defining how American geopolitics differed in substance from German geopolitics. Instrumental in this process was the careful re-interpretation of Mackinder for an American audience. While he had often been treated in Britain as unreconstructed organic nationalist and ignored in both Britain and America during the interwar years, a veritable Mackinder revival started with the outbreak of war in 1939.[67] For American writers on the topic during the war, Mackinder became the icon of a legitimate humanistic geopolitics; a figure whose views were continually contrasted with the views of the now demonized Haushofer. Charles Kruszewski in 1954 could thus make the claim on the pages of *Foreign Affairs* that:

> With the extension of the Nazi shadow over Europe, maps illustrating Mackinder's Heartland conception began to appear in American publications, and Americans became aware of the importance of global thinking and the need of maps for the air age showing the skyways over the top of the world and the distances of American cities from other parts of the globe.[68]

The tradition laid down by Mackinder and his work allowed American commentators to show that an objective geopolitics was possible. This position, however, overlooked the deeper values Mackinder and Haushofer (and, by extension, their collective heirs) shared concerning the virtues of an organic conservatism and its concomitant geo-social paradigm.

Another element involved in the changing geographic self-understanding of Americans had to do with the type of map projections used to convey this new view of America. There was a widely held view in the American wartime literature surrounding geopolitics that a "map gap" of sorts existed between America and Germany. R. E. Harrison and Strausz-Hupé, authors of an article entitled "Maps, Strategy, and World Politics," argued that:

> The psychological isolationism of the United States can be in large measure traced to our failures in map-making and the teaching of geography—the prerequisites of education in international relations. The world is round. By the skillful presentation of its 'roundness' strategic realities are made clear.[69]

Part of the problem, according to those who believed in a map gap, had to do with the continuing dominance of Eurocentric Mercator map projections in American classrooms and publications. Harrison and Strausz-Hupé maintained that "Mercator's world is the world of sea power" that did not graphically capture the geopolitical goal of equating great power status in the twentieth century with the possession of great areas of landspace. This "antiquated 'vision' of the world" in their view, promoted the "psychological isolationism" that was helping to prevent the United States from fulfilling its destiny to define "the American century."[70] Happily, for the authors' purposes, commentators on American foreign policy such as Spykman were leading the way in preparing an environment in which the "assault on map traditionalism" could be unobtrusively carried on "mainly by American magazines and newspapers in their search for visual aids to reports from the theater of war."[71]

The mark of the well-informed citizen of the brave new era of American cartographic consciousness was, ideally, to be found in his mental "flexibility." This would be appropriate after World War Two when, given the extent of America's global commitments, enemies to American interests might appear at any point on the globe. Harrison, whose new maps appeared in such magazines as *Fortune* and *Life*, influenced the training of the armed forces and offered technical advice to the State Department and OSS. He believed during the war that it was a problem that "we have not learned so far ... to adopt a constant flexibility in the process of forming a world view."[72] Part of this new "flexibility" in America's cartographic consciousness was to involve an awareness of how such new projections as the polar azimuthal equidistant (which was designed, among other things, to make Americans aware of their nearness to Eurasia) highlighted shifting areas of the earth deemed worth fighting for in the national interest. For many of its enthusiasts, this projection, by centering on the North Pole, would help Americans see themselves situated at the center of things, rather than on the periphery of world events.

By the end of the war, many concluded that the effort to make Americans aware of the new geographic realities of world affairs had been a success. There was, first, the feeling that "Victory was won because our side committed fewer geographical blunders than the enemy."[73] Second, there was the prevailing sense (as expressed by Hans Weigert) that history itself "has taught us that geographical ignorance in the twentieth century is a crime."[74] To paraphrase an old expression, ignorance of geopolitics in the postwar world would be considered worse than a crime, it would be a mistake; a mistake in the chess-like game of world politics where every realistic calculation counted.

Containment and Geopolitics

There was officially sanctioned support for Weigert's view that by 1944 "Geographical sense and geographical vision are now weapons in our arsenal."[75] In the *Army Services Forces Manual* of 1944, one could find the role of geography highlighted as follows: "if a political system is ever to be devised which can offer real promise of [eradicating] ... the roots of war, the men who design it and those who implement it will need an intimate and full understanding of geography in its relation to human affairs."[76] The torrent of literature about geopolitics coming out of World War Two would thus have lasting effects in official American thought about the Cold War, even after Haushofer and German *Geopolitik* faded into the past.

Often, the geopolitical conceptualization of postwar American foreign policy would assume a taken-for-granted quality in government documents and official public pronouncements relating to Containment of the Soviet Union. Even before George Kennan wrote the "Long Telegram" and "Sources of Soviet Conduct," the U.S. military was already showing by the fall of 1945 concern with Soviet influence over Eurasia.[77] Prominent civilian strategists, including such colleagues of Spykman as F. S. Dunn, E. M. Earle, W. T. R. Fox, A. Wolfers, G. L. Dirk, D. N. Power, and H. Sprout argued for the necessity of a politically fragmented Eurasia in a study called "A Security Policy for Postwar America." The Foreign Secretary of Britain in the early postwar period, Ernest Bevin, made reference at one point to his fear that "physical control of the whole World-Island [Mackinder's term for Eurasia] is what the Politbureau is aiming at."[78]

Well-before the enunciation of the Truman Doctrine and the Marshall Plan in 1947, geopolitics offered an influential lens through which to understand the new postwar international system then coming into being. Kennan's articulation of the famous Containment policy in 1947 itself bore—if not a direct—at least a homologous relationship to Mackinder's fears of a too powerful heartland and Spykman's fears of "rimland" powers dominating Eurasia.[79] As Kennan reflected in his *American Diplomacy*, a central premise in American foreign policy must include the recognition that "It [is] essential to us, as it was to Britain, that no single continental land power should come to dominate the entire Eurasian land mass."[80]

Containment, it could be argued, was simply a refined articulation of this central principle as it related to the specificities of Russian culture and history (specificities which would be forgotten in many later ahistorical accounts of Soviet behavior). The emphasis, however, on the geographic dimensions of this new paradigm of American foreign policy was striking. A famous passage of Kennan's "Sources of Soviet Conduct" article, for example, reads:

> Soviet pressure against the free institutions of the western world is something that can be contained by the adroit and vigilant application of counter-force at a series of constantly shifting geographical and political points, corresponding to the shifts and manoeveres of Soviet policy, but which cannot be charmed or talked out of existence.[81]

Kennan, like Mackinder, had discerned long-term "Russian expansive tendencies" that threatened British, and now U.S., interests in the political fragmentation of the Eurasian continent."[82] Long unrecognized has been the affinity between Kennan's social beliefs and Mackinder's beliefs. Just as both believed in a natural balance of power abroad, both favored an organically conservative social order at home.

The domestic views of Kennan and Mackinder were not as influential as their foreign policy views, however. The danger that the geographical nuances in Kennan's conception of Containment would be missed by those responsible for implementing it worried him greatly because, in his view, over-preoccupation with the enemy would lead to decay at home. Kennan believed that "The greatest danger that can befall us in coping with this problem of Soviet communism is that we shall allow ourselves to become like those with whom we are coping."[83] His greatest fears about the uses to which his ideas on the Containment of the heartland power would be put were amply realized in the well-known Cold War security document NSC-68 (1950). The fundamental assumption in this document was that the Soviets were, for the foreseeable future, *the* implacable foe of the U.S. A "fundamental design" was attributed to the U.S.S.R.; the design of destroying America on the way "toward the domination of the Eurasian land mass."[84] Worse yet—from the point of view of those who thought that ideas and values were ultimately more important than unchanging geographic facts and various quantifications of military strength—was the sentiment expressed in NSC-68 that, "In coping with dictatorial governments acting in secrecy and with speed, we are also vulnerable in that the democratic process necessarily operates in the open and at a deliberate tempo."[85] This distrust of democracy was always endemic in geopolitical thought.

Eurasia on the Mind: American Preoccupation with the Heartland after NSC-68

One leading student of American national security policy in the postwar period discerns a consistency over time in the foreign policy assumptions of successive presidential administrations in the postwar period. J. L. Gaddis offers the belief that "There exist for presidential administrations certain 'strategic' or 'geopolitical' codes, assumptions about American interests in the world."[86] These codes might encompass the seeming diversity in the Truman administration's concern with "points" and "lines"; the domino theory that haunted the Eisenhower and Kennedy administrations; the reliance on regional power structures by the Nixon administration; and the delineation of an "arc of crisis" (reminiscent of Spykman's rimland theory) during the Carter administration.

The geographic scope of Containment policy was as far reaching as the geographic framing of these geopolitical codes. Not too long after the original advocacy of the Containment policy, a kind of "pactomania" swept the thinking of government officials until, by 1955, America had guaranteed the defense of some forty-seven countries on five continents. The military cooperation spelled out in the NATO, SEATO, ANZUS, and CENTO pacts could not have fulfilled Spykman's dream of securing the rimlands against a dominant Eurasian land-power any better. The problem was that in trying to contain the Soviets in a geographic straitjacket there was always the danger that such an implementation of Containment would only help produce the very aggressive behavior it was designed to preempt. The Russian view of geopolitics was, not surprisingly, negative. J. N. Semjonow, a leading Russian observer of the western geopolitical theory that informed Containment doctrine, believed that this theory was a geographic expression of capitalism in its imperialistic stage of development.[87] The assumptions of geopolitics, which had helped mobilize the cartographic consciousness of Americans into the country's new worldwide obligations, would continue to inform America's Cold War thinking through the 1980s. Such influence would remain relatively quiescent for two reasons. First, as one observer of this issue puts it, "geopolitical interpretation and analysis continued, but sailed under such other colours as strategic studies or even political geography" because of the term's lingering connotations with Nazism.[88] Second, geopolitics encompassed ideas that fit what the historian of ideas A. O. Lovejoy defines as those "beliefs which are so much a matter of course that they are rather tacitly presupposed than formally expressed and argued for ... ways of thinking which seem so natural and inevitable that they are not scrutinized with the eye of logical self-consciousness."[89]

That the educational establishment supported the institutionalization of such beliefs in the nation's educational system as well is shown in the fact that while there were few courses on political geography in the 1930s listed in American college catalogs, by 1960 the number had increased to 300.[90] As has been shown, the leading political geography textbook of this period was marked by a positive appraisal of (by that point) mainstream geopolitical ideas. For scholar-strategists such as Spykman, the development of a unified geopolitical world view in popular American consciousness was part and parcel of the domestic aims of geopolitical theory. With the rise of "public education and new technological developments," Spykman saw the need to proselytize in behalf of a correct interpretation of international politics given, as he thought, that it was now "easier to influence the thinking of the masses."[91] In this view, little could be left to chance to what Mackinder had called the "half-educated" majority in modern democracies.

The campaign to educate America about geopolitics during the war and the subsequent popularity of cold war era political geography courses in the nation's schools led Charles Kruszewski to observe in the pages of *Foreign Affairs* that "Today, Statesmen, generals, seamen and airmen everywhere see the round world through Mackinder's eyes. And they see the Soviet Union in control of what he described as its heartland."[92] Conflict between the Soviet Union and the United States was now defined geographically as a conflict between the "West" (now assumed to be dominated by the U.S.) and the "East" (now assumed to be dominated by the U.S.S.R.). On maps, both East and West could be caricatured as undifferentiated monoliths. For example, the Soviet Union and China were lumped together as a unified political force on many Cold War maps. On such maps the borders between these states were elided by a great expanse of red coloration in order to symbolize monolithic communism. This coloration, of course, conveyed a political harmony that did not, in fact, exist between these states. It is not surprising that Richard Hartshorne, a leading American geographer, declared in 1954 that Mackinder's pivot thesis provided the most popularly influential—if not the most truthful—view produced by modern geography.[93]

America in the Cold War assumed Britain's previous function of warding off threats to Europe's (and now the whole of Eurasia's) balance of power. This involved the United States in an updated and expanded version of the old "great game" Britain had once played with imperial Russia. Only now, as Stephen

Ambrose writes, "The United States had military alliances with fifty nations, over a million soldiers, airmen, and sailors stationed in more than 100 countries and an offensive capability sufficient to destroy the world many times over."[94] NSC-68 offered such a narrow interpretation of Containment that the State Department geographer G. Pearcy could say without modification in 1964 that "No segment on the face of the earth is sufficiently remote or unimportant not to attract some sort of attention from the U.S. Government or from sectors of its citizenry."[95] Such talk would lead to serious concern with who was "ahead" in the Cold War based on the criterion of which side appeared to dominate more of the map than the other. This, too, was reminiscent of the heyday of European imperialism when imperial powers measured their rank by the area of a world map filled in with their national colors.

The appearance of NSC-68 and the outbreak of the Korean War in 1950 helped to make Pearcy's comment seems uncontroversial. The Joint Secretaries of the military had already in 1950, for example, interpreted the outbreak of war on the Korean peninsula in that same year to signify the need for an "urgent and frank re-appraisal of the global position of the United States' military potential. The geo-political security of the United States requires diplomatic, psychological and military coordination of the highest order."[96] This reappraisal led to the defining of national security in brittle and unimaginative ways. Mechanistic spatial representations of the enemy and his geographical drives would increasingly substitute for answers to the harder questions regarding the heartland enemy's culture, history, and disparate motivations. By the late 1950s, the objectification of the enemy into an undifferentiated geographic mass (as undifferentiated a mass as the color used to represent communism on most maps) led America to view countries such as Vietnam as mere geographic extensions of a Russian communist monolith.

Geopolitical arguments were then advanced in America to support the idea that countries on the "rimland" of the Soviet Union must be made to hold back the tide of communism emanating from its heartland source. As General Willoughby put in testimony before the Senate in 1958:

> This Southern Barrier [consisting of Thailand, Indo-China, and Malaysia] ...
> has already been vaulted by the Russians. Like the Middle-East where they
> vaulted the Baghdad Pact and are now in the rear of it in Syria-Egypt, they
> appear to have done so in the south-east in vaulting our line ... [now they] have
> reached Indonesia.[97]

Given such evidence of official sanction for a geopolitical conceptualization of world politics, it was nearly inevitable that the U.S. would become a victim of its own geopolitical rhetoric when Vietnam came to symbolize an attempt to save the "rimlands" from encroachment by the heartland power.

By the 1960s, commitment to Vietnam was, in large measure, deemed necessary in order to demonstrate the credibility of America's multitudinous security guaranties against Soviet expansion. Even so reflective a student on diplomacy as George Ball argued in a 1966 issue of the Department of State *Bulletin* stated that:

> To succeed in that struggle [with Vietnam] we must resist every communist effort to destroy by aggression the boundaries and demarcation line established by the post-war arrangement. We cannot defend Berlin and yield Korea. We cannot recognize one commitment and repudiate another without tearing and weakening the entire structure on which the world's security depends.[98]

In effect, President Kennedy had already declared in 1961 that the U.S. was prepared to "bear any burden and pay any price" to ensure that the Soviets would remain geographically contained by nations supportive of American interests. Kennedy declared, after all, that "Our frontiers today are on every continent."[99] Since determination of who was "ahead" in the Cold War was so hard to measure, recourse was had to measuring winning momentum in terms of the quantity of men and weaponry and in terms of crude control of strategic territory. Lyndon Johnson continued the tradition of presidential fascination with the geographical lines separating friend from foe. On 7 October 1964, for example, Johnson vowed to continue Kennedy's concern with maintaining the integrity of America's extended frontiers when he stated that:

> every President, and the leaders of both parties have moved with courage and firmness to the defense of freedom. President Truman met Communist aggression in the Formosa Strait. President Kennedy met Communist aggression in Cuba, and, when our destroyers were attacked, we met Communist aggression in the waters around Vietnam.[100]

State Department geographer G. Pearcy made explicit in his 1964 article on geopolitics and foreign policy some of the assumptions underlying Johnson's comments. Pearcy is an interesting figure in the history of geopolitical thought for developing a geopolitical world view that attempts to synthesize into one whole all the main trends in the history of geopolitics. He took from Mackinder the ur-geopolitical concern with the status of the heartland and its controlling power's inherent potential to dominate the whole of Eurasia. From the German geopolitical tradition, he derived powerful visual techniques for use in his maps which allowed him to objectify the enemy into a faceless mass of expansive evil.

Where the acolytes of *Geopolitik* in Germany had produced provocative maps picturing the British Isles as an octopus spreading its controlling tentacles throughout the world, Pearcy used the same imagery in an attempt to define the essential nature of the Soviet Union. The Russians, in his words, continuously resorted to the "octopus-like tactic of communist aggrandizement of control of territory."[101] Finally, Pearcy utilized Spykman's rimland concept in reducing Containment into a mere extension of a larger geopolitical doctrine. Geopolitical language and rhetoric, as we have seen, had the power to conjure up foreign policy crises where none needed to exist. Pearcy unwittingly spoke volumes about the mindset of the foreign policy elite of his time when he wrote in his article that "the Southeast Asia bloc represents a potential 'leak in the dike' of

Western Containment. Its northern reaches approach a section of the rimland and therefore are inclined to pressure of the Communist masters of the Eurasian landmass stronghold."[102]

The uniquely American twist Pearcy gave to an applied geopolitics is one that we have seen before in reference to Bowman and Spykman. His article showed how geopolitics could support the realism in American foreign policy; a realism raised in reaction to the idealism and isolationism that were viewed as having once led to abject appeasement of a geopolitically informed opponent at Munich. For this to work in an American context, geopolitics would have to be presented as a neutral field of analysis rather than as just another partisan, *engagé* European ideology. Pearcy summed up this attitude by commenting on the methodological foundations and aspirations of an American geopolitics as follows:

> geopolitics must be generally accepted as a realistic discipline capable of revealing many needed relationships between our physical surrounding and our political behavior. To damn it would be like damning the science of medicine because certain doctors chose to use drugs to degrade and destroy human beings. Medicine must be a strong science to cope with the ills of the human body; a strong science of geopolitics offers an understanding of some of the ills of the body politic and helps point the way toward remedial action.[103]

After the debacle in Vietnam (an adventure that Pearcy and most other avatars of geopolitics supported), Secretary of State Henry Kissinger tried to resurrect the case for the necessity of Containment in the face of a doubting American public. It could no longer be assumed that Americans would continue to offer uncritical support for the maintenance of a Byzantine network of geographic dikes around the Soviet heartland. Kissinger perceived that the public would have to be convinced that many of its instincts were overly emotional and not good for the long-term interests of the country, geopolitically understood. In his memoirs he defines his understanding of geopolitics by stating that:

> By 'geopolitical' I mean an approach that pays attention to the requirements of equilibrium ... Nixon and I wanted to found American foreign policy on a sober perception of permanent national interest rather than on fluctuating emotions that in the past had led us to excesses of both intervention and abdication.[104]

Elsewhere, he suggested the need to "achieve domestic support for a long term conception of our national interest."[105] Even Kissinger's superficial understanding of formal geopolitics belies his profound attraction to the doctrine's underlying and reactionary geo-social program.

The pursuit of *détente* and arms control with the Soviet Union in the 1970s resulted in a neo-conservative reaction on the part of some members of the American foreign policy elite. Representative figures of this movement—such as the influential strategist Colin Gray of the Hudson Institute—argued that "appeasement" of the Soviets in the wake of Vietnam was pointless since the

Soviets were deemed to be irredeemably bent on achieving military superiority and geographic expansion. For figures like Gray in the 1970s and 1980s, it was taken as a fundamental axiom that "East-West conflict is ... a permanent feature of international relations."[106] One of Gray's books, *Geopolitics of the Nuclear Era*, maintained that nuclear weapons did not eliminate the possibility of victory in a hypothetical war with the Soviets. If the U.S. was to prepare adequately for the eventuality of such a war, it would have to make sure the Russians were sufficiently contained geographically lest they exploit even more of the resources of Eurasia for the purposes of achieving "escalation dominance" in any future struggle with the United States.

Most interesting was the role Gray accorded geopolitics in achieving domestic consensus on a "realistic" foreign policy. Gray's book was introduced as a warning to the U.S., whose "neglect of geopolitical analysis may cause the United States to underestimate the magnitude of the current Soviet threat."[107] Indeed, the virtue of geopolitics for neo-conservatives like Gray was that it "directs attention to factors of enduring significance."[108] From Spykman to Gray, Americans influential in the shaping of a powerful geopolitical rhetoric maintained a constant distrust of the democratic process because of its perceived inability to stick with realism in foreign affairs. The only way the fickle demos might be constrained to follow the logic of an unemotional foreign policy would be to have the unchanging facts of geopolitics aggressively arrayed before it. The leading personages of the Soviet Union, as well as their idiosyncrasies and aspirations, would come and go for thinkers like Gray, but the facts of geography stayed the same, as Spykman had once put it. Spykman had long been dead, in fact, but three decades of Cold War history had not changed Gray's mind that the Cold War was essentially about "control/denial of the Eurasian-African 'rimlands.'"[109]

President Carter's National Security Advisor, Zbigniew Brzezinski, echoed Gray's neo-conservatism in his development of the "arc of crisis" concept to describe instability along Spykman's rimland (an area stretching from Pakistan to Bangladesh) after the Soviet invasion of Afghanistan in 1979. Such geopolitical rhetoric would be necessary to fortify a democratic people who, in Brzezinski's words, "are short on historical memory and who tend to view peace as natural and war ... as an aberration."[110] In his *Game Plan* (1986), Brzezinski, as many a geopolitically-minded commentator had done, felt compelled to quote Mackinder to support his contention that democracies need to be constantly reminded on the importance of pursuing a certain kind of realistic foreign policy. Mackinder, after all, had once stated that "Democracy refuses to think strategically unless and until compelled to do so for purposes of defense."[111] Also, Brzezinski mirrored his geopolitical predecessors by upholding a simplified image of the Soviets as a people marching in lockstep toward the long-term goals of their own version of a realistic foreign policy based on their geographic location. According to Carter's national security advisor, the Soviets had an important edge over the U.S. because of their "persistence against our impatience and lack of constancy."[112]

National security intellectuals such as Gray and Brzezinski—wedded as they were to the geopolitical assumption of constant Russian expansion—themselves had an interest in seeing "a historical rivalry [between the U.S. and U.S.S.R.] that will long endure."[113] For such thinkers, this rivalry—one that had "been transformed into an endless game" in Brzezinski's words—constituted an intellectual and sporting challenge of the highest order. Again, the game involved for Brzezinski a "geopolitical struggle for the dominance of Eurasia."[114] In the minds of these security intellectuals, the U.S.S.R. had inherited the mantle of the threatening land power once represented by Germany while the U.S. had taken on Britain's role as the leading seapower seeking nobly to contain this threat.

Notes

1. *New Statesman and Nation*, August 26, 1939.
2. Robert Strausz-Hupé, *Geopolitics: The Struggle for Space and Power* (New York: G. P. Putnam, 1942), viii.
3. W. T. R. Fox, *The Super-Powers: The United States, Britain, and the Soviet Union* (Harcourt, Brace and Co., 1944).
4. Frederick Sondern, "Hitler's Scientists," *Current History and Forum* 53.1 (1941): 10.
5. Gearóid Ò'Tuathail, *Critical Geopolitics* (U. of Minnesota Press, 1996), 121.
6. Frederick Schuman, "War for Time and Space," *Saturday Review of Literature* (June 27, 1942): 4.
7. Joseph Roucek, "Geopolitics of the United States," *American Journal of Economics and Sociology* 14.2 (1955): 206.
8. P. Hutchinson, "The Father of Geopolitics," *Christian Century* 59 (1942): 1216.
9. Isaiah Bowman, "Geography Versus Geopolitics," *Geographical Review* 32.4 (1942): 652. Mackinder tried to help this process along when he stated in an interview with *Time* (11 Jan. 1943, pp. 95-96) that "As I understand that word [geopolitics], which I myself never employ, it is the name given by Germans to a political theory which by exploiting the geographical pattern of the globe, will lead to a world empire under German control. I have always felt, and am still of the opinion, that the grouping of lands and seas is such as to lend itself to the growth of empires and, in the end, to a single empire. If I'm right, it is the duty of the allied nations to take the threat seriously."
10. G. T. Renner, "Map for a New World," *Collier's* (June 6, 1942): 15.
11. Hans Weigert, *Generals and Geographers: The Twilight of Geopolitics* (New York: Oxford U. Press, 1942), 250.
12. Frederick Schuman, "Let Us Learn Our Geopolitics," *Current History* 2.9 (1942): 164.
13. Schuman, "Geopolitics," 163.
14. "Case for Geopolitics," *Business Week* (Aug. 1, 1942): 68.
15. The research of Peter F. Coogan on this topic is summarized in Ò'Tuathail, 133.
16. Quoted in Ò'Tuathail, *Critical Geopolitics*, 133.
17. N. Smith, "Isaiah Bowman: Political geography and geopolitics," *Political Geography Quarterly* 3.1 (1984): 71.
18. Nicholas Spykman, "Geography and Foreign Policy," *American Political Science Review* 32.1 (1938): 30.

68. Charles Kruszewski, "The Pivot of History," *Foreign Affairs* 32.3 (1954): 399. Strausz-Hupé was representative among these writers in expressing his confirmation of most of Mackinder's early prognostications. Strausz-Hupé felt the war only confirmed, for example, the idea that "The history of our times appears to reflect, with malignant fatality, the trend toward empires and super-states predicted by the Ratzels, Spenglers, and Mackinders." Strausz-Hupé, *Geopolitics*, 191. Mackinder's *Democratic Ideals and Reality* was reissued with a foreword by E. M. Earle. *Makers of Modern Strategy* (1942; ed. by E. M. Earle), was notable for the wide attention it gave to Mackinder's ideas and to other geo-strategists.

69. R. E. Harrison and R. Strausz-Hupé, "Maps, Strategy and World Politics," *Infantry Journal* (Nov. 1942): 43.

70. Weigert and Stefansson, *Compass of the World* (1944), 74.

71. Harrison and Strausz-Hupé, "Maps, Strategy," 43.

72. Weigert and Stefansson, *Compass of the World*, 77.

73. *New Compass of the World*, xi.

74. Weigert, *Generals and Geographers: The Twilight of Geopolitics* (New York: Oxford U. Press, 1942), 7.

75. Weigert and Stefansson, *Compass of the World*, 88.

76. Quoted in *New Compass of the World*, vii.

77. M. Leffler in "The American Conception of National Security and the Beginnings of the Cold War, 1945-48," *American Historical Review* (vol. 89, no. 2, 1984): 357 notes that "By the autumn of 1945, military planners already were worrying that Soviet control over much of Eastern Europe and its raw materials would abet Russia's economic recovery." Leffler further notes (p. 366) on this point that in January 1946 "the Joint War Plans Committee observed that the long-term objective [of the Soviet Union] is deemed to be establishment of predominant influence over the Eurasian land mass and the strategic approaches thereto." Overall, while not stressing the point being made here that the official American use of geopolitical rhetoric and assumptions was uncritical and half-understood, Leffler's research never the less supports the idea that geopolitics was of some importance in official self-understanding of the causes and consequences of the Cold War. He comments on this issue that, "Postulating a long term Soviet intention to gain world domination, the American conception of national security, based on geopolitical and economic imperatives, could not allow for additional losses in Eurasia, could not risk a challenge to its nuclear supremacy, and could not permit any infringement on its ability to defend in depth or to project American force from areas in close proximity to the American homeland." *New Compass of the World*, vii.

78. Quoted in G. Parker, *Western Geopolitical Thought in the Twentieth Century* (New York: St. Martin's Press, 1985), 136.

79. Kennan informed the geographer S. B. Jones that his understanding of containment policy bore no direct relationship to Mackinder's heartland thesis. S. B. Jones, "Global Strategic Views," *Geographical Review* 45.4 (July 1955): 497.

80. George Kennan, *American Diplomacy* (Chicago: U. of Chicago Press, 1984), 10.

81. Kennan, "Sources of Soviet Conduct," reprinted in T. H. Etzold and J. L. Gaddis, *Containment: Documents on American Policy and Strategy, 1945-1950* (New York: Columbia U. Press, 1978), 87.

82. Kennan, "Sources," 87

83. Kennan, "Long Telegram," reprinted in T. H. Etzold and J. L. Gaddis, *Containment: Documents on American Policy and Strategy, 1945-1950* (New York: Columbia U. Press, 1978), 26.

84. NSC-68, reprinted in T. H. Etzold and J. L. Gaddis, *Containment: Documents on American Policy and Strategy, 1945-1950* (New York: Columbia U. Press, 1978), 387. In this document, the view was also offered that "Soviet domination of the potential power of Eurasia, whether achieved by armed aggression or by political and subversive means, would be strategically and politically unacceptable to the United States." NSC-68, Etzold and Gaddis, *Containment*, 438.

85. NSC-68, 403.

86. J. L. Gaddis, *Strategies of Containment* (New York: Oxford U. Press, 1982), ix.

87. Quoted in P. Scholler, "Die Geopolitik im Weltbild des Historischen Materialismus," *Erdkunde*, Band XIII: 88.

88. Hepple, "Revival," 23.

89. Quoted in Henrikson, "Mental Maps," 509.

90. H. Sprout, "Geopolitics," *Encyclopedia of the Social Sciences* (1968), 116-117.

91. Spykman, *America's Strategy*, 203.

92. Kruszewski, "Pivot," 388.

93. Quoted in Parker, *Geopolitical Thought*, 120.

94. Stephen Ambrose, *Rise to Globalism: American Foreign Policy Since 1938* (New York: Penguin, 1991), vi.

95. G. T. Pearcy, "Geopolitics and Foreign Relations," *Department of State Bulletin* (March 3, 1964): 322.

96. *Memorandum by the Secretaries of the Army, Navy, Airforce Defense*, 1 Aug. 1950, from *Foreign Relations of the United States* 1950, Vol. I, Washington, 357.

97. Quoted in G. R. Sloan, *Geopolitics in United States Strategic Policy, 1890-1987* (New York: St. Martin's Press, 1988), 149.

98. G. Ball, "The Issue in Vietnam," *Department of State Bulletin* (Feb 14, 1966): 244.

99. Quoted in Sloan, *Geopolitics*, 151.

100. Quoted in Sloan, *Geopolitics*, 157.

101. Pearcy, "Geopolitics," 319.

102. Pearcy, "Geopolitics," 323.

103. Pearcy, "Geopolitics," 319.

104. H. Kissinger, *White House Years* (London: Weidenfeld and Nicolson, 1979), 79, 914.

105. Quoted in Sloan, *Geopolitics*, 185.

106. Gray, *Geopolitics*, 5.

107. Gray, *Geopolitics*, viii.

108. Gray, *Geopolitics*, 5.

109. Gray, *Geopolitics*, 14. Gray also continued the tradition of invoking Mackinder's name for his specific policy recommendations by saying (p. 4) at one point that "Mackinder was the intellectual father of U.S. containment policy after World War II."

110. Z. Brzezinski, *Game Plan: A Geostrategic Framework for the Conduct of the U.S.-Soviet Contest* (New York: Atlantic Monthly Press, 1986), 8.

111. Quoted in Brzezinski, *Game Plan*, 194.

112. Brzezinski, *Game Plan*, 239.

113. Brzezinski, *Game Plan*, xiii.

114. Brzezinski, *Game Plan*, xiii.

Conclusion

The Soviet invasion of Afghanistan and the Iranian seizure of American hostages helped to usher in, by the end of the 1970s, what some observers have called the second Cold War.[1] Correspondingly, the term "geopolitics" came back into wider use in the 1980s.[2] On the other hand, while it could once have been assumed that the American public and foreign policy elite would be largely uncritical of bedrock geopolitical assumptions about how international politics worked, beginning in the late 1960s many of those assumptions were put into question.

The Reagan administration gave official sanction to this neo-conservative effort to revive the old consensus. In April 1988 the *Department of State Bulletin* published Reagan's address on the "National Security Strategy of the United States," an address that summed up the eight-year-old administration's belief in the merits of the old geopolitical framing of American foreign policy. This document stated the new administrations two core convictions on foreign policy: 1) U.S. national security strategy is "grounded in unchanging geographic considerations" that "dictate basic dimensions" of this strategy; and 2) that national security strategy must stress "realism. We have sought to deal with the world as it is, not as we might wish it to be."[3] The underlying geopolitical philosophy informing these beliefs:

> includes the conviction that the United States' most basic national security interests would be endangered if a hostile state or group of states were to dominate the Eurasian landmass—that area of the globe often referred to as the world's Heartland. We fought two world wars to prevent this from occurring. And, since 1945, we have sought to prevent the Soviet Union from capitalizing on its geostrategic advantage to dominate its neighbors in Western Europe, Asia, and the Middle East, and thereby fundamentally alter the global balance of power to our disadvantage.[4]

Thus the Reagan administration did all it could to take advantage of post-Vietnam confusion about the ends and means of American foreign policy by offering reassurances based on the apparently solid policy foundations provided by geopolitics. Little thought, therefore, was given during the renewal of the Cold War in the 1980s to the possibility that "the mellowing" of Soviet power might have much to do with its internal domestic politics rather than from a strengthening of geographic dikes surrounding the U.S.S.R.

But geopolitical thought had always been appealing for its unambiguous and even eschatological qualities. Once a certain territory was labeled as possessing predominant strategic advantages simply because of its location by an "objective" community of defense intellectuals, it would not take long before the particular culture and state dominating that area would begin to fulfill its assigned role of destined enemy. Geopolitical theory led its believers to be resigned to the necessity of violent international conflict and the indefinite continuance of the geopolitical era. For all their differences, geopoliticians such as Halford Mackinder, Karl Haushofer, and Nicholas Spykman agreed that it was incumbent upon non-heartland states either to balance the inherent power of the heartland area, or to strive for the political fragmentation of the heartland. In this sense, geopolitics should be understood as an ideology of the nation-state whose patina of legitimacy depended on the belief that territory ultimately trumped other variables of international relations in terms of relative importance. When the social forces that had once limited European interstate competition broke down by the end of the nineteenth century, geopoliticians (influenced by Darwinism and organic conservative philosophies) offered geopolitics as the saving philosophy of mid-sized European nation states experiencing the threatening rise of Russia and the U.S., both competitive continental challengers to European hegemony in the world. Modern geography itself was a product of the nation at this particular level of development. As Kenneth Boulding once said, modern "history and geography are devised to give 'perspective' rather than truth: that is to say, they present the world as seen from the vantage point of the nation."[5]

Geopolitics was perfectly suited to an age that took for granted the notion of the autarchic and territorially "satisfied" nation state. If geopoliticians had their way, only attention to the *measurable* "hard facts" of international life (including geography, weaponry, and manpower) would count as factors in the calculation of power. The birth and efflorescence of geopolitical theory also is historically specific to the era 1870-1945 because geopolitics depended on a competitive and hierarchical political culture (coupled with a level of pre-nuclear economic and technological development) that made the pursuit of territory appear a rational goal for the old and new elites of the day seeking to maintain their social positions (a position to some extent defended recently by the political scientist Peter Liberman in his recent work *Does Conquest Pay?*). As Hans Speier put it in his warning about the seductiveness of German *Geopolitik*, "The use of maps in propaganda is dependent upon highly developed techniques of map making and reproduction, a certain minimum of mass education in reading cartographic symbols and a specific organization of society."[6] The power of geopolitics was—and to some extent remains today—based on its ability to depoliticize through scientific-sounding rhetoric what are at heart deeply political and subjective choices regarding foreign and domestic policies.

The founding fathers of geopolitics—Mackinder, Haushofer, Spykman—took refuge from the truly scientific and democratic evaluation of such policies. Lay citizens—whether of democracies such as Britain and America or dictatorships such as Nazi Germany—could not, in their view, be entrusted to uphold the eternal geopolitical verities concerning a realistic foreign policy. In this sense, geopolitics failed its own highest objective of providing a realistic understanding of foreign policy precisely because it discounted the real and powerful effects idealism and irrational elements play in international affairs. Only a "higher" realism with fewer pretensions than traditional geopolitics could have encompassed the realm of values and the element of the unpredictable in the world. Unfortunately, geopolitics was never simply an innocuous tool of national power. Instead, its assumptions about how the world worked and the political rhetoric it shaped helped to produce the calamities of World War One, World War Two, and the Cold War. Harold Sprout once commented on the fact that "erroneous geographical conceptions may be just as 'influential' as notions that do correspond to the 'facts' of the 'real world.'"[7]

With the exception of critiques provided by thinkers such as E. Reclus, Peter Kropotkin, and Karl Wittfogel, geopolitical descriptions of reality were rarely criticized between the time of the Franco-Prussian war and the beginning of World War Two. While the voyages of discovery beginning in the late fifteenth century had elevated the status of seafaring nation-states in terms of international prestige, by the nineteenth century such prestige was beginning to be accrued by continental landpowers now able to exploit their resources through the tools provided by the industrial revolution. The race for colonies in the era of high imperialism—and the subsequent attempt by Germany to colonize large parts of Europe itself in the twentieth century—attest to the perception among elites that world power status demanded a "first class" territorial foundation for the advancement of national goals.

Although considerations of territorial possession played a large role in the Cold War (as witnessed by American interest in containing the Soviets from dominating Eurasia), as the decades-long struggle wound down by the late 1980s, it became apparent that possession of continental space by either the Soviet Union or the United States was counting for less and less. Leo Amery, in his early critique of Mackinder's heartland thesis ("he who rules the Eurasian land mass rules the world") in 1904, had already anticipated such a situation. Amery responded to Mackinder's thesis by arguing that "The successful powers" of the future would be "those which have the greatest industrial basis." He continued by saying that it would "not matter whether they are in the center of a continent or on an island; those people who have the industrial power and the power of invention and science will be able to defeat all others."[8] As nuclear weapons inhibited the outbreak of war between the superpowers, geoeconomics began to gradually supersede purely geopolitical concerns among the elites of the leading economic powers by the end of the Cold War. Thus one may discern beginning in 1945 a geoeconomic social consensus in Europe that sacrificed territorial ambition for the promise of legitimation through an ever-increasing GNP. In terms of military strategy as well it has been noticed that, in the words of G. Segal on the relationship between geopolitics and nuclear weapons, "In the nuclear age of microchips and small, powerful, weaponry, size counts for much less."[9]

For all the talk in the 1980s and early 1990s about the rise of multinational corporations at the expense of national sovereignty, the geography in "geoeconomics" is still important. As Edward Luttwak notes:

This new version of the ancient rivalry of states, I have called 'geo-economics.' In it, investment capital for industry provided or guided by the state is the equivalent of firepower; product development subsidized by the state is the equivalent of weapon innovation; and market penetration supported by the state replaces military bases and garrisons on foreign soil as well as diplomatic 'influence.' ... as bureaucracies writ large, states as a whole are impelled by the urge to preserve their importance in society to acquire the geo-economic substitute for their decaying security role.[10]

Therefore prestige in the new world order will—according to the emerging geoeconomic master narrative—derive from the power of a nation's investment capital (the equivalent of firepower in the old geopolitics), product development (equivalent to the old emphasis on weapons development) and market penetration (analogous to the old geopolitically-based interest in the maintenance of overseas military bases). While nations still—at one level—define themselves geographically, their power is increasingly perceived in de-spatialized economic terms. Where once geopolitical theorists such as Mackinder, Haushofer, and Spykman argued for the primacy of spatial capital, the geoeconomic paradigm gives primacy to industrial policies that ignore previous preoccupations with the heartland or rimlands of Eurasia (unless, of course, they provide new targets for market penetration). Indeed the territorially based nation-state finds itself being questioned from above by the forces of border-ignoring multinationals and from below by non-governmental organizations and various regionalization initiatives.

From the work of recent American writers on geopolitical and geoeconomic themes, one can discern three dominating trends. First, there is of course the geoeconomic preoccupation with China. The Pentagon's controversial defense guidance policy of early 1992 argued that it was in America's interest to prevent the rise of a new power that could threaten American hegemony won after the collapse of the Soviet Union and the defeat of Iraq. One can expect in the future attempts to use the legacy of geopolitics (as it is now embodied in geoeconomics) to argue the case that China is America's strongest threat and must be contained in some way. A second concern of the longer term is over the role of outer space in international politics. Zbigniew Brzezinski and like-minded thinkers consider that "Space control is likely to become tantamount to earth control" in the long run.[11] Finally, there is the potential for Islam to become geopolitically defined as a primary enemy of the West. As the geographer P. Taylor recently wrote, "Here is a new geopolitical 'Islamic rimland' from North Africa to Southeast Asia in which 'fundamentalism' is equally a threat to Western security."[12]

Geopolitics may have given way to geoeconomics as an orienting ideology among foreign policy elites in the economically advanced nations of the world, but the legacy of Mackinder, Haushofer, and Spykman continues to affect the world today. Just as the parochial European balance of power system lived on vestigially in the geopolitical age (1870-1945), so too will geopolitics survive vestigially in a geoeconomic age so long as there are national security interests to be rationalized and national powers to be measured.

Notes

1. See Fred Halliday, *The Making of the Second Cold War* (London: Verso, 1986).

2. L. W. Hepple, "The Revival of Geopolitics," *Political Geography Quarterly* 5.4 (1986): 22.

3. "National Security Strategy of the United States," *Department of State Bulletin*, (April 1988): 3.

4. "National Security," 2.

5. K. Boulding, "National Images and International Systems," *Journal of Conflict Resolution* 3.2: 122.

6. Hans Speier, "Magic Geography," *Social Research* 8.3 (1941): 310. In this context, Carl Troll observed that "in the age of the masses caution on the part of men of learning is all the more needed in the formation of public opinion." Carl Troll, "Geographic Science in Germany During the Period 1933-1945: A Critique and a Justification," trans. by Eric Fischer, *Annals of the Association of American Geographers* 39.1 (1949): 135.

7. Harold and Margaret Sprout, "Geography and International Politics in an Era of Revolutionary Change," *Journal of Conflict Resolution* 4.1 (1960): 148.

8. Quoted in Sprout and Sprout, "Geography," 148.

9. G. Segal, "Nuclear Strategy: The Geography of Stability," *Political Geography Quarterly*, Supplement to 5.4 (1986): 43.

10. Edward Luttwak, *The Endangered American Dream: How to Stop the United States from Becoming a Third World Country and How to Win the Geo-Economic Struggle for Industrial Supremacy* (New York: Simon & Schuster, 1993), 35-36, 314.

11. Z. Brzezinski, "America's New Geostrategy," *Foreign Affairs* (1988): 681.

12. P. G. Taylor, "Tribulations of Transition," *Professional Geographer* 44.1 (1992): 12.

Bibliography:
Primary Sources

1) Halford Mackinder and British Geopolitics

Archival Material:
Cabinet Records 1919-1920 (Public Records Office).
C.O. 885/17, 19, 21, 22, 23. Visual Instruction Committee (PRO).
F.O. 800/251 Russia: Private Papers of H.J. Mackinder relating to his mission to
    South Russia (Oct. 1919 - Feb. 1920) (PRO).
Mackinder Papers, School of Geography, Oxford:
    M.P/A/ Miscellaneous photographs and prints.
    M.P/B/ Miscellaneous maps, pamphlets and journals.
    M.P/C/ Autobiographical fragments.
    M.P/D/ Correspondence relating to Mackinder papers.
    M.P/E/ to M.P/J/ Kenya materials. Also M.P/L/ and M.P/M/.
    M.P/K/ Fragments of articles.
    School of Geography, Scrapbook 1.
Royal Geographic Society.

Printed Sources:
Parliamentary Debates (1910-1922), 5th series, House of Commons (Hansard).
Woodward, E.L., and Butler, R., eds. *Documents on British Foreign Policy
    1919-1939*. London: HMSO, 1949.

Works by Mackinder:
"On the Scope and Methods of Geography." *Proceedings of the Royal
    Geographical Society, New Series* 9 (1887): 141-160.
"The Physical Basis of Political Geography." *Scottish Geographical Magazine* 6
    (1890): 78-84.

With M. E. Sadler. *University Extension: Past, Present and Future.* London: Cassell, 1891.

"Reports on Geography at the Universities: Oxford." *Geographical Journal* 4 (1894): 29-30.

"Modern Geography, German and English." *Geographical Journal* 6 (1895): 367-79.

"The Great Trade Routes." *Journal of the Institute of Bankers* (1900).

"A Journey to the Summit of Mt. Kenya, British East Africa." *Geographical Journal* 15 (1900): 453-86.

Britain and the British Seas. London: Heinemann, 1902.

"Higher Education." *The Nation's Need.* Ed. by S. Wilkinson. London: Constable, 1903.

"The Geographical Pivot of History." *Geographical Journal* 23 (1904): 421-437.

"Man-power as a Measure of National and Imperial Strength." *National Review* 45 (1905): 136-43.

Our Own Islands; an Elementary Study in Geography. London: George Philip, 1906. [14th ed., 1921]

Address delivered on 10 Jan., 1907, on the occasion of the opening of the class for the administrative training of army officers. London: HMSO.

Britain and the British Seas, 2d ed. Oxford: Clarendon P., 1907

"On Thinking Imperially." In *Lectures on Empire.* Ed. by M. E. Sadler. London, 1907.

The Rhine: Its Valley and History. London: Chatto and Windus, 1908.

"Geographical Conditions Affecting the British Empire, I: The British Islands." *Geographical Journal* 33 (1909): 462-76.

India. Eight Lectures Prepared for Visual Instruction Committee of the Colonial Office. London: George Philip, 1910.

"This Unprecedented War." *Glasgow Herald,* 4 Aug. 1917.

Democratic Ideals and Reality: A Study in the Politics of Reconstruction. New York: Holt, 1919.

"Geography as a Pivotal Subject in Education." *Geographical Journal* 57 (1921): 376-84.

The World War and After: A Concise Narrative and Some Tentative Ideas. London: George Philip, 1924.

"The English Tradition and the Empire: Some Thoughts on Lord Milner's Credo and the Imperial Committees." *United Empire* 14 (1925): 1-8.

"The Music of the Spheres." *Proceedings of the Royal Philosophical Society,* Glasgow 63 (1937): 170-81.

"Geography, an Art and a Philosophy." *Geography* 27 (1942): 122-30.

"The Round World and the Winning of the Peace." *Foreign Affairs* 21 (1943): 595-605.

Speech at the presentation of the medals at the American embassy by the American ambassador. *Geographical Journal* 103 (1944): 132-33.

2) Karl Haushofer and German Geopolitics

Archival Material:
Bundesarchiv, Koblenz.

Works by Haushofer:
Grenzen in ihrer geographischen und politischen Bedeutung. Berlin-Grunewald, 1927.
Der natinalsozialistische Gedanke in der Welt. Munich, 1933.
Die Grössmachte vor und nach dem Weltkriege Deutschland (K. Haushofer, ed.) Berlin: Kurt Vorwinckel, 1930.
Geopolitik des Pazifischen Ozeans. Berlin: Kurt Vorwinckel Verlag, 1924.
"Geopolitische Einflüsse bei den Verkorperungsversuchen von National Sozialismus und sozialer Aristokratie." *ZfG* 1 (1924): 127-34.
With E. Obst, H. Lautensach, and O. Maull, eds. *Bausteine zur Geopolitik.* Berlin: Kurt Vorwinckel, 1928.
"Das asiatische Antlitz der Sowjets." *ZfG* 8 (1931): 473-81.
Geopolitik der Pan-Ideen. Berlin: Zentral-Verlag, 1931.
Wehr-Geopolitik; geographische Grundlagen einer Wehrkunde. Berlin: Junker und Dünnhaupt, 1932.
"Atemweite, Lebensraum un Gleichberechtigung auf Erden!" *ZfG* 11 (1934): 1-14.
Weltpolitik von Heute. Berlin: "Zeitgeschichte" Verlag, 1934.
"Pflicht und Anspruch der Geopolitik als Wissenschaft." *ZfG* 12 (1935): 443-8.
Der Kontinentalblock, Mitteleuropa, Eurasien, Japan. Munchen: F. Eher Nachf., 1941.
"Das vielerlei der 'Ost'-Begriffe." *ZfG* 19 (1942): 144-7.

3) Nicholas Spykman and American Geopolitics

Archival Material:
Derwent Whittlesey Papers, Harvard University Archives.

Printed Sources:
Department of State Bulletin, Washington: USGPO.
Foreign Relations of the United States: Washington: USGPO.

Works by Spykman:
"Geography and Foreign Policy." *American Political Science Review* 32 (Feb. 1938): 28-50; 32 (April 1938): 213-36.
With Abbie A. Rollins. "Geographic Objectives in Foreign Policy." *American Political Science Review* 33 (June 1939): 391-410; (Aug. 1939): 591-614.
America's Strategy in World Politics: The United States and the Balance of Power. New York: Harcourt Brace, 1942.

Bibliography

"Frontiers, Security, and International Relations." *Geographical Review* 32 (July 1942): 436-47.
The Geography of the Peace. New York: Harcourt Brace, 1944.

Bibliography:
Secondary Sources

Ambrose, Stephen. *Rise to Globalism: American Foreign Policy Since 1938*. New York: Penguin, 1991.

Ashley, R. K. "The Geopolitics of Geopolitical Space: Toward a Critical Social Theory of International Politics." *Alternatives* 12 (1987): 403-434.

Banse, E. *Raum und Volk im Weltkriege: Gedanken Uber Eine Nationale Wehrlehre*. Oldenburg: Stalling, 1932.

Bassin, M. "Imperialism and the Nation State in Friedrich Ratzel's Political Geography." *Progress in Human Geography* 11 (1987): 473-495.

———. "Race Contra Space: The Conflict Between German 'Geopolitik' and National Socialism." *Political Geography Quarterly* 6 (1987): 115-134.

Bell, Morag, ed. *Geography and Imperialism 1820-1940*. Manchester U. Pr., 1995.

Berger, J. *Ways of Seeing*. Viking Press, 1995.

Berger, P.L., and Luckman, T. *The Social Constructon of Reality: A Treatise on the Sociology of Knowledge*. Garden City, NY: Anchor P., 1967.

Beukema, H. "School for Statesmen." *Fortune* 27 (Jan. 1943): 108-109+.

Boggs, S. W. "Cartohypnosis" *U.S. Dept. of State Bulletin*, 15 (Dec. 22, 1946): 1119-1125.

Bowman, I. *The New World*. Yonkers on Hudson: World Book Co., 1921.

———. "Geography Versus Geopolitics." *Geographical Review* 32 (1942): 646-658.

———. "Political Geography of Power." *Geographical Review* 32 (1942): 349-352.

Brown, F. and E. Herlin. *The War in Maps: An Atlas of "New York Times."* New York: Oxford UP, 1944.

Brzezinski, Z. *Game Plan: A Geostrategic Framework for the Conduct of the U.S.-Soviet Contest*. Boston: Atlantic Monthly Press, 1986.

————. *The Grand Chessboard*. Basic Books, 1997.

Burleigh, Michael. *Germany Turns Eastward: A Study of Ostforschung in the Third Reich*. Cambridge, 1988.

Burnham, J. "Coming Rulers of the United States." *Fortune* 24 (Nov. 1941): 100-101+.

Business Week. "Case for Geopolitics." 674 (Aug. 1942): 68.

Chaliand, G. and Rageau, J.-P. *Atlas Strategique*. Paris: Librairie Artheme Fayard, 1983.

Clarke, I. F. *Voices Prophesying War: 1763-1984*. London: Oxford UP, 1966.

Cohen, S. B. *Geography and Politics in a World Divided*. New York: William Morrow, 1963.

Cohn, C. "Sex and Death in the Rational World of Defense Intellectuals." *Signs* 12 (1987): 687-718.

Committee on the Present Danger. *Alerting America: The Papers of the Committee on the Present Danger*. Washington, D.C.: Pergamon Brassey's, 1984.

Cox, R. W. "Gramsci, Hegemony and International Relations: An Essay in Method." *Millennium: Journal of International Studies* 12 (1983): 162-175.

Crampton, A., and Ó'Tuathail, G. "Intellectuals, Institutions and Ideology: The Case of Robert Strausz-Haupé and 'American Geopolitics.'" *Political Geography*, vol. 15, no. 6/7: 533-555.

Dalby, S. "Geopolitical Discourse: The Soviet Union as 'Other.' " *Alternatives* 13 (1988): 415-442.

————. "American Security Discourse: The Persistence of Geopolitics." *Political Geography Quarterly* 9 (1990): 171-188.

Dalby, S., and Ó'Tuathail, G., eds. *Rethinking Geopolitics*. Routledge, 1998.

De Bres, K. "George Renner and the Great Map Scandal of 1942." *Political Geography Quarterly* 5 (1986): 385-394.

Dehio, L. *The Precarious Balance: Four Centuries of the European Power Struggle*. New York: Vintage Books, 1965.

De Landa, M. *War in the Age of Intelligent Machines*. New York: Zone Books, 1991.

Demangeon, A. *Le Declin de L'Europe*. Paris: Payot, 1920.

DerDerian, J., and Shapiro, M. J., eds. *International/Intertextual Relations: Post-modern Readings in World Politics*. Lexington, MA: Lexington Books, 1989.

De Seversky, A. P. *Victory Through Air Power*. New York: Simon and Schuster, 1942.

Deudney, D. *Whole Earth Security: A Geopolitics of Peace*. Washington, D.C.: Worldwatch Institute, 1983.

Diner, Dan. "'Grundbuch des Planeten' Zur Geopolitik Karl Haushofers." *Vierteljahrshefte für Zeitgeschicte* 32 (1984): 1-28.

Dorpalen, A., ed. *The World of General Haushofer: Geopolitics in Action*. New York: Farrar and Rinehart, 1942.

Dunnigan, J. F. *The Complete Wargames Handbook.* New York: William Morrow, 1992.

Earle, E. M., ed. *Makers of Modern Strategy: From Machiavelli to Hitler.* Princeton, NJ: Princeton UP, 1944.

Edley, M. H. *Mapping an Empire: The Geographical Construction of British India, 1765-1843.* U. of Chicago. Pr., 1997.

Etzold, T., and Gaddis, J. L., eds. *Containment: Documents on American Policy and Strategy, 1945-1950.* New York: Columbia UP, 1978.

Fahlbusch, M., Rossler, M. and Siegriest, D. "Conservatism, Ideology and Geography in Germany 1920-1950." *Poltical Geography Quarterly* 8 (1989): 353-367.

Fifield, R., and Pearcy, G. E. *World Political Geography.* New York: Thomas Y. Crowell, 1949.

Freedman, L. *The Evolution of Nuclear Strategy.* St. Martin's, 1983.

Friedberg, A. *The Weary Titan: Britain and the Experience of Relative Decline, 1895-1905.* Princeton, NJ: Princeton UP, 1988.

Gaddis, J. L. *Strategies of Containment: A Critical Appraisal of Postwar American National Security Policy.* New York: Oxford UP, 1982.

Genovese, Eugene, and Hochberg, Leonard, eds. *Geographic Perspectives in History.* Blackwell, 1989.

Gilpin, R. *War and Change in World Politics.* New York: Cambridge UP, 1981.

Glassner, M. I. *Political Geography.* New York: John Wiley and Sons, 1992.

Godlewska, Anne, and Smith, Neil, eds. *Geography and Empire.* Oxford, 1994.

Gombrich, E. H. *Art and Illusion: A Study in the Psychology of Pictorial Representation.* Princeton, 1972.

Gottmannn, J., ed. *Centre and Periphery: Spatial Variations in Politics.* London: Sage, 1980.

Gray, C. S. *The Geopolitics of the Nuclear Era: Heartland, Rimland and Technological Revolution.* New York: Crane, Russak, 1977.

————. *The Geopolitics of Superpower.* Lexington, KY: UP of KY, 1988.

————. "A Debate on Geopolitics: The Continued Primacy of Geography." *Orbis*, Spring 1996: 247-259.

Grimm, H. *Volk Ohne Raum: Ein Roman.* Munich: Langen-Muller, 1933.

Gulick, E. *Europe's Classical Balance of Power.* Ithaca: Cornell UP, 1955.

Gyorgy, A. *Geopolitics: The New German Science.* Berkeley: U. of Calif. P., 1944.

Halliday, F. *The Making of the Second Cold War.* London: Verso, 1986.

Hamilton, J. D. *The Truth About Rudolf Hess.* London: Mainstream Publishing, 1993.

Harley, J. B. "Deconstructing the Map." *Cartographica* 26 (1982): 1-19.

Hennig, R. "Geopolitik und Rassenkunde." *Zeitschrift fur Geopolitik* 13 (1936): 58-63.

Henrikson, A.K. "The Geographical 'Mental Maps' of American Foreign Policy Makers." *International Political Science Review* 1 (1980): 495-530.

Hepple, L. W. *The Revival of Geopolitics. Political Geography Quarterly* 5 (4) Supplement (1986): S21-S36.

Herb, G. Heinrik. "Persuasive Cartography in Geopolitik and National Socialism." *Political Geography Quarterly* 8 (1989): 289-303.

Herf, Jeffrey. *Reactionary Modernism: Technology, Culture and Politics in Weimar and the Third Reich.* Cambridge, 1984

Herken, G. *Counsels of War.* New York: Oxford UP, 1987.

Heske, H. "German Geographic Research in the Nazi Period: A Content Analysis of the Major Geography Journals." *Political Geography Quarterly* 5 (1986): 267-281.

———. "Karl Haushofer: His Role in German Geopolitics and in Nazi Politics." *Political Geography Quarterly* 6 (1987): 135-144.

Heyck, T. W. *Transformation of Intellectual Life in Victorian England.* Lyceum Book, 1989.

Hildebrand, Klaus. *The Foreign Policy the Third Reich* (trans. By A. Fothergill). Berkeley: U. of California P., 1973.

Hooson, D. "A New Soviet Heartland?" *Geographical Journal*, 128 (March, 1962): 19-29.

Howard, M. *War in European History.* Oxford UP, 1976.

Hunt, L., ed. *The New Cultural History.* Berkeley: U. of California P., 1989.

Jacobsen, H.-A. *Karl Haushofer: Leben und Werk. Vols. 1 and 2.* Boppard am Rhein, 1979.

James, P. *All Possible Worlds: A History of Geographical Ideas.* New York: The Odyssey P., 1972.

Jones, E. L. *The European Miracle: Environments, Economies, and Geopolitics in the History of Europe and Asia.* Cambridge U. Press, 1981.

Kaplan, F. *The Wizards of Armageddon.* New York: Simon and Schuster, 1983.

Kearns, G. "Closed Space and Political Practice: Frederick Jackson Turner and Halford Mackinder." *Environmental and Planning* D (Society and Space) 2 (1984): 23-34.

Kennedy, P. *The Rise and Fall of the Great Powers.* New York: Random House, 1987.

Kern, S. *The Culture of Time and Space: 1880-1918.* Cambridge: Harvard UP, 1983.

Kidron, M., and Smith, D. *The War Atlas: Armed Conflict-Armed Peace.* New York: Simon and Schuster, 1983.

Kissinger, H. *A World Restored: Castlereagh, Metternich and the Restoration of Peace, 1812-1822.* Boston: Houghton Mifflin, 1957.

———. *Diplomacy.* New York: Simon and Schuster, 1994.

Kjellén, R. *Der Staat als Lebensform.* Leipzig: S. Hirzel, 1917.

Kolkowicz, R. "The Strange Career of the Defense Intellectuals." *Orbis* (1987): 179-192.

Korinman, Michel. *Quand L'Allemagne Pensait le Monde: Grandeur et Décadence D'une Géopolitique.* Paris, 1990.

Kost, K. "Begriffe und Macht: Die Funktion der Geopolitik als Ideologie." *Geographische Zeitschrift* 74 (1986): 14-30.

———. "The Conception of Politics in Political Geography and Geopolitics in Germany Until 1945." *Political Geography Quarterly* 8 (1989): 369-385.

Kristoff, L. K. D. "The Origins and Evolution of Geopolitics." *Journal of Conflict Revolution* 4 (March 1960): 15-51.

LaCapra, D. *Modern European Intellectual History: Reappraisals and New Perspectives.* Ithaca: Cornell UP, 1982.

Lange, K. "Der Terminus 'Lebensraum' in Hitlers 'Mein Kampf.'" *Vierteljahresheft für Zeitgeschichte* 13 (1965): 426-437.

Lewis, Martin and Wigen, Karen *Myth of Continents: A Critique of Metageography.* U. of California Pr., 1997.

Liberman, Peter. *Does Conquest Pay?: The Exploitation of Occupied Industrial Societies.* Princeton U. Pr., 1996.

Life. "Maps: Global War Teaches Global Cartography." 13 (Aug. 3, 1942): 57-65.

Livingstone, David. *The Geographical Tradition.* Oxford: Blackwell, 1992.

Louis, W. R. *Imperialism at Bay: the United States and the Decolonization of the British Empire, 1941-1945.* New York: Oxford UP, 1978.

Lowe, James Trapier. *Geopolitics and War: Mackinder's Philosophy of Power.* Washington, D.C., 1981.

Luttwak, E. N. *Strategy: The Logic of War and Peace.* Belknap Press, 1990.

Mahan, A. T. *The Influence of Seapower Upon History, 1660-1783.* Boston: Little, Brown, 1980.

Mandelbaum, M. *The Fate of Nations: The Search for National Security in the Nineteenth and Twentieth Centuries.* New York: Cambridge UP, 1988.

Maull, O. *Politische Geographie.* Berlin: Borntraeger, 1925.

Mayer, A. J. *The Politics and Diplomacy of Peacemaking: Containment and Counterrevolution at Versailles 1918-1919.* London: Weidenfeld and Nicolson, 1968.

———. *The Persistence of the Old Regime: Europe to the Great War.* Cambridge, MA: Harvard UP, 1983.

McNeill, W. *The Pursuit of Power: Technology, Armed Force, and Society Since A.D. 1000.* U. Chicago P., 1982.

Mitchell, B. R. *European Historical Statistics: 1750-1970.* Columbia UP, 1978.

Modelski, G. *Long Cycles in World Politics.* Seattle: U. of Washington P., 1987.

Monmonier, M. *How to Lie With Maps.* Chicago: U. of Chicago P., 1991.

———. *Map Appreciation.* Englewood Cliffs, NJ: Prentice-Hall, 1988.

Mowrer, E. A. and M. Rajchman. *Global War, an Atlas of World Strategy.* New York: William Morrow, 1942.

Murphy, David Thomas. *The Heroic Earth: Geopolitical Thought in Weimar Germany, 1918-1933.* The Kent State U. Pr., 1997.

Nathanson, C. "The Social Construction of the Soviet Threat: a Study in the Politics of Representation." *Alternatives* 13 (1988): 443-483.

Naumann, Friedrich. *Mitteleuropa.* Berlin, 1915.

Norton, D. H. "Karl Haushofer and the German Academy, 1925-1945."*Central European History* 1 (1968): 80-99.

O'Loughlin, J. *Dictionary of Geopolitics*. Westport, Conn.: Greenwood P., 1994.

O'Loughlin, John and Van Der Wusten, Herman. "Political Geography of Panregions." *Geographical Review*, vol. 80, no. 1: 1-18.

Ó'Tuathail, G. "Putting Mackinder in His Place." *Political Geography* 11 (1992): 100-118.

Ó'Tuathail, G., and Agnew, J. "Geopolitics and Discourse: Practical Geopolitical Reasoning and American Foreign Policy." *Political Geography* 11 (1992): 190-204.

Paret, P., Craig, G, and Gilbert, F., eds. *Makers of Modern Strategy: From Machiavelli to the Nuclear Age*. Princeton U. Press, 1986.

Parker, G. *Western Geopolitical Thought in the Twentieth Century*. New York: St. Martin's P., 1985.

———. "French Geopolitical Thought in the Interwar Years and the Emergence of the the European Idea." *Political Geography Quarterly* 6 (1987): 145-150.

———. *The Geopolitics of Domination*. London: Routledge, 1988.

Parker, W. H *Mackinder: Geography as an Aid to Statecraft*. London: Clarendon Press, 1982.

Paterson, J. H. "German Geopolitics Reassessed." *Political Geography Quarterly* 6 (1987): 107-114.

Pearton, Maurice. *The Knowledgable State: Diplomacy, War, and Technology Since 1830*. London: Burnett Books, 1982.

Perkin, H. J., *The Rise of Professional Society: England Since 1880*. London: Routledge, 1989.

Ratzel, F. *Politische Geographie*. Munich: Oldenbourg, 1897.

Renner, G. T. "Maps for a New World." *Collier's Magazine* 533 (June, 1942): 14-21.

———. *Global Geography*. New York: Thomas Coswell, 1944.

Rich, Norman. *Hitler's War Aims: Ideology, the Nazi State and the Course of Expansion*. Vol. 1. London: W. W. Norton & Co., Inc., 1974.

Rorty, R. *Philosophy in the Mirror of Nature*. Princeton U. Press, 1981.

Sandner, G. "Recent Advances in the History of German Geography." *Geographische Zeitschrift* 76 (1988): 120-133.

Schnitzer, E. W. *German Geopolitics Revived*. Santa Monica: RAND Corp., 1954.

Schultz, H.-D. "Fantasies of 'Mitte,' 'Mittellage' and 'Mitteleuropa' in German Geographical Discussion in the 19th and 20th Centuries." *Political Geography Quarterly* 8 (1989): 315-339.

Searle, G. R. *The Quest for National Efficiency*. Berkeley: U. of California Pr., 1971.

Selden, R. *A Reader's Guide to Contemporary Literary Theory*. University Press of Kentucky, 1989.

Semmel, B. *Imperialism and Social Reform*. New York: Anchor Books, 1968.

Sharp, J. P. "Publishing American Identity: Popular Geopolitics, Myth and The *Reader's Digest.*" *Political Geography* 12 (1993): 491-503.

Short, E. H. *Handbook of Geopolitics.* London: Allen and Unwin, 1935.

Sloan, G. R. *Geopolitics in United States Strategic Policy, 1890-1987.* New York: St. Martin's P., 1988.

Smith, J. A. *The Idea Brokers: Think Tanks and the Rise of the New Policy Elite.* New York: The Free P., 1991.

Smith, N. "Isaiah Bowman: Political Geography and Geopolitics." *Political Geography Quarterly* 3 (1984): 69-76.

————. "Bowman's 'New World' and the Council on Foreign Relations." *Geographical Review* 76 (1986): 438-460.

Smith, W. D. *The Ideological Origins of Nazi Imperialism.* New York: Oxford UP, 1986.

Sondern, F. "Thousand Scientists Behind Hitler." *Reader's Digest* 38 (June 1941): 23-27.

Speier, H. "Magic Geography." *Social Research* 8 (Sept. 1941): 310-330.

Sprout, H., and Sprout, M. *The Ecological Perspective on Human Affairs.* Princeton: Princeton U. Press, 1965.

Stoddart, D. R., ed. *Geography, Ideology, and Social Concern.* Totowa: Barnes and Noble, 1981.

————. *On Geography.* New York: Basil Blackwell, 1986.

Stone, N., ed. *The Times Atlas of World History.* Maplewood, NJ: Hammond, 1989.

Strausz-Hupé, R. *Geopolitics: The Struggle for Space and Power.* New York: Putnam, 1942.

Summers, H. G. *On Strategy: A Critical Analysis of the Vietnam War.* New York: Dell, 1984.

————. *On Strategy II: A Critical Analysis of the Gulf War.* New York: Dell Publishing, 1992.

Symonds, R. *Oxford and Empire.* St. Martin's Pr., 1986.

Taylor, A. J. P. *The Struggle for Mastery in Europe: 1848-1918.* London: Oxford UP, 1971.

Taylor, Peter. (ed.) *Political Geography of the Twentieth Century: A Global Analysis.* Belhaven Pr., 1993.

Taylor, P. J. *Political Geography: World-System, Nation-State and Locality.* 2nd ed. London: Longman, 1989.

————. *Britain and the Cold War: 1945 as a Geopolitical Transition.* New York: Guilford P., 1990.

Time. "Mysteries of Geopolitics." 41 (Jan. 11, 1943): 92-96.

Troll, C. "Die Geographisch Wissenschaft in Deutschland in dem Jahren 1933 bis 1945. Eine Kritik und eine Rechtfertigung." *Erkunde* 1 (1947): 3-47.

United States. Office of War Information. *A War Atlas for Americans.* New York: Simon and Schuster, 1944.

————. War Department: *A Graphic History of the War.* Washington, D.C.: 1942.

U.S. Air Force. *Military Aspects of World Political Geography.* Alabama: USAF Academy, 1958.

U.S. Army. Field Circular 100-34, Operations on the Integrated Battlefield. Field Circular 101-34, Command and Control on the Airland Battlefield. Fort Leavenworth, KS: U.S. Army Command and General Staff College, 1984.

Van Valkenberg, C. *Elements of Political Geography.* New York: Prentice-Hall, 1940.

Vasquez, J. A. *Classics of International Relations.* Englewood Cliffs, NJ: Prentice-Hall, 1990.

Vigor, P. "The Soviet View of Geopolitics." In C. Zoppo and C. Zorgbibe (eds.), *On Geopolitics: Classical and Nuclear*, pp. 131-139. Dordrecht: Martinus Nijhoff.

Walsh, E. J. *Total Power: A Footnote to History.* Garden City, NY: Doubleday, 1948.

Weigert, H. W. *Generals and Geographers: The Twilight of Geopolitics.* London: Oxford UP, 1942.

————. *Principles of Political Geography.* New York: Appleton-Century Crofts, 1957.

White, H. *Metahistory: The Historical Imagination in Nineteenth-Century Europe.* Johns Hopkins, 1990.

Whittlesey, D. S. *The Earth and State: A Study of Political Geography.* New York: Henry Holt, 1939.

Whittlesey, D. S., C. C. Colby, and R. Hartshorne. *German Strategy of World Conquest.* New York: Farrar and Rinehart, 1942.

Williams, W. A. *The Tragedy of American Diplomacy.* New York: World Publishing, 1959.

Wirsing, G. *The War in Maps, 1939-40.* New York: German Library of Information, 1941.

Wittfogel, K. A. "Geopolitics, Geographical Materialism and Marxism." trans. by G. Ulmen. *Antipode* 17 (1985): 21-72.

Wood, D. *The Power of Maps.* New York: The Guilford P., 1992.

Zoppo, C. E., and Zorgbibe, C. *On Geopolitics: Classical and Nuclear.* Dordrecht: Martinus Nijhoff, 1985.

Index

About the Author

Mark Polelle is an assistant professor of history at the University of Findlay in Ohio. He obtained a B.A. in history at the University of Chicago before receiving his Ph.D. in history at Rutgers in 1995. He has also earned his M.L.S. and J.D. from Rutgers. His teaching and research interests are now focused on world history and modern European history.